Praise for David Pitkin's recent books

Haunted Saratoga County

"...brings the invisible in from the void, gives voice to the muted, and lights a candle for every playful, elusive, angry and mischevious soul that has been hiding in eternity's shadow..."
THE SARATOGIAN

Ghosts of the Northeast

"...a stylish glossary of ghost stories...a wonderful book to take along on a country drive up and down NY State's open roads. The stories are told with honesty and an open mind, never attempting to capitalize on the "fright" factor, but instead bringing common sense to the stories, although there were one or two that had me sleeping with the night light on...truly one of the BEST books on true hauntings that I have read to date..."
VANCE L. KIBE on AMAZON.COM

"... one of the best true ghost books that I've ever read, and I've read many. I would rank it high in my top ten. I thrilled to every page and had a terrible time trying to put it down...the information was presented concisely and deliciously, and I savored every chilling drop."
BB "NOVELIST13" St. Joseph, MO on AMAZON.COM

Spiritual Numerology: Caring for Number One

"In the last five hours I have DEVOURED the whole book. It is lucid, synthetic in the best sense of that word, humane and inspiring. It's moving and instructive. I really like the quotations from major religions. I am so grateful on behalf of everyone the book reaches that you have done this work and communicated it so manageably."
VAUGHN WARD, Adirondack Editor, GREENFIELD PRESS

"This is a most unusual book in that (1) it's a great read the first time through, (2) is a "must have" reference manual for the subject and (3) is very down-to-earth and practical. In essence, this is a very well written manual on how to use numerology in identifying your strengths and weaknesses, as well as the cycles in your life. This is the "owner's manual" we should have gotten at birth! Thanks for providing something on numerology that's sensible and useful for everyone."
"SKEAR" on AMAZON.COM

Haunted
Saratoga
County

ALSO BY David J. Pitkin

Ghosts of the Northeast

Spiritual Numerology: Caring for Number One

Saratoga County Ghosts

AURORA PUBLICATIONS e-mail address:
pitkinaurora@aol.com

Haunted Saratoga County

David J. Pitkin

AURORA PUBLICATIONS
CHESTERTOWN, NEW YORK

Copyright © 2005
by David J. Pitkin

Printed in the U.S.A.

AURORA PUBLICATIONS
P.O. Box 690
Chestertown, NY 12817

Publication Data
Pitkin, David J. 1939-
Haunted Saratoga County
Includes Index
ISBN 0-9663925-3-1 (trade pbk.)
1. Ghosts. 2. Saratoga County, NY
Library of Congress Control Number:
2004114035

Cover: The Old Wilton Academy

Table of Contents

Preface

The decision to compile my first book on ghosts in 1996 arose from my experiences in the 1960s, when I taught American History in Oneida County, NY. By 1964, my former idealism had been shattered by a succession of assassinations of national political figures. These events motivated me to begin seeking more profound answers to human dilemmas. Perhaps politics (my field of teaching) wasn't the ultimate answer to the human condition, I had begun to think.

My favorite haunt in the 1960s was the Jervis Library in Rome, NY, where I loved to browse the "new book" shelves. One autumn evening I spotted a strange title, *Ghosts That I've Met* by a Dr. Hans Holzer. Unfamiliar with the man's work, and skeptical of its subject matter, I took the book from the shelf and skimmed its pages. The author seemed to sincerely believe in ghosts. Until that time, I'd considered ghosts as something akin to the Tooth Fairy or Santa Claus, figures meant to charm or frighten children. I had never met or read of an adult who took such stories seriously. Tantalized, and ready for some bizarre material, I signed out the book and left for home.

A lover of enlightening talk radio at the time, I tuned my car radio to KDKA in Pittsburgh when I left the parking lot. It was a "clear channel" station whose talk shows often intrigued me. Weaving my way into traffic, I suddenly recognized that the talk show host and his guest were discussing ghosts! How coincidental, I mused. The guest, whose name I didn't immediately hear, related the tale of a ghost priest in a Roman Catholic church in Millvale, outside Pittsburgh. This sudden combination of folklore and my religious denomination focused my attention. At 9 p.m., the host cleared the decks for the news and urged listeners to call in and speak to that night's guest—Hans Holzer! An hour before I had never heard of the man. Now I was headed home with his book on my car seat and his voice in my ears. Later, astounded by the concepts in his book, I subsequently read every title he had in print, and though I didn't believe all Holzer's ideas, the rethinking of my life had begun.

My former narrow understandings about life and death now became modified and expanded. Weren't ghosts essentially dead? But, if so, how could they interact with the living? I began to think of variations in what is called "life." Holzer wrote of people called "mediums" who were capable of putting consciousness aside and permitting disembodied spirits to use their vocal cords for communication. He called himself a "psychologist for ghosts," a man who would listen to the spirit's problem, then help the entity to resolve it, sending the specter on its way into eternity. Soon after encountering these ideas, I began to wonder just when eternity began; aren't we already *now* in a part of that dimension? I had a Masters Degree in history and was well versed (I thought) in Christianity, but I had never heard educated people treat the phenomenon of ghosts as genuine, or even as worthy of study. Hundreds of questions about the afterlife begged for answers now, and I began to read every book on the subject that I could find.

In later years I read works by Dr. Carl G. Jung, a psychoanalyst, who was fascinated by what is termed *synchronicity*—two or more seemingly related events that arise or occur at the same time. Jung felt the simultaneity of such experiences was intimately connected to the soul's search for more profound levels of understanding. Fascinated to find a potential connection between religion, psychology and subjects now considered parapsychological, I read voraciously. Only later did I first hear a phrase that I now know to be true, "When the student is ready, the teacher appears." My church was undergoing a regeneration at that time, and I had thrown open my own inner doors and windows, confronting my formerly simplistic religious philosophy.

In 1968, I moved to another public school district in central New York State, and began to teach African and Asian Culture Studies, a new curriculum in the state's public school syllabus, containing information and concepts in which I'd had little college preparation. One day, the lesson plan required me to show a film about an East African village where the cows had stopped giving milk and the wells were drying up. The village shaman was summoned and revealed that an elderly woman who had died recently was not happy with her funeral ceremony and was making mischief to let the villagers know. The shaman ordered a new, more lavish ceremony to be performed in order to "lay her ghost." Following the new funeral, the village wells filled and village women were shown returning from the fields with gourds of milk. End of film! I didn't know how to make any sensible commentary.

With my parochial American understanding of the world, all I could do was laugh and joke about the primitive people and their superstitions. After class, a student approached me and said, "You shouldn't make fun of ghosts, Mr. Pitkin. They're real. We have one in our barn and you ought to come over and hear him sometime." Poor girl, I mused, even though she is an A student, she shouldn't automatically assume she had a ghost. Whatever she's experiencing, I thought, it's certainly some easily explainable event, and I can help her find the scientific cause. A few weeks later, I went forth to provide a facile explanation and save this bright student from ignorance.

On a cold November afternoon we entered the barn and could see the building might fall on us at any moment. It was old, poorly supported, and one could see the sky through many holes in the roof. A hayloft had once graced the interior, but had long ago been removed. Only its ladder remained behind me, against the wall. I became edgy about explaining away any phenomena because I could see there was no place where even a barn cat could hide—no hollow wall where some wild animal could produce a sound. If a noise was heard I'd be hard pressed to explain it. After an hour of waiting, we heard slow, heavy footsteps on a wooden floor seemingly four feet over our heads...*clump, clump.* Startled, I looked up. But there was no hayloft floor there for any being to walk on! *Clump, clump,* it continued, moving away from us toward the center of the barn. I believe there were about ten to twelve "footsteps." There was nothing moving in the barn. I was stupefied. Then the footsteps stopped. The girl and I looked at one another. She had a *See?* look on her face. My goose bumps were gradually subsiding. "What else does he do?" I asked. "That's it—he just walks," she replied. Slowly I regained my courage. I'd heard and seen much worse in old Hollywood movies—this wasn't that scary. We left the barn, but I was very uneasy. *Something* had made that noise. The student was sure of its cause; I was very perplexed and slowly losing my former certainties.

Familiar with some of Holzer's investigative techniques by now, the next day in school I asked the student what she knew of the barn or farm's history. She knew little but promised to ask her parents. From a neighbor she learned that, forty years before, the former owners had had a mentally ill adult son who, one day, went up into the hayloft, crossed to its edge, placed a rope around his neck, and jumped. I was astonished. My private study of such matters through the books of Holzer and other investigators seemed to suggest that here, in those footsteps, was the animated soul of a suicidal man who kept repeating his last act. But why? And more importantly, *how*?

I didn't know in what context to place these events and, as with most people, I filed the episode away. For two more years I had no more such experiences, heard no more stories about ghostly events, and had no informed person to query. Still, I was certain of what I'd experienced, and could no longer suppress my curiosity and *need* to know more.

In 1971, I took a teaching position in Saratoga Springs, NY, and very soon made the acquaintance of several individuals interested in ghosts, e.s.p., water dowsing, hypnosis, UFOs and a great range of hard-to-explain phenomena. In 1972, we formed a parapsychology study organization, Parapsychology Study and Investigations (PSI), holding monthly meetings and an annual convention that drew hundreds of curious seekers. I felt honored to make the acquaintance of Dr. Joseph Rhine of Duke University, father of e.s.p., and Dr. Alexander Tanous from Portland, ME, an outstanding psychic and a bi-locator. The latter term indicates he could be seen to interact with people in two far-distant locations, an activity attributed to some saints and yogis. Tanous, a devout Catholic, had no problem integrating his faith and extraordinary talents. I met two wonderful psychics from Warren County, Millie Coutant and Gail Putnam, both of whom inspired and expanded my understanding. When investigating houses with these two women, I sometimes found *my* psychic sensitivity enhanced.

In summers I worked as a historic tour guide for Saratoga Circuit Travel and Tours in Saratoga Springs, and it wasn't long before I conspired with owner Mary Reed to script a ghost tour of haunted sites I'd heard of in the Racing City. I had kept notes of interviews and rumors through the years, and when I retired from teaching in 1996, I proposed to write about twenty such stories in what became my first book, *Saratoga County Ghosts*. As I worked, I discovered help coming to me most fortuitously, as if there were beings "on the other side" assisting me to find people, places and personal experiences that would offer readers a well-rounded education about the world of ghosts. Before it went out of print in 2001, the book sold 15,000 copies, quite a feat for a first-time, self-published author.

In the process of compiling that book, with at least one ghost in each of the county's towns and cities, I realized how very *common* ghosts were, as my pursuit uncovered many people's experiences that had never before been disclosed. I also relished the opportunity to visit out-of-the-way places and travel many of Saratoga County's back roads that I'd never visited during my growing up years in Corinth. I ask your indulgence if some of these locations aren't readily identifiable. Many people shared their stories with the understanding that their home would remain anonymous. Wherever possible I've tried to check the history of these buildings to see if the ghost behaviors can be attributed to a specific former resident or event at that place. And, often, I was successful.

Since 2001, there has been a clamor for a new ghost book for Saratoga County, which I believe to be the "most haunted of American counties." Some theorize it is the mineral waters in Saratoga Springs that attract such haunts. Others suspect, with some scientific support, that ghost noise and light phenomena are more frequent in areas having a geological fault line, a feature Saratoga County does have. My historical investigations many times helped these ghost experiencers and myself understand the more profound activity surrounding death. This book, then, offers new insights on old stories and good new stories for old ghost story fans. Although some of these tales are historical, and thus encapsulated in time, others are still wide open and the phenomena at such sites continue to this day.

On its day of publication this book will already be out of date, because new ghosts are continually coming into being in Saratoga County, as they are all over the world. Many individuals continue to pass into death with issues not faced, with goals or desires frustrated, with relationships in distress, and with responsibilities or commitments broken. Unresolved issues of body, mind, emotions and spirit are simply carried over for resolution into The Beyond, and many souls must begin this soul task *here* before releasing their attachments to the material world.

David J. Pitkin
January 2005

Introduction

Ghost stories and contacts with the dead were common long before Man began to record his history. In ancient times, folk music, legends and religion proclaimed much more intimate connections with the world of the dead than modern people enjoy. Primitive people had to prepare their own family members for burial, and gradually evolved ethnic funeral customs, many of which are still followed thousands of years later. As formal religions emerged, more elaborate ceremonies were established, and many prohibited contact with the spirit world, lest the pious person be misled. Both primitive shamans and religious clerics warned, correctly, that not everything seen or said by spirits should be taken at face value. Institutional religions throughout much of the world have divorced the dead from the living, deeming such contacts "sinful." Yet, in many places on earth, there *are* civilized people who retain intimate, if not daily, contact with the dead, and consider deceased family members as part of an extended family. Such cultures retain respect for those dead ancestors and the contributions they made to the foundation of the family, village or nation. Because the deceased are loved and not feared in such cultures, their members believe that ancestors' spirits are capable of assisting the living in life's affairs.

In the 1600s, when Europe entered the Age of Reason, and many ancient superstitions vanished under the scientist's microscope, chemistry, or scientific formulae, it became unfashionable to believe in things which couldn't be replicated at will in a laboratory. Ghosts were treated as figments of the imagination or mental disorders. As religions became ever more dogmatic, believers were told that a spirit world existed, but beyond earth life, not inter-penetrating this world. Church members were enjoined *not* to contact it. Many sincere contactees were forced to stifle stories of their personal experiences for fear of being castigated as outcast sinners in league with the devil.

Only recently, as science has produced an array of electronic devices to register subtle energies, have some researchers begun the serious study of death and the hereafter. Compounding the difficulty in understanding the reality of ghosts, the entertainment industry (with its eye focused solely on thrills for profit, not education) has inundated Modern Man with films and videos that exploit people's uneasiness with, and fear of, the unknown.

My folklore collecting and investigation have yielded only an occasional instance of what may be termed an "evil spirit." As I interviewed people throughout Saratoga County, I was struck with how *human* most ghosts seem; after all, when they lived they *were* human. Essentially, a ghost is the memory and emotional energy of an individual who no longer has a physical body. I discovered that what separated them from me, was my capacity to make decisions and resolve problems by *acting* on them. Ghosts, I found, are usually fixated at some place in time, still attempting to resolve uncompleted work. Some remain overcome with guilt for deeds done or avoided in life. And many, I have found, are locked in a limbo of space and time because they cannot forgive themselves for apparent failures during their just-passed lives.

Eventually, I discovered that one can (and probably should) talk to such spirit entities, perhaps with the purpose of assisting them to leave a place and move into eternity, thus completing the original purpose of their life. I have often empathized with the disembodied individual, unable to bring its concluded life experience to finality. And I discovered that my compassion usually over-rode any fear for myself or those working with me when I visited haunted sites.

Investigating a haunted place, often with the assistance of gifted psychics, I have been more moved by the mystery of who remains in a place, why, and how, seldom finding a family that lives with ghosts in fear. Those who inhabit a haunted property are often irked by the ghost's behavior, but most also learn to co-exist with the spirit. And, as the relationship deepens, both sides learn to better tolerate one another. Very few people who have related their experiences to me seem to want their ghost removed, and many people today find that "having a ghost" is a quaint topic of conversation with guests. Sometimes, houses with a ghost can command a premium re-sale price.

In the almost fifty years in which I have collected stories, I have come to believe that almost every home or place of business *is* haunted, if only briefly, by some deceased resident or worker. Many of the strange phenomena experienced in such places can be clearly linked to a specific individual who has died. The ghost's consciousness can be no more or less than it was during the person's life.

I have collected many tales of such phenomena from widows and widowers, who continue to sense the departed spouse for some time after his or her death. In one such case, a widow kept up a relationship with her dead husband for almost three years. In the end, as she felt him rising from the bed one morning, she opened her eyes to see a brilliant purple light on the other side of the bed. The illumination remained for several minutes before vanishing. And, with the light, vanished the sounds that had lingered in the three years since the man's death. Soon after this leave-taking, the widow began dating again. It seems the dead husband stayed around to comfort his spouse for the period of time it took to resolve her grief and begin looking forward to a new life. More often than not, these are stories of love and human endurance, and sometimes there is a reward for those who take such contacts seriously.

In presenting Saratoga County's ghost stories, I'm honoring the hard working people in the county's past, some of whom have remained working following body death. Also, I honor those living folks who brushed aside "what the neighbors might think" to relate their experiences. Such truthful behavior is a part of cosmic "truth," which people must adhere to if they are to be happy. Creating this book also gives me an opportunity to impart some of the county's rich historic past. I hope you enjoy reading these tales as much as I enjoyed collecting them.

TOWN OF

BALLSTON

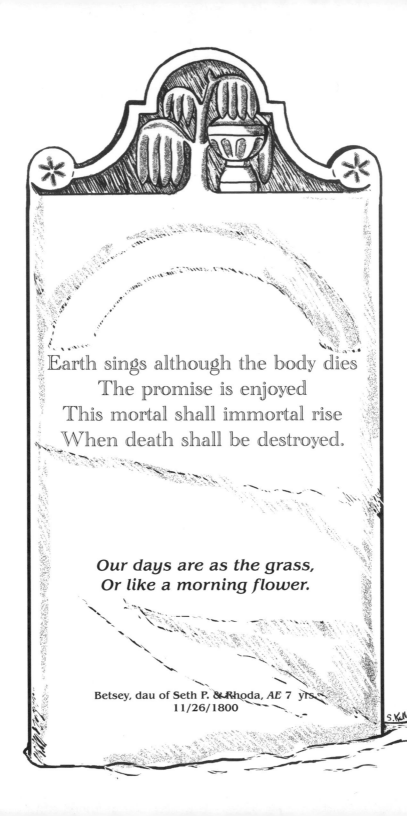

Earth sings although the body dies
The promise is enjoyed
This mortal shall immortal rise
When death shall be destroyed.

Our days are as the grass,
Or like a morning flower.

Betsey, dau of Seth P. & Rhoda, *AE* 7 yrs
11/26/1800

S. Kelly 05

Town of Ballston

S eparated from the Town of Saratoga in 1775, the Town of Ballston was named after an early settler, the Rev. Eliphalet Ball. Mineral springs had been discovered within the township as early as 1769, prompting an influx of visitors and entrepreneurs by the end of the Revolutionary War. A hamlet grew up west of Ballston Lake and around the Ballston Springs, offering the benefits of a small health resort to visitors in the years before neighboring Saratoga Springs gained pre-eminence. The Sans Souci Hotel, center of the village's resort activities, became world famous as an elegant attraction for famous Americans such as Henry Clay, Daniel Webster and Washington Irving, who left his initials engraved in a window at another old hotel now called Brookside Museum. Ballston Spa eventually became the seat of county government, and today attracts artists to the Glass Blowing Museum and other creative facilities.

The Burned Hills

Before permanent settlement began south of the Ballston Springs many white traders and trappers moved through the land of the Mohawks. There is a legend that, in those early wilderness contacts, an incident occurred that gave the settlement of Burnt Hills its name. Two greedy white trappers were quick to spot the ready riches of the fur pelts already laboriously gathered by local Indians in the woods and waters around Ballston Lake. The pair decided that "trapping Indians," who had already done the hard work, was more profitable to them. Finding some local Indian trappers encamped south of Ballston Lake, they stealthily approached the campfire. The Indians were killed quickly and their packs of pelts were stolen away.

To cover the crime, the two men set fire to the campsite and surrounding woods, obscuring the site of the murder forever. The fire spread throughout several miles of forest before burning itself out. It is said that travelers crossing that area for years afterward saw ghosts of dead Indians moving over the burned hills of south-central Saratoga County. Fearing the evanescent wraiths, most travelers moved swiftly through the area, not wishing to spend the night in a haunted region. Today, Burnt Hills is a

3

suburban village and the ghosts have long passed on to the Happy Hunting Ground. White settlers, however, have created enough ghosts of their own since that time.

The Spy

As farmers and settlers poured into Saratoga County in the middle 1700s, and small scale industry began, friction with Great Britain was becoming heated. Farm families and business people became separated according to their loyalty to King George or to a new country that was not well represented, and thus heavily taxed, in the British Parliament. As war became a strong possibility, many on both sides took desperate measures to insure that their side would win the struggle.

A well-bred stranger named Jones came to the Long Lake area of the county (now called Ballston Lake) and built a substantial home on the north shore, near what is now called The Outlet. No rough-sawn lumber for Mr. Jones—only the finest in building materials were used, transported overland from Albany and the Hudson River at considerable expense. Then he landscaped the grounds, an art almost unknown to the struggling farmers of the region. Once established at this luxurious home site, however, Jones and his family took little part in the community activities. No wonder that local gossips attempted to unravel the intrigue that the stranger posed in their lives.

Once war was declared in 1775, armies began marching, and by spring of 1777 it became known that a great army, led by British Gen. John Burgoyne, was headed for Albany via Lake Champlain, Lake George and the Hudson River Valley. Throughout New York State and New England local patriots established "committees of safety" to see to their families' defense, and, especially, weeding out the Loyalists in the region. Vigilant observers noted that Jones, who had been absent from his home for months, had recently reappeared. By then, the Jones family had radically altered their lifestyle—servants had been dismissed and the grounds went unkept. What business had Jones been tending to?

In July a local man returning from Albany brought a handbill that branded Jones as a traitor, a royal spy. He was wanted for attempting to infiltrate American General Gates' defensive lines near Stillwater, where the Continental Army was erecting its defense against Burgoyne's invasion. The handbill noted that Jones had been briefly held by American sentries but had then escaped. When the Committee of Safety of the Town of Ballston accosted Mrs. Jones, she protested that she didn't know where her husband had gone.

One early August night, a local man, Mr. Wright, when paddling home across Long Lake, spotted a dark figure running along the eastern shore and slipping into the darkened Jones house. Realizing that the spy had eluded patrols and returned home, Wright summoned friends that arrived swiftly and entered the building, arresting Jones, who struggled in vain to escape. Though his wife and children wept and begged for mercy, Jones remained silent, giving his captors no information. He was transported by wagon to an Albany court where he was quickly tried and then hanged for treason. The next day, as Burgoyne began his assault on the American positions ten miles to the east of Long Lake, Jones' body was returned to his family for burial. He was interred in a small cemetery a few miles north of his home, and his family, perhaps fearful of retaliation, vacated the once sumptuous house and fled the area. Mr. Wright received a reward for aiding in Jones' capture and the State of New York auctioned the house for funds to fight the Revolution. But, for some strange reason, the buyer never occupied the house, which sat and decayed over the years.

Mr. Wright continued his nocturnal paddling to his fiancée's house across the lake. Late one night, as he returned home, he was surprised to spot a shadowy form moving stealthily through the brush toward the abandoned Jones house. The figure entered and soon a dim light shone inside the window. Wright paddled to shore, furtively approached the house and peered inside. He could see nothing in the dim candle light, and entered the open doorway. As he did so, the light was extinguished, though Wright encountered no living person inside. He concluded that this was the unquiet soul of Jones, still attempting to thwart the Patriot cause.

When this story, written by Ballston Spa businessman Joel Lee, appeared in *The Philadelphia Album* newspaper in 1827, the article noted that Wright remained so shaken by his experience that he never crossed the lake at that spot again. In the village of Ballston Spa, some wags figured that Wright's vision was induced by liquor, which he had purchased with his reward money. But for the most part, locals felt he'd really encountered the ghost of Jones, the man who guessed wrong about his country's future.

The Ghosts of V-Corners

At the south end of the village of Ballston Spa is a busy intersection, a v-shaped historic crossroads of the town's commerce. Beside the V-Corners Greenhouse is a Victorian structure built as a summer home by a New York City man in the late 1800s. After World War II it was used as a boarding house, then, in 1969, the Schultz family purchased it and began a landscape and greenhouse business there. The house was a pleasant place to raise a family, said Rosemary, as her children could roam the nearby forest and streams. "We didn't know we were getting a former resident or two when we bought that house, however," she added.

During the first six months of their residence the Schultz family experienced many disturbances. Soon after they occupied the house, Rosemary escorted an elderly aunt through the interior, where, at the rear of the first floor the door to the attic stairway stands next to a bedroom door. When the aunt neared the doorways, she sprang back startled, as if some person or force had repelled her. "There's something bad in there! Never use this room for a bedroom," she exhorted. But there was only so much space within the house, and eventually Rosemary designated that room as her son's bedroom. Curiously, the boy never related anything alarming during the fifteen years he slept there. Rosemary recalls, however, that as she approached *that* doorway one day, she spied what appeared to be "a black dust" swirling in the hallway. The cloud then quickly vanished through the bedroom door at the end of the hall. Just my imagination, she thought at the time. Only years later, in a conversation with her son, did she discover that *he* remembered watching many shapes and forms moving about the bedroom as he lay in bed. "But they never bothered me, so I didn't talk about them," the boy said.

When Warren and Rosemary's daughter was thirteen, she threw a sleepover party for her girlfriends. The teens chatted late into the night, and then gradually dropped off to sleep. Suddenly the daughter was roused by the sound of tapping on her bedroom door. She opened it only to find nobody there; the entire house was quiet. All her girlfriends, who knew nothing of the house's reputation, remained asleep. When the girl told her mother about the incident the next morning, Rosemary was willing to believe it had been a ghost, though other family members rolled their eyes.

Oftentimes at night the family heard strange noises that were never heard during daytime. Many times, in the morning they found furniture or small objects moved from their customary positions. Still, as with most residents of haunted houses, the Schultz family was not greatly disturbed by these strange events, as they were all tolerable. And there was a business to run.

One day, as Rosemary worked on a project indoors, the children were in school and Warren was busy in the greenhouses. "Mommy, Mommy!" a small child's voice called. Engrossed in her work, Rosemary replied, "It's okay, honey, I'll be there in a minute." A second later she did a reality check. That wasn't *her* child—the kids were in school! She searched the house thoroughly but found no youngster who could have called her.

By the 1980s their children had grown and the Schultz's decided to sell the old house and business. Warren and Rosemary recalled the happy days they had spent there. "Only you never experienced all the strange things going on here, did you, Warren?" Her husband surprised her when he admitted that he had heard and seen many strange things, but remained silent because fathers were supposed to safeguard their families, and he never could figure out what to do with a ghost.

Eventually, Janet Levine opened "Janet's V-Corners Gift Shop" in the old home. One day she was startled to notice a lady on the attic stairs. The woman smiled pleasantly at her then suddenly disappeared. Later, Janet discovered that most of her clerks had experiences with a spirit whom they believed to be female. One of the employees complained that no matter how carefully the store was picked up and ordered at closing time, the next morning objects were found in the middle of the downstairs hall and inventory in the upstairs was also found moved.

One day a customer visiting the store said she had seen a strange woman looking out the second floor window. Janet informed her that nobody was upstairs. Intrigued by this response, the woman said she had a psychic sister and asked Janet's permission to return to the store later that day with the sister, to investigate the strange woman's identity and purpose. Around dusk, the pair arrived and went upstairs to the empty storage space. "They saw a filmy woman looking out the window and then felt the temperature

7

drop twenty degrees. The hair on their necks rose and they returned downstairs shaken," said Janet.

Wanda LaRock, who became store manager in 1992, heard footsteps in the attic when she knew no one else was up there. "I knew it was a ghost of some sort, because they told me the building had a spirit when I came to work there. But, I'd had ghost contacts in other places and wasn't really afraid. From time to time the wind chimes we sold would ring spontaneously, though there was no breeze in the store. Over the years that I managed the gift shop, I was never afraid. Once I went down to the village library and did some research on the house. I discovered that in the 1800s, when it was a summer home for a New York City man, a woman lived in the house year round, likely as a mistress to the New Yorker.

"One day I heard a woman's quick steps in the hallway, and looked up to see a sandy-haired woman in a long, white lacy dress walking away from me toward the front door. After that I saw her numerous times, always in the same garment. But she was more like a companion and never made me feel uncomfortable. I often wondered if she had wanted a marriage that never took place, and appeared to us in a wedding dress that she never got to wear. Whatever end she came to, I believe she was angry at the New Yorker for not marrying her, and simply never left the house after her death."

John was a handyman at Janet's gift shop, and one day as he worked at the foot of the stairs to the second floor, looked up just in time to avoid a wooden box plummeting down the stairs directly at him. He wondered if the woman ghost, whom everyone, by now, called "Mary," disliked men. Wanda, remembering some of the house's history, thought Mary probably had good reason to do so. On another occasion, John encountered a filmy adult woman in what appeared to be a wedding dress, though the figure quickly vanished.

Paula also worked as a store clerk at Janet's and was startled one day to hear the floor beside her creak. She looked up from her work to see a man and boy standing nearby, though they quickly vanished. On another occasion she heard a voice whispering in her ear. Expecting it to be Janet, she looked up, but nobody was there.

In 2000, shortly before the store closed, two strange events occurred. Clerks saw a woman dressed in black inside the store—a ghost they had never seen before. Then, the owners of a neighboring house told Janet that they, also, had been troubled with the ghost of a small girl, but had arranged a house blessing. After that, the little girl apparently left.

When Janet closed her business, the structure was converted to residential use once more. The tenant family that moved into the house had a small daughter who was four years old at the time. Befuddled, the child never could understand why, when she looked in a mirror, she could see another little girl, dressed in old fashioned clothes, looking back at her. Apparently the child that fled the neighbors' house had moved into Janet's old store, seeking new playmates.

Children Return

Shepherd's Hill rises on the western side of Ballston Spa. Today, automobile traffic noisily crests the hill and drivers seldom take time to study the beauty of the old Lee house near its top. Joel Lee, mentioned in the earlier spy story, was a successful village businessman in the early 1800s and built a magnificent house on the hill to catch the summer breezes and offer a vista across what was rapidly becoming a village of mills, small hotels and shops.

Years later, the Gilson family bought the house and raised two sons there. At the beginning of World War II, both sons enlisted in the military service, and it is said that one of the boys died in battle, though I was unable to confirm this. In the early 1970s the Gilsons put the historic property on the real estate market. The new owner raised an inquisitive eyebrow when Mr. Gilson, in turning over the keys to the property, said mysteriously, "You'll like this house, there's always *something* happening here."

And the new family found that to be very true. Parents and children alike often experienced cold spots in the house, even during summer's heat. The scent of perfume often was encountered in rooms where it had never been used. "We really don't believe in the supernatural," said the mother, "but around holidays, especially, we have an increase in strange experiences." She recalled that near Christmas in 1996, as she and her husband relaxed in front of the family room television, the sounds of laughing and playing children could be heard in the kitchen. Their children weren't home—who could it be? Both rose from their chairs and went to investigate. The kitchen was empty and the door was closed. "All I could figure is that this was a flashback, maybe emotionally, to happy Christmas times that other families had enjoyed here," the wife said. Or was this perhaps what this author terms a "house memory, projected by the ghosts," or a playback of vibrations and noises of the past, elicited by the family for just a moment in time?

The new family's children remember many small annoyances during their growing up years in the house. One son awoke during the night to feel something on the left side of his body, then that something brushed against him lightly. He opened his eyes to see a wispy image but was unable to focus his eyes. As it became clearer—a figure about five feet tall, possessing no distinct features, manifested. Thinking it was his mother, he called, "Mom?" His voice awoke his brother sleeping nearby. "Who you talking to? There's nobody here," mumbled the brother. By then, the figure had vanished. Both daughters slept in an adjoining room and both of them experienced a filmy figure standing alongside their beds at night. One girl described the figure as "tapering outward toward the floor, as if it wore a nightgown." All family members have heard the footsteps on the wooden floor of the hallway, but the walker is never seen.

In the early 1990s the mother had what seems to have been the strangest experience. On a warm summer's day she stood washing dishes at the kitchen sink, which overlooks the back yard and part of the driveway. The windows over the sink were cranked open to allow the pleasant breeze to blow through. "For a moment I glanced up at the beauty of the back yard, and caught nature's peace reflected in the glass of an opened window," she said. "Then a movement caught my eye. There was my parked car reflected in the glass, and next to it, a young man in a tan or khaki uniform stood unmoving. He seemed to have a faraway look on his face. We have a visitor, I concluded."

She rushed to the back door to welcome the stranger, but nobody was outside. Opening the door, she saw no one in the back yard either. She returned to the sink, suspecting that her mind had played a trick on her. Again looking up from the sink, a minute later, she again saw the uniformed man, still in the same location near her car. "I must have missed him, I thought, so I went quickly to the door and looked outside. Nobody was around. When I returned once more to the sink, I could still see him reflected in the window glass, but I knew another trip to the door would be futile, so I just looked at him. He seemed to have a little smile on his face, but he didn't move. It was if he were taking in the house and grounds, maybe just remembering. He stood there for a full five minutes. Then he just dissolved. I never saw him again."

My research indicated that one of the Gilson boys was in the Army Infantry and the other in the Army Air Force during World War II. One of them may have been near death at that time the housewife observed his youthful appearance some 35 years after the war. The man's mind or spirit may have returned to survey the scene of happy childhood memories before venturing on to the next stage of Life.

Carney's

On September 14, 1901, just before noon, when the southbound train stopped in Ballston Lake, a grim group of men ushered Vice President Theodore Roosevelt from the train to the nearby Shendahora Hotel. President McKinley had been shot and Roosevelt needed both a meal and up-to-date news via the telegraph at the D&H train station. Eating rapidly, the party departed on the next train from the north. This was perhaps the most distinguished guest in the community up to that time. Roosevelt went on to Washington to become a notable American president. The Shendahora Hotel evolved more slowly as a famous eating place.

Patrons of the nearby trolley connecting Ballston and Schenectady, as well as travelers arriving at Briggs' Livery Stable behind the hotel, created a steady stream of customers at the ten room establishment. Between 1911 and 1936, the hotel had several owners. One of these, a Mr. Murphy closed his hotel's bar during the years of Prohibition, spurring illegal still operators to increase their production to fill the void. In 1936 Tom and Katherine McDonough purchased the building and kept a very orderly house, having a "swear box" on the bar for any offensive speaker to pay a fine. Then, after the hotel function ended in 1971, the bar and restaurant experienced a fairly rapid succession of turnovers in ownership until, in the late 1970s, owner Bruce Allen renamed the building, "Cousin Bruce's Empty Arms Hotel." Allen seems to have invested his heart in the place, a factor that may well explain some of the present day phenomena.

Although ill for some time, Allen was nevertheless energetic with many "irons in the fire." He died suddenly at age 36, leaving many dreams unfulfilled. For a few years, the building was known simply as The Main Street Tavern, and the glory of yesteryear seemed to wear thinner.

11

Then, Bob and Rosemary Carney, newcomers to Ballston Lake, brought an Irish theme to the old hotel, expanding the dining room and doing extensive interior and exterior redecoration. Seven upstairs bedrooms became a single large meeting room, and the Gaelic atmosphere downstairs lured many first-time diners into what had previously been a dive. The original tin ceiling was repainted and the original large oak bar was re-varnished, and the first customers were served in October 1982.

Not long afterward, at the end of a successful business day, Bob remained after hours, checking out each room and turning off the lights. Emerging from the liquor storage room, he was startled to see a large man hunched over the jukebox, which provided most of the light in the dining room. "It sure looked like Bruce Allen to me," Bob observed with a twinkle in his eye. "Rosemary and I had known him when we first came to Ballston Lake. He vanished almost as soon as I looked at him. Then, a year of so later, our bartender Kathy looked toward the rear windows of the dark dining room and was surprised to see the filmy silhouette of a man. She knew all customers had left and that the door was locked, so the sight startled her. Thankfully, the spirit vanished again quickly—fast enough for Kathy to suspect, this first time, that the entire episode had been her imagination." Kathy no longer thinks that's true.

Several people have seen the ghost man, and a few have spoken to him, though he doesn't reply, and vanishes if they do. He is always quiet and seldom moves; it's as if he is simply observing his old business place. The dining room was added after Bruce's tenure, and one suspects he is checking out the posters of Ireland and the historic pictures that the Carneys have used in decoration. More than likely, his spirit self is thinking, "Gee, I shoulda thought of that!"

TOWN OF CHARLTON

To us for
sixteen anxious months,
Her infant smile was given.
And then she bade farewell to earth
And went to live
in heaven.

"Our loved ones we gave"

Calliel & Cordire
Twin daut's of B.D. & C.A. , died 1863
AE 1 yr. 8 mns.

Town of Charlton

I n 1770, the first Europeans arrived in western Saratoga County and Thomas Sweetman formed the first settlement there four years later. Indian raids were a hazard to the first settlers, an issue not resolved until after the Revolutionary War. With peace came an influx of hardy farmers who built the hamlet of Charlton. Today, many of those original houses and stores are preserved along County Route 51.

The Veterans of Blue Corners

Old Farmer Tretiak didn't have to look; he knew they'd be there— the same figures he saw from his barn door each evening at twilight. But he *did* look down Old Route 67 again this night and, sure enough, there they were. Performing their usual activities, two soldiers dressed in blue uniforms, walking arm in arm, crossed the road from the old Brotherson Cemetery to the opposite shoulder, where they disappeared. One of the soldiers seemed stronger than the other, supporting his companion by the elbow or forearm. Over time, Tretiak had come to refer to them as his "Civil War Ghosts," because of their uniform color.

As usual, the farmer entered the house and told his family what he'd seen, and again, they smiled and nodded, only half hearing him and completely disbelieving him. But as the situation was so abnormal, he felt impelled to share his experience each night. A few years later Tretiak died and the story slipped from the memory of all but a few. One young man, Andy, who had heard this tale and knew of my interest in the Civil War, told it to me. I was intrigued enough to interview the family and neighbors. Something in the tale led me to believe it was more than just one elderly man's hallucination.

Visiting the Brotherson Cemetery, I found a burying ground that had seen better days. Only the tombstones of recent vintage still stood erect. Older stones were cracked, fallen or had partially disappeared. My research showed that the cemetery had once been the burial site for congregants of St. Mary's Episcopal Church, which had been razed a hundred years earlier, and of which no sign remains today. The issue presented to me was this: if

15

two soldiers had been buried there, why did they still walk each night? What was the fascination for getting to the other side of the road?

A great research tool for local historians is the microfilmed record of Saratoga County cemeteries, compiled by a man named Durkee in the late 1800s. All the gravestone epitaphs and dates from the County's graveyards at that time were recorded, and the document was placed on microfilm in the 1960s for researchers to examine. As I viewed these records I scanned the burials in the Brotherson Cemetery, as it is now called. Only one military burial was recorded—that of a Capt. Philip Brotherson who served in the 32nd N.Y. Militia in the War of 1812. No Civil War burials, though many veterans of that conflict might still have been alive when Durkee made his notes. Scanning to the bottom of the listings, I had found only one soldier. My finger remained on the "down" button of the microfilm viewer and the Brotherson records left the screen. Next up was the Fosburgh Cemetery. I wondered where *that* one was located. I stopped the film and read. The Fosburgh Cemetery was *right across the road*! But I had visited the site, and hadn't observed another cemetery. Moving through the Fosburgh burials I found just one soldier interred there: Colonel Samuel Richards, who served in the 32nd N.Y. Militia in the War of 1812. It seemed likely that Brotherson and Richards had known one another. Maybe these two men, whose military uniforms were also blue, were the night walkers, and not Civil War veterans. On my next trip to the ghost apparition site, downhill behind a cow pasture, near a creek, I located the remnants of a cemetery, with broken and scattered gravestones.

I researched these men at the N.Y. State Archives in Albany, and discovered that there are few histories of The War of 1812 military units to read. However, I did find enough history on the unit I wanted. Composed of civilian soldiers, the 32nd was quickly trained and rushed to the northern borders of New York State to face the invasion of battle-hardened British soldiers attacking from Canada. The unit was deployed both at Ogdensburg on the St. Lawrence River and at Sackett's Harbor on Black River Bay near the mouth of Lake Ontario, where a fort had been constructed to guard the outlet into the St. Lawrence. Fierce fighting erupted at both sites. Throughout the period from 1812 to 1814 the Americans held their ground, though the British units were fresh from the fields of Waterloo, where they had vanquished Napoleon's armies.

Brotherson and Richards were mustered out at war's end and returned home to Saratoga County. I found no record of either man having been wounded or applying for a veteran's disability pension, making me curious

16

as to the infirmity of the one who leaned on the other along Old Route 67. Both of the men eventually went on to become successful businessmen and both were elected Justices of the Peace in the Town of Charlton. In 1850 Col. Richards died and was interred in the Fosburgh Cemetery. Brotherson followed him four years later and was buried across the road.

Here then, lost to living memory, was a tale of comrades-in-arms, two men that had served their new nation in a time of danger, and who later kept the peace in rural western Saratoga County. They finished their earthly sojourn buried less than three hundred yards apart along a road that is now seldom traveled. Blue Corners has lost its church, stores, tavern and mills, and today it is a residential and pastoral area. At the quiet time of dusk, on this back road, those sensitive to the world beyond might also occasionally see these old friends, still living in the 1800s, and taking an evening stroll in the Town of Charlton.

The Church

Those traveling west from Ballston Spa and Harmony Corners on Route 67 cannot miss its spire, as the church was built high on a hill. Known today as "Scotch Church," a name that spread to the crossroads on which it is built, the Presbyterian Church was the house of worship for hardy Scots who settled the Town of Charlton. Built in the 1880s, the structure still houses a vigorous congregation.

Readers seldom think of churches as prime locations for hauntings, but some energy seems to remain in this building, giving us all an opportunity to think more broadly about ghosts. These spirits at Scotch Church seem to remain in a happy state, even greeting a solitary sensitive visitor. The experiences of several church members led me to examine the building and inquire into the events reported there. Mind you, these informants were not sensation seekers, but simply congregants wondering who the entities are, and why the mysterious phenomena persist.

About twenty years ago a young college student agreed to clean the church on Saturdays in exchange for a stipend with which to pay his college loans. "I used to clean on Saturdays, and it was a big job that used to take most of the day," he said. "Something funny, though, I felt *observed* from the minute I entered the church alone—not threatened, but just that someone was watching what I did. I never felt it at Sunday services, though." On quiet Saturday mornings he'd often hear noises emanating from the Pastor's Study, though he never found the pastor (or anyone else, for that matter) in the room. "Then, from the Nursery, there was always the sound of children playing happily. When I looked in, everything was still—nobody there! I tried to believe it was my imagination."

He cleaned as best he could, although "the vacuum cleaner plug would sometimes jump from the wall socket, even when I wasn't pulling on the cord. Or, at other times, the vacuum would turn itself on or off when I wasn't anywhere nearby!"

After cleaning the Sanctuary, he turned off the lights and went on to another room. If he looked back, however, the overhead Sanctuary lights were once more ablaze. It often took him more than one trip to the breaker box before those lights would remain off.

When the student became engaged, he found his fiancée interested in expediting his cleaning, as the two could finish in a half day and have the remaining time to spend together. His fiancée occasionally babysat a little girl, and on those mornings brought the child to the church, where the child played happily in a Nursery filled with toys. "One day we heard her let out a scream and come scrambling back into the Sanctuary to us. We asked, 'What's wrong, honey?' and she responded that 'Those other kids—they scared me!'" A check of the Nursery found no one else there, especially children. "So, we said, 'That's enough for today!' and got our coats and left. As we drove out of the parking lot, the little girl raised herself up in the back seat of the car and waved out the rear window to someone.

"We asked who she was waving at, and she said, 'The other kids. I don't understand it, we used to play so nicely, but today they scared me.'" The child said no more and the adults let the matter drop, but still wondered how to understand these events. It is entirely possible that the child witnessed ghost children dissolving in mid-air. But what children, and from where?

I considered that such events can often be traced to an epidemic somewhere in the past, where large numbers of children in the congregation or living nearby, might have perished. I interviewed a 90 year-old member of the congregation, who assured me that no such mass death had occurred within her memory, which went back almost to the construction of the building. There is a large cemetery kitty-corner across the road. Might the spirits of the children have originated there, and assemble at the nearby church where so many toys and tricycles are unused most days?

And how do we think about the noises in the Pastor's Study and the electrical phenomena which took place in the Sanctuary? It would not be out of line to suspect these might emanate from the timeless, ongoing work of a pastor or elder from days gone by who still keeps watch over the building that he loved so well. Whoever the adult(s) or children are, they have found a place of deep meaning and happiness at Scotch Church Corners, certainly one of the best criteria for the establishment of any church.

TOWN OF
CLIFTON PARK

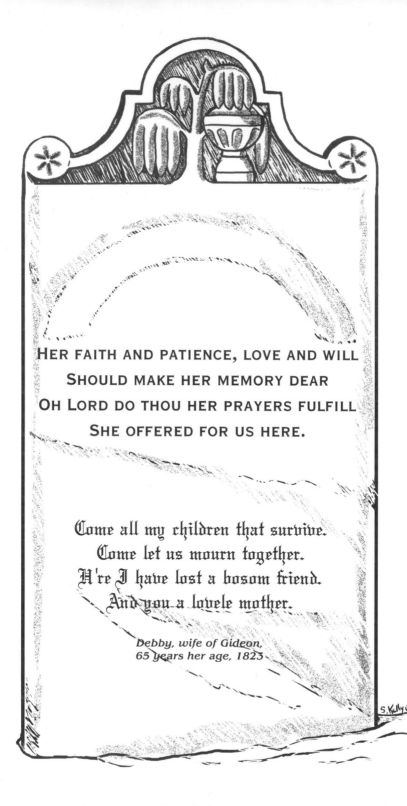

HER FAITH AND PATIENCE, LOVE AND WILL
SHOULD MAKE HER MEMORY DEAR
OH LORD DO THOU HER PRAYERS FULFILL
SHE OFFERED FOR US HERE.

Come all my children that survive.
Come let us mourn together.
H're I have lost a bosom friend.
And you a lovele mother.

*Debby, wife of Gideon,
65 years her age, 1823*

Town of Clifton Park

I n 1828, the Town of Halfmoon was subdivided and the Town of Clifton Park created. Known at first as "Clifton," the name had "Park" appended in 1829. A rural area, the town had a famous academy in Jonesville in 1841, attracting business people beyond those already involved in the Erie Canal activities along the town's southern borders. Today, the community has blossomed and is a commercial and residential center with easy access to the Interstate, permitting many in the town to work in the Capital District.

The Lady in the Robe

Prior to 1910, a number of "newer" homes were built along Riverview Road overlooking the Mohawk River Valley. George Ward, a musician, and his late wife Vaughn, a folklorist, author and musician, purchased one of these homes in 1972, when both were in their thirties. The previous owners had done little modernization of the structure, so Vaughn spent her first hot summer there doing interior redecoration before she and George occupied the house.

Whenever she opened the closet doors, it became apparent to Vaughn that the previous owners had been smokers, as the smell clung to the old wooden shelves. She therefore decided to completely repaint the closet interiors to freshen the house by eliminating odors. One hot July day, she worked on a particular closet and, hearing a faint sound behind her, turned abruptly to see an older woman wearing a blue bathrobe standing there. "It was as if she had tears on her cheeks," said Vaughn, feeling at once empathetic. "Because of all my folklore collecting, I suspected she might be a ghost, but she seemed solid enough to me. Then I heard her speaking to me in what must have been telepathy, because I didn't see her lips move. 'Oh, I am so glad that someone is *finally* fixing things up! I wanted to do this for so long, but I was unable to,' she exclaimed, and then she just faded out."

23

Tantalized by such intimate contact with a former resident, Vaughn decided to investigate to ascertain if her vision was accurate. She discovered that the previous woman owner had been ill in her final years, and had died there.

As many residents of Riverview Road in the 70s were newcomers, the Wards initiated a custom of 'open house' to welcome other young families such as theirs. This permitted older and younger residents to mingle and share stories of their past, while providing a new intimacy for the neighborhood.

Vaughn asked an old-timer if the figure of a woman in a blue bathrobe meant anything to him. "If I saw her, *that* would be the day I gave up drinking," he proclaimed with a scowl, and strode away, leaving his wife to continue the conversation. The wife explained to Vaughn that the old woman who had lived in the Ward house seldom got out of her nightclothes during her final years of illness, and often roamed her house and yard clad in a blue bathrobe. "That made a believer out of *me*," Vaughn chuckled.

Sadly, Vaughn Ward, who became my good friend and mentor, has now passed beyond the vale. I suspect she has set up her own field station and is joyously researching the interesting stories of others who have passed into The Beyond while she makes beautiful music.

The Ghost of Riverview Road

Crossing to the eastern part of Riverview Road, one soon encounters The Riverview Country Club and its extensive golf course. Few moderns know that the site was once the Zoller farm, owned by Frank and Jessie Zoller. The land was first developed for dairying by the Knowlton family during the early 1800s, but the Zollers turned it into a showplace that was the envy of neighboring dairy farmers. The Zollers called it 'Walhalla Dairy' and its purebred cows produced legendary amounts of milk. The farm was well known even in Europe, where Frank exported many prize bulls.

In 1932, Frank made a mistake in handling one of his temperamental breeding bulls and was gored by the animal. Carried to the house, he was dead within hours. Jessie made every effort to carry on the business after Frank's death, hiring a Mr. Magnusson as overseer of dairy operations. The farm was prosperous until the 1960s, when a turn of fortune forced Jessie to sell the entire operation.

Buyers from all over the world descended on Walhalla Dairy for the great auction, and the livestock were sold quickly, then the house, barns and land. The new owners had plans for the property—a new golf course, so the buildings were bulldozed, except for the house, which became a clubhouse for Walhalla Country Club. Verdant pastures were reconfigured for fairways and putting greens. *But*, the new operation seems to co-exist with the former one in space and time.

Golfers arriving for an early tee-off on Saturday mornings sometimes see an old man trudging along the roads and paths that once marked Walhalla Dairy. Those who knew him swear it's Frank Zoller. He seems to be in a world of his own, walking to sites where the old barns were likely located. The head groundskeeper arrives early, about 5 a.m., to ready the Club for early golfers, and he often sees footprints made in predictable work patterns in the dew-wet grass. The early-rising Frank Zoller may have moved over to another plane, on which he continues the work he enjoyed for so long. And if he sees a duffer "cutting grass" with a driver or iron, Frank likely scoffs and would remind the golfer—if he had time—that he could accomplish much more with a grass cutter and tractor. Then he'd probably add, "And that's no bull!"

Hollie

One of the town's pioneers was Edward Rexford, who purchased 300 acres of land in the Apple Patent in 1763, a time when Clifton Park was the frontier, where settlers were fearful of Indian attacks. As with many other local frontiersmen, Edward constructed a log cabin from timber cut on what became known as Rexford Flats. As the Revolution approached, there were increasing numbers of Indian attacks, aided and abetted by Loyalists to the north and along the Mohawk River to the west. By staying on his land, Rexford, a Lieutenant in the Albany Militia's Eighth Regiment, knew he was in danger of capture or death, but in the end, survived all the hazards of war with his property intact. After the war, he aspired to much more than rude frontier life, and began to amass a commercial bankroll, which he expanded in business ventures.

Eleazor Rexford, his descendant, erected a tavern on Rexford's hill, which overlooks the Erie Canal. There, he did a brisk trade among the 'canawlers,' especially after an aqueduct was constructed at the river ford below his tavern. After some years, the tavern was replaced by a Greek Revival home on the crest of the hill. Much of the American westward movement in the early 1800s began on the Erie Canal, carrying passengers and freight to the newly opened lands of the Midwest and Trans-Mississippi regions. The Rexfords were fierce abolitionists and often provided shelter for escaped slaves from the South along The Underground Railway.

Eleazor's son, Cyrus, turned his father's house into a fashionable Victorian "stick architecture" mansion. He had a spirited daughter, Fannie Hollister Rexford, called "Hollie" by her friends and admirers. Though she was expected to be a lady and adopt bourgeois manners, her spirit was too rambunctious to be held in check. Knowing this, Cyrus packed her off to a Philadelphia finishing school for girls. It wasn't long, however, before Hollie was expelled "for showing her skirts to the boys." Intelligent and attractive, she was courted by many Saratoga County businessmen, of whom William Graves, a prosperous merchant, emerged victorious. Upon her parents' deaths, William and Hollie inherited the estate, known then as Elmcrest.

When William died in the 1920s, Hollie ran the mansion and grounds as her castle. Her favorite grandson, Fritz Schaus, married in the 1930s, and Hollie invited him and his bride, Doris, to live in a small servant house on the property. Living in the small house behind Hollie's, the Schaus's got to know Grandmother well. Near Christmas in the early 1940s, Doris went next door to Hollie's house to hide her children's presents safely until the big day.

It was after dark as she passed through the spacious front rooms, which were illuminated only by a distant streetlight. Doris was amazed to see that all the chairs and sofas were occupied by people in old-fashioned clothing. No one moved or spoke—it was as if they were on display or, even worse, waiting for her! Quickly retrieving her presents, she fled. In later years, reminiscing with a friend about the scary incident, she said, "Well, *that* was a chapter in my life!" The wise friend retorted, "No, Doris, you were a chapter *in the house's life!*"

After Hollie's death in 1974, Fritz and Doris took possession of Elmcrest and began a puzzling series of experiences with missing and moved objects. Although most of the disappeared items were later found or "returned," it took several years for Doris to understand the true significance of the events. Hollie, it seems, was going to *retain* her dominance at Elmcrest and direct its goings-on. A post-funeral party was held in Hollie's honor, as she had *so* loved parties. A party guest using an upstairs bathroom could not get the light to work and 'made do' in the dark. As she turned the knob to open the bathroom door, the light popped on. Doris recalls that most of the lights in the house did this at times, turning on and off without reason. Electrical inspections could never find anything amiss.

Fritz's brother brought his wife to visit one summer, and the pair stayed at Elmcrest for several nights. During that time, a white cat, never before seen in the neighborhood, often appeared, clinging to the screen door. If the house occupants opened the door, the cat shot past them and into the interior of the house, running frantically through the rooms making a strange "He-e-e-n" noise, very unlike any cat sound that the Schaus's had ever heard. It spooked everyone in the house, as the cat's noise sounded so like the name 'Helen' who had been Hollie's old housekeeper. As suddenly as it had appeared, the cat disappeared and was never seen again.

Fritz and his brother decided to look up some old friends further down the hill, to reminisce about shared childhood experiences on the hill at Elmcrest. As they strolled, they heard a series of two sharp whistles. Could it be some neighbor's exotic bird? "It gave them the willies," Doris said, "because it was their grandmother's old whistling signal for them to return home." Fritz was a G.E. engineer and would not accept this sound as a supernatural event. With his brother, they set out to explore the neighborhood, to find the source of the sound. Near the foot of Rexford Hill they finally found a parrot, caged on a porch, making the noises. Still, this find did not entirely explain the phenomenon. Why had Fritz never before heard the sound when walking alone? And why did he and Doris never hear the sound again? It was a sound that made sense only to the two men, and it seemed to have occurred only when they had walked together that one afternoon.

Beside their bedroom, there was a stairway into the attic, and Fritz and Doris often heard heavy stomping footsteps ascending the stairway. They would rush to the foot of the stairs, but never saw anyone. In time, they learned that servants once slept in the attic, and a relative suggested that the attic space might also have been a shelter for the runaway slaves.

Fritz became ill in the 1980s, limiting his ability to work, so he and Doris decided to open Elmcrest as a Bed & Breakfast, a delightful accommodation for visiting engineers at the General Electric Company. An executive's wife came down to breakfast one morning, casually inquiring if they had a ghost. Doris inquired why the woman asked, and received a wonderful story in return.

The wife said she and her husband had gone to bed and turned off the bedroom lights the previous night. Soon, the bedroom door opened softly and a woman entered wearing a long white nightgown and accompanied by a similarly dressed child. The intruder came directly to the bed, tucked the comforter beneath the wife's chin, and left the room, closing the door silently as she left. Charmed by this Hollie appearance, Doris responded to the executive's wife, "It was just Grandma and one of her girls, trying to make you comfortable!"

Doris recalled that passersby often claimed to have seen Hollie's ghost in an upstairs window. She usually scoffed at such a thought, and told the person that she had placed Hollie's wedding dress on a mannequin in an upstairs bedroom. But, as the house sits back a bit from the road and the second floor is fairly high up, one wonders just what elements of the room's interior *are* visible from the street, and if it *was* the mannequin.

After Fritz died, Doris strewed his ashes around the grounds of the old Rexford House, as they had agreed. Coming to the end of the container, she tossed the remaining ashes straight up in the air. "As they fell, they fell at an angle, as if avoiding a space that looked just like the outline of a man," she recalls, wondering if Fritz's energy or spirit had not, likewise, stayed around Elmcrest, if only for a brief time after his passing.

A few years later, Doris became reacquainted with Deac Stauffer, a friend from childhood. They married and Deac became a new resident of the old house. Because of the great cost of upkeep, they eventually decided to put Elmcrest up for sale. At the conclusion of the sale process, the two prepared for their exit. Doris, realizing she was the last of the Rexford line, accepted that now, "strangers" would occupy the house. Deac finished some last details in the kitchen and dropped the house keys onto the counter. A minute later, when he turned, they were gone. The couple prepared to tell Hollie, "Okay, you're still boss here," and opened the kitchen door. There were the keys on the sill between the doors!

The Andersons took over Elmcrest and decided to continue the house as a B&B. Throughout their years there, as Judy Anderson says, they've experienced many "little things." Looking for her dust mop one evening, she could not find it in its accustomed place in the closet. It had simply disappeared. The next day, there it was—back in the closet. One day, as she cleaned an upstairs bedroom, she heard the sounds of music and dancing coming from the attic. But the old stairway to the attic had long ago been sealed off, and there was no way to enter the space. Knowing of Doris's experiences there, Judy yelled, "It's okay. We're taking good care of it, Hollie!" And, as usual, when she yells out those words, the phenomena stop.

Mr. Anderson, whose vision is poor, once traveled on business to California. He makes it a practice to take his glasses off only once he is *in* his bed, placing them on the nightstand, where he can reach them first thing in the morning. On his first morning at the Embassy Suites Hotel in California, he could not find his glasses. They just were nowhere to be found! He had a terrible time seeing until he crunched his foot against the frames *in an adjoining room of the* suite! He never figured how they got there, and the Andersons long suspected that Hollie's reach was much further than Saratoga County.

One night the town Historical Society met at Elmcrest for a meeting and tour of the house. One of the members reminisced about talking with Hollie shortly before her death. Hollie had expressed concern that she was either misplacing objects or, her fear, that *someone else* was taking them on her. So, perhaps another less-dominant spirit also lives at Elmcrest, but whether Hollie, or another quiet spirit, continues to hide objects, the borrowed items are always returned. Perhaps all that is needed now is the obligatory, "Please" and "Thank You."

In any case, it seems that gentility has finally settled on Cyrus Rexford's daughter.

A Nest of Robin's

"We leased this old farmhouse, which had been vacant for a while, in 2002 and had a lot of renovation work to do in order to get it in shape," Robin Kravetz told me. "Before us, there had briefly been one other business after the Niskayuna Elks Lodge moved out. The Elks had purchased the property from the family of the original owners and changed or removed some of the original features, such as the stairway to the second floor. It was our intention to restore as much of the 1840s flavor as we could, while creating an early American theme for our café and gift shop that are on the first floor."

Her husband, Mike, added, "There were a lot of little frustrations right off the bat. For example, my favorite screwdriver kept disappearing. I discovered that when this occurred, the tool would usually turn up in our office room three days later. I wondered why Robin was taking my tools, but she denied using them. And when her scissors disappeared, she thought I was the culprit, though I denied it. At first it was little things, but the saw incident had us both bug-eyed. I have this power saw," he said, showing me the saw in a carrying box. "One night we worked long hours of strenuous work and at the end, I decided I'd leave the saw on the floor where we were working, though I'd normally store it in its box. The next morning, the saw was missing, frustrating us no end, because we had so much work to do. We later discovered the saw *in its carrying box*, tucked into a little cupboard way at the back of the storage closet. Robin denied putting it away, and besides, she can't fit it into the box."

A short time later, Mike saw a grey, shadowy woman in a floor-length Victorian style dress flutter through the room. He asked, "Robin, is there someone else in here?" "Of course, we were working and the doors were locked," Robin interjected, "and I told him nobody had come into the building."

A few weeks after they opened for business, a customer eating at "The Robin's Nest," called Robin over to her table. Speaking confidentially, the lady asked, "Did you know, there's an old woman standing over there watching you? Whenever you go into the kitchen, the woman disappears, but as soon as you come out, the grey lady takes up her position—hovering—not standing, outside that closet door." Now, Mike *knew* there was a spirit there! When she paid her check, the customer told Robin that she knew some intuitive friends and would like to return after closing some evening and hold a "circle." Circles are intuitive gatherings in which the participants share their psychic impressions.

"I was okay with that," Robin said, "as long as they didn't do any séances or other bad stuff." So, in 2003, several ladies entered and sat in the café, relaxed, and began to share their impressions with one another. Then, they asked to go to the second floor, where they felt a great deal of energy. "They shared their impressions with us afterward," Robin said. "There are a number of spirits here, but not all of them are related to this house, the group told us. One woman described seeing the Victorian woman that Mike had seen."

The women of the circle informed Robin and Mike that there was the spirit of an American Indian present, though he didn't stay long. His message was to inform them that the nearby creek once served as a boundary between local Indian tribes or villages. After delivering this information, he left.

"The group also told us about a little girl," Mike said. "She appeared lost, alone and scared, and they told us to address this child every day, reassure her and encourage her to go back through the light to her family. We did what they recommended for a few weeks, though we don't know if the little girl is still here or not." The group informed Robin and Mike about a small boy who rode his hobby horse or stick pony from room to room upstairs, reciting some words that none of them could make out, and which seemed to be spoken in a "sing-song tone." The group members believed that if the children ever came downstairs, they never did so during the daytime.

None of the visitors could determine the children's names or the period of history they came from. They *were* sure, however, that the Victorian woman had no connection to the house, but had come with the Kravetz family from Scotia the year before! "I was never aware of a spirit in our old Scotia house," Robin said, "but the ghost lady doesn't seem to cause us any problem now that we've totally moved in and have our shop open. Maybe she's comfortable with the Colonial and Victorian style items I sell."

The circle also told the Kravetz's that deceased members of their families often visited them at the store. Robin's father was described precisely and one of the ladies gave Robin two messages from her father—issues that only Robin could authenticate. One of the group spoke of an older woman spirit making an unusual, affectionate gesture, and Robin's daughter, Melisa, immediately recognized Grandma Kravetz.

Intrigued with the intrusion of past history into their lives, Robin and Mike sought help from local historians and learned about many of the former residents. Built in 1845, the building had originally been the farmhouse of Jonas Southard, who had come to Clifton Park about 1800. He and his sons had a very large farm on the property at Rexford Flats, and much of their produce was sold to the old McLane Hotel located about one mile south along the Mohawk River—a landmark near Rexford Bridge that was torn down in the early 1970s. For over a century that hotel had served those traveling along the Erie Canal, as well as those traveling north and south between Saratoga County and Schenectady County. It was believed that the McLanes were related to the Southards by marriage and, later that year, Robin met one of the McLane descendants. Asking the woman if she

31

knew of any sudden deaths in the house, the woman joked that lots of horses and cows had died on the land and were buried there, but she knew of no family members dying in the building during the 1900s. Sometime later, the woman informed Robin that she had heard a rumor of a farmhand's daughter dying on the property, though she couldn't confirm it.

"I have a thing that I say," Robin confided. "As I approach a customer, I ask, 'Is there anything I can help you with?' and I say it a dozen times in the course of a day." One day recently I caught sight of the back of a woman wearing a long dark coat browsing in the front of the shop. There was something odd about the woman, as her coat was unfashionably long and dark. I gave my usual greeting, but she didn't answer. She kept her back turned to me, so I walked into the room, but she had disappeared. The room was empty. The part of the room where she had been standing was much cooler than the rest of the shop. I knew I'd encountered something uncanny.

"A few weeks later Melisa, who was seated in the café, looked into this mirror, which reflects the front display room. She told me we had a customer in the front room. Strange, I thought, I hadn't seen anyone enter. And, sure enough, when I went to the doorway, nobody was there."

Another time, a chef friend visited and offered to create a surprise for the Kravetz family in the café kitchen. A half hour later, Melisa and Robin heard the microwave timer chime, and told their friend that the timer had gone off in the kitchen. "It can't be," he retorted, "I never use a timer; instead, I use my watch." Melisa and Robin looked at one another dumbfounded—they both knew what they'd heard, but, as it turned out, the oven creation *was* ready to take out.

"We've had other things happen in the shop," Mike continued. "We have the radio set to a particular FM channel, but someone changes it, and Robin and I used to accuse each other of switching it. One day it even changed over to the AM dial!"

Robin and Mike thought over all their experiences for the past two years, then simultaneously grinned, remembering a rather boisterous and grouchy woman customer who did nothing but complain loudly from the minute she entered the shop. "At one point, she marched over to the bathroom door and tried the knob. It was locked, so she almost screamed, 'Come out of there. I have to go!' But there was not a sound from inside," Robin explained. "We didn't know what to do because we'd never locked that door and couldn't even remember where the key was. After further insults and loud complaints, the customer left. About ten minutes later Mike found the key and we unlocked the door, only to confirm that nobody was inside.

We looked at one another and asked, 'The grey lady?' We said a big 'thank you' to her for her mischievous loyalty to us."

Mike and Robin respect all the spirits who continue to live in the house. "They have never done any harm to us. Their unusual activities are mischievous at most," they told me.

Each year the Kravetz family opens the Robin's Nest grounds for a public education day relating to early American history. On such occasions one would probably meet costumed Indians or colonial soldiers. One might visit their newly-built replica frontier cabin and see how butter was churned or herbs were dried. "There are many things about our ancestors that we, today, forgot or never knew. They had to make do with so little," Robin reminisced. "We try to bring it alive for our customers and visitors and expect school groups to visit us starting in late 2004. Mike looked at Robin, gave a mischievous grin, and said, "Maybe we'll even tell them about the *real* historical characters that help us out here."

TOWN OF CORINTH

35

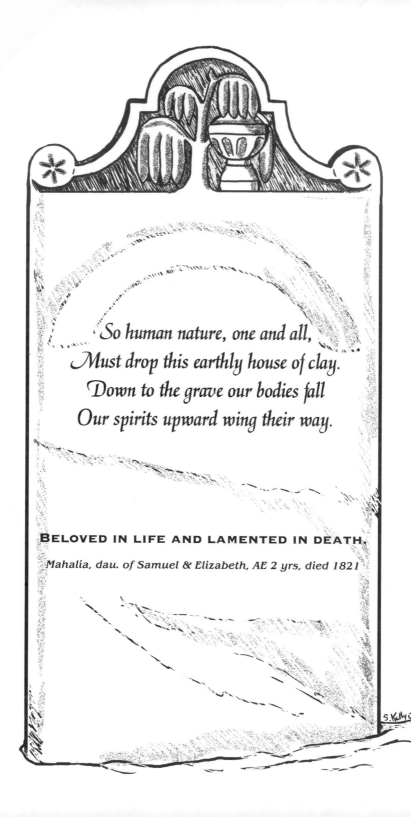

So human nature, one and all,
Must drop this earthly house of clay.
Down to the grave our bodies fall
Our spirits upward wing their way.

BELOVED IN LIFE AND LAMENTED IN DEATH.

Mahalia, dau. of Samuel & Elizabeth, AE 2 yrs, died 1821

S. Kelly 05

Town of Corinth

The good fishing and powerful waterfalls first brought Indians to "Ka-ben-de-cook," as Corinth was once known. Later called "Jessup's Landing," after a Tory (and before the Revolution), the town was eventually renamed by a minister's wife opening the Bible to the Book of Corinthians and choosing that name. Formed as a town in 1818, the community soon had dams at both waterfalls. Then, the Hudson River Paper Mill became the leading industry at the Palmer Falls in the late 19th Century. Purchased by International Paper Company, the mill provided employment for thousands over the years. Cluett-Peabody Shirt Company also operated a factory in the village for over sixty years. Both companies are now closed, victims of the continual "bottom line" profit margins sought by global business.

"Davenaws"

One can find the names Davignon Road and Davignon Pond in the northwest corner of the Town of Corinth. Up-staters have a propensity to mispronounce French Canadian names, and over the years have come to phonetically pronounce Davignon as "Davenaws."

An old timer in the area, now deceased, had two ghostly experiences in that locality. In the 1940s, as a young man, he walked along County Route 10, between Shippee Road and Davignon Road. His path carried him toward the Great Sacandaga Lake at Brooks Bay. As he strolled along the wooded road he noticed a woman wearing a long white dress, moving rapidly in his direction from the woods.

The young man knew everyone in his neighborhood and this lady was unknown to him. Something about the experience frightened him also, as he knew *nobody* would be in that dense forest. As she advanced, he could see her anguished face. She seemed to scream at him, though he heard no sound. Was she shouting his name? It seemed so. Just as she neared the road where he stood, she vanished! He had never had such an experience before, and his fear propelled him down the road to find friends he *did* know. Apparently no one ever saw the ghostly woman but him.

37

Another thrilling spot at Davenaws was the old "haunted house" on Davignon Road. The abandoned old red house had stood there for years, and was a curiosity for the young people of the neighborhood in the early 1900s. An elderly woman on Shippee Road told me, "When the ghosts were out, people would hear iron-rimmed wagon wheels crunching along Davignon Road and into the house's cobblestone driveway. But no wagon was ever seen."

There were times when the ghosts were quiet in the old house, and at such times the youngsters of the neighborhood used to play hide and seek there, often frightening one another with pranks. If anyone is running near the old house's foundation today, it is likely fishermen rushing over to Daly Brook on the first day of Trout Season. New York State Environmental Conservation officials annually stock the brook with trout and it's a fisherman's paradise. Others seek recreation by zooming uphill in their 4x4s on Davignon Road. What once was a scary site for youngsters of yesteryear is now a recreation area for their grandchildren.

Stuck!

Bob had had a long walk out to West Mountain Road. He was tired and needed help to recover his Jeep, which was stuck fast in the forest mud off Mesacosa Road. Now he headed into the Village of Corinth to get his buddies to help him rescue his vehicle, and he knew he'd have to face plenty of jibes about the stupidity of his off-road venture into a muddy forest road, but, in the end, he knew they'd help him. Before long, he hitched a ride into Corinth and dropped off at the Star Hotel bar. His friends roared at his predicament, then finished off their beers, went outside and assembled their towing chains, and soon a small convoy of vehicles headed back up West Mountain and over to Mesacosa Road.

Bob's Jeep was found three miles back in the forest, with mud higher than the wheel wells. With only a few flashlights to illuminate the site, it was demanding work even for husky young men whose courage was boosted by alcohol. They had to rock the Jeep, and then, rock it some more, all the while straining backs and muscles to propel the jeep forward. Finally, it rose from the ooze, and Mike, one of the friends, leapt into the driver's seat.

"Once she pops free, you *gun* that engine," were the instructions, "keep the pedal to the metal until you get out onto the blacktop." As soon as the Jeep was freed, Mike sped out of the bog and zoomed up the road, but only to the next rise on the trail, where the group saw his brake lights come on and the vehicle stopped. The group groaned, as they figured they'd have to push the Jeep again.

Mike sat, waiting for his grumbling friends to catch up. Rain began to fall and the group slipped and fell as they started up the rise toward the Jeep. Then Bob and the others saw something that frightened them—the Jeep started to rock! The back of the vehicle began to bounce up and down and it took all Mike's concentration to stay in the driver's seat. It was as if he were aboard a bucking bronco! It seemed some invisible force was copying their vigorous Jeep-rocking of a few minutes ago. Mike *stood* on the brake pedal, but the bouncing continued.

All at once, Mike regained control and floored the accelerator, and the Jeep sped down the trail and out of the woods. Slowly the rescuers got their ropes and chains together and slogged out of the rainy forest. An hour and a half later they returned to Corinth and sat on the steps of the now-dark Star Hotel. They knew they'd been through something extraordinary, but how could they talk about it? Bob says that even today, some twenty years later, the members of the group are afraid to discuss the experience they shared. Is it possible that there is some spirit, some force in nature or a ghostly energy back in the woods? How did it get there? And who is going to encounter it next?

The House on Miner Road

Herbert Loeffler lived in Greenfield, NY, for decades and knew many stories that I call "head-scratchers." Few of them involved *seeing* ghosts, but he did recall *experiencing* spirits that went 'bump' in the daytime! I'll leave it to the reader to decide what forces were at work here.

Herbert and his brother once owned a house on Miner Road, on the southern border of the Town of Corinth. When they bought the property after World War II it was already abandoned, and apparently had been so for some time. The two brothers believed they could fix up the house and gain some rental income from the property. In the course of their renovation, Herbert had strange experiences.

When he'd enter the house he'd always hear voices, as though in conversation upstairs. When Herbert went to check on the phenomenon, there would never be anyone there. All he would find in the upstairs was dust on the floor, but no footprints except his own. Yet, upon returning downstairs, he'd hear footsteps overhead, then voices in quiet conversation, though he never could make out individual words. Once or twice he sprinted back up the stairway but could never discover anyone hiding there. On one occasion he distinctly heard a baby crying upstairs, but his search for the child was fruitless.

The brothers left off their renovation of the building, thinking they should take the time to ponder all ramifications. "I don't think we ever thought of the words 'haunted house,'" he told me. Suddenly, in 1950, the house burned to the ground, ending the brothers' option to restore and create a rental property.

In our conversation, we agreed that old, abandoned houses are usually a signal that someone has given up on some hope or dream. Perhaps the former residents were personally haunted by financial or personal problems and left. It is my belief that such experiences of failure, sorrow or remorse are often the raw material for what many experience as a "haunting."

Gold!

A remarkable former resident of Lake Luzerne, Dick Richards lived many years in and around the Town of Corinth. He collected tales which he often told with a grin. "*Most* of what I tell is true," he'd say. But listeners were reminded that "Daddy Dick" was a charter member of The Adirondack Liar's Club, a group of tall-tale-tellers which regularly entertains in upstate New York. Dick was missing an arm, but that never interfered with his wonderful Bluegrass band and square dance fiddling.

He told me about an abandoned house on Comstock Road years ago in the time of Prohibition. "A stranger came to town one day and rented the old house. He seemed down on his luck, maybe a tramp, who knows? He kept pretty much to himself so most of us never got to know him well. And it was a mystery to us, some months later, where and how he got the money to buy the house from an estate.

"One night he showed up at Julius Craig's speakeasy in South Corinth and paid for his drinks with a gold coin! The regulars there were awestruck—where could this apparent drifter get gold coins in such hard times? To loosen his tongue, they began to buy drinks for him—hard stuff. Soon, the stranger began to spin his tale.

"He told of hunkering down in the old house and being frightened the first night by a ghost that swept through the front room. Each night about the same time, the ghost flashed past his chair and into the kitchen. Gaining courage, one night he followed the ghost's path and saw it disappear into the cellar. A few days later, summoning all his strength and courage, he took a flashlight and went into the cellar to watch for the ghost's next appearance. Right on schedule, the wraith came flying down the cellar stairs and disappeared into the stone foundation. Night after night the specter repeated the action, until the stranger finally figured the ghost was relentlessly trying to tell or show him something.

"After enough of these nighttime experiences, he gathered the courage to take a shovel and begin digging into the foundation at dawn. He tugged and pulled at the loose cobblestones in the wall where the ghost had disappeared, and, in the lantern-lit cellar, a clay pot soon came into view. Retrieving it, the man found the pot filled with gold coins! So, that was the end of the story—here he was at Craig's having a few drinks, which he could now well afford."

The tale made the rounds in Corinth, and in a few days the stranger was served with a summons—former heirs to the property were suing him to recover the apparently valuable land. They claimed the stranger had purchased the land fraudulently, and they hired Mr. Dunham, a top lawyer in town, to defend their avarice. The judge, however, found no legal grounds for the suit and tossed the case out of court.

Some days later, villagers noted that the stranger had left town. Vandals ransacked his house and literally tore the foundation wall apart, stone by stone, seeking more riches, though nothing more was discovered. Down the road, a smiling stranger moved on, thoroughly enjoying his brief, but profitable, sojourn in the Town of Corinth.

The Store

Barbara Reed, proprietor of Eno's Store in South Corinth, had a strange experience back in 1992. Living upstairs over the old country store afforded her a vantage point from which to keep a close watch on the business. Her apartment had a hall door that had always worked well; it never had rubbed on the floor or caught on the doorframe. "It was even a bit higher than it needed to be, with about an inch of clearance on the bottom," she said. "One day, when I tried to open it, it stuck fast after opening only about a foot. I giggled and said loudly, 'Come on, Gram, knock it off!' and the door opened fully."

Barbara's grandmother died six years before in a nearby house, but Barbara had felt her presence in *this* apartment. "I'd have thought it might be my grandfather or another female relative, as they both died in this apartment," she said. She related that her grandmother had had a wonderful sense of humor, so the "little things" that went on around the building, Barbara attributed to her.

Many strange incidents happened during that time in her life; some not easily explainable. Barbara kept a metal T-square inside the store's front door. In cold winter weather she used it to cut straight edges on polyethylene sheets that she fastened over the large store windows. It kept some of the cold out. The square leaned against a front wall for the rest of the year.

In the fall of 1997, after cutting the plastic sheets, she placed the square in its usual place. A minute later she looked over and it was gone! Over the next few weeks she turned her store inside out, genuinely provoked by the strange disappearance of a valued tool. It was nowhere to be found. A customer entering or exiting the store would normally not have seen or taken it. Barbara began to wonder if Gram was up to her humorous tricks again.

On the day I came to interview Barbara and her mother, shortly after New Year's Day in 1998, the owner was laughing. "I just got my square back—out of nowhere, there it was, returned to its old spot. But *now* my hole-puncher has disappeared—right off the counter! So, I'm back to negotiating with Gram again," she said with a smile.

Mulleyville

Just west of South Corinth, in what is now a thick woods, one can still find old cellar holes and evidence that a small hamlet once existed there. It was called Mulleyville, and was home for farmers, laborers and craftspeople. The population of Mulleyville was composed of woodsmen and their families, all hard-working people, but also lovers of entertainment that brought relaxation, community, and enjoyment to their laborious lives. In the days before radio, television or movies in the early 1900s, most rural folks had to entertain themselves.

One of the most famous entertainers in Mulleyville was Pete Baker, a noted fiddler and square dance caller. He had no formal music instruction, but acquired his art through constant work, though many said he began life with "the gift." "House dances" were a favorite diversion on Saturday nights, and Pete was usually fiddling away into the wee hours of the morning. Walking home in the early morning dew and mists was sometimes unnerving, because he never knew whether a ghost or a bear would jump from the woods. So as he walked along, he fiddled. And the sound of his music always alerted his family that Dad was returning home.

Pete used to tell of *seeing* a ghost only once, as he tried to drive his wagon across Sultz's Bridge, and that was enough to scare him for the rest of his life. As he reached the bridge, a ghostly form shot across the far end of the bridge. His team of horses stopped in their tracks. Whatever he did, Pete could not get the team to move. Taking burlap sacks from his wagon, he had to blindfold the horses and walk them across.

Remembering these events, Daddy Dick Richards, no mean fiddler himself, said that for months after Pete Baker died, his fiddle music could be heard along the roads leading to and from Mulleyville. Pete was undoubtedly adding to his musical resume by playing for dances in Heaven.

Fenton's Flats

Southeast of the Village of Corinth, County Route 24 will take you to Fenton Road, a side-road that heads toward the Hudson River. Dick Richards remembered a now-demolished Fenton homestead that once stood at the south side of that intersection. An even earlier family home stood farther north on the road, and it was a strange one, he said. Dating from the early 1800s, the home had been built entirely of chestnut wood, which was common then.

The family abandoned this older house in favor of the newer one near the County Road, and local children amused themselves for hours on end in the now vacant house. It might be a fort or a castle, a prison, cave or even a sailing ship in the youngsters' minds. Dick remembered, "We had much fun there, because there was always something *mysterious* taking place inside. One day when we were there, a picture fell off its nail on the wall, though the nail was slanted steeply upward. At other times the interior doors would be heard to slam, even though the air was heavy and there was no breeze blowing. And nobody else was inside the house. There was an air of mystery there—a free treat for all youngsters in the neighborhood. We never saw any ghost, though."

The old house had already "given up the ghost" by the time of Dick Richards's childhood, though, as with many old houses, it still retained the energies of long ago family life.

TOWN OF DAY

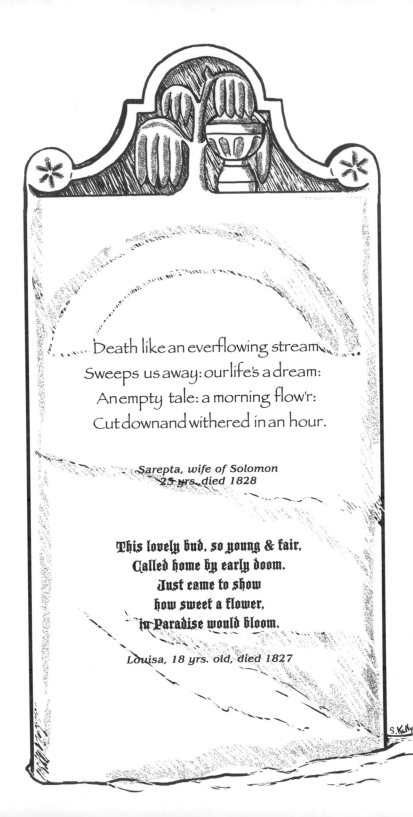

Death like an everflowing stream
Sweeps us away: our life's a dream:
An empty tale: a morning flow'r:
Cut down and withered in an hour.

Sarepta, wife of Solomon
25 yrs. died 1828

This lovely bud, so young & fair,
Called home by early doom.
Just came to show
how sweet a flower,
in Paradise would bloom.

Louisa, 18 yrs. old, died 1827

S. Kelly 05

Town of Day

T he Town of Day is one of the three towns in northern Saratoga County that lost real estate when the Sacandaga Reservoir (now called The Great Sacandaga Lake) was formed in 1930. In order to prevent devastating floods downriver along the Hudson, properties in these towns were bought by a regulating commission, then demolished, along with large trees, to form a water catchment basin for Adirondack Mountain runoff, which was especially heavy, and often dangerous, in the spring. A great earthen dam was built at Conklingville, and several old communities vanished under the filling waters, along with their histories and unique memories. Many residents moved away with broken hearts, defeated in a sorrow of lost homes and friends that persists even into the 21st Century. Don Bowman worked on the demolition crews and I am indebted to him for the memories he has carried all these years.

The Ghosts of Boulder Bay

Near old Conklingville there was a major landmark called Boulder Bay. When the glacier retreated from the area some 12,000 years ago, its massive size and weight carved out valleys and left a residue of huge boulders at this spot along what became the Sacandaga River. A creek once flowed into Boulder Bay, a juncture which was a wonderful fishing spot for years.

David Allen built a sawmill at that spot, and profited greatly from the ready supply of hemlock and Adirondack pine cut locally. Families that worked as log skidders, woodcutters and horse team drivers in his operation built small houses or shacks near the sawmill, and a small community sprang up. Don recalls that "One windy night, two of the shacks with overheated stovepipes took fire and burned to the ground. The folks in the second shack got out safely, except for some smoke trouble. But the folks in the first shack, father, mother and son, all died.

"On the next windy night, people in the camp began to hear a deep moaning sound, something they'd never heard before at Allen's Sawmill. 'Surely, it must be the wind blowing through the cracks in these old buildings' walls,' they said. But, though they tried very hard to devise rational

47

explanations, they had to discard them when the white, wispy shapes appeared. Often, at twilight, these forms flitted through Boulder Bay." Local people soon abandoned attempts to rationalize the eerie sounds and flitting, evanescent figures. They accepted that this phenomenon was truly the spirits of the dead logger family.

Soon, Allen's little settlement gained a regional reputation as a "haunted camp." A couple of well-educated men from Albany used to fish in the area and determined to end what they considered a local superstition. "Marsh gas," they said. "Just some freak of nature caused by wind hitting those boulders just right," they rationalized with weak smiles on their faces. But none of the locals fell for that reasoning. Why had they never heard those sounds in the many years they had lived there before the fire? How could these strangers speak of marsh gas when there were no marshes along the swift river? And the boulders had been there for thousands of years— why had nobody seen spirits or heard moaning before the tragic fire occurred?

The little settlement of Huntsville (now known as West Day) retained the folktale of the poor family killed in the fire, whose souls had somehow become trapped in Boulder Bay. Had the reservoir waters not closed over the site in the early 1930s, perhaps fishermen and recreational boaters might still be able to hear the sounds and see the sights of the deceased family. Gone now are the people who knew this tale, even Don Bowman himself. Just about gone are the memories of the small communities that were demolished so the people of Troy and Albany, downriver, could be safe from spring floods.

The Ghost of Horse Race Rapids

Early settler Gordon Conkling gave his name to the settlement known as Conklingville, fated to be the site of a great dam. The community grew in two locations, one on the north side of the Sacandaga River and the other one on the south shore. When the Reservoir was built, much of the southern community was torn down, though some buildings were jacked up and tediously moved to the northern shore, where they remain today.

Don Bowman remembered a particularly pretty girl named Christina who lived in Conklingville. Her parents had died of the flu, and a couple named Gordon and Alfreda took her in, raising her as their own child. There were two brothers, also, in the family: Mickey and Alan. The three children grew up playing as friends with one another. However, as they reached adolescence Alan developed an obsessive crush on Christina. Mickey, unaware of the attraction, treated the girl as a loved sister. Christina, for her part, loved the boys equally.

In her early 20s, Christina fell in love with Bernard, a neighbor boy, and accepted his engagement ring. The wedding went happily for everyone except Alan, who became crazed by the loss of Christina to someone else. After the wedding ceremony, he rushed the married couple, seized Christina's arm and pulled her away. At first, the assembly thought it a light-hearted prank, but Mickey could see the glare in his brother's eyes. Wedding guests surrounded Alan and Christina, wresting her from his strong arms. Alan spun away toward the river, fleeing the outraged throng. He headed directly to Horse Race Rapids, a dangerous spot below Conklingville on the river.

When the sad day concluded, witnesses couldn't agree just what *had* happened. Alan had jumped out onto a rock in the river, lost his balance (or was he feigning a dance?) and fell into the tumultuous waters. His body completely disappeared and wasn't seen for days, when body gasses forced the corpse to the surface in more placid waters downriver. The searchers took his remains to Mr. Talbot, the local undertaker, who also served as community barber and carpenter. It was a gruesome sight that Dick Talbot faced, and he quickly built a wooden coffin and nailed it shut for the funeral.

A tragic story—one that remained unfinished after the burial. People strolling near the Sacandaga River just a few days later reported seeing a ghost floating in the air over the rapids. The hovering spirit seemed to have just a skull on its shoulders. Over at Talbot's and in the local store, people debated just what the others could have seen—it had to be Alan's ghost! Those who had retrieved the corpse noted that Alan's body had been savaged by snapping turtle bites, walleye pike nibbles, and countless bashings against rocks in the rapids, and, when found, the body had no flesh above the neck.

For many years to come, people told of the apparition of Alan, the boy who couldn't let go of Christina, even when she was married. In time, the southern part of the valley floor was cleared of its buildings, trees and cemeteries, and the foundations of southern Conklingville disappeared beneath Sacandaga's flow. And Horse Race Rapids, along with its gruesome specter, was seen no more.

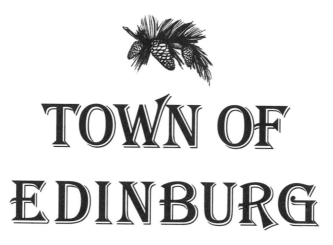

TOWN OF
EDINBURG

So the bird of my bosom
fluttered up to the dawn,
A window was opened
-my darling was gone!
A truant from time,
from tears,
and from sin,
For the angel on watch
took the wanderer in.

Yet never let our hearts divide
Nor Death dissolve the chain

For Love and Joy
were once alloyed

and must be joined
again.

S.Kelly 05

Town of Edinburg

C reated as the Town of Northfield in 1801, the township rapidly attracted loggers and farmers from southern parts of Saratoga County. When residents realized that there was already a Northfield in New York State, community leaders chose the name Edinburg, perhaps because of so many residents' Scottish roots. Here was forested and cheap fertile land available to the many veterans of the Revolutionary War who came to homestead. Sawmills and wooden-ware factories sprang up, exploiting the abundant supplies of Adirondack timber. Settlements sprang up at Batchellerville and Beecher's Hollow. Most of the mills are now gone, victims of fires, and other old buildings were razed to make way for the shores of the Sacandaga Reservoir.

Old Caleb

One of the eeriest Edinburg tales comes from a place called Crazy Loon Cove that once existed near Batchlerville before the 1930s. Farming on the river's flood plain was excellent, as was the river fishing. Though life wasn't idyllic, one could make a good living on the flats. Don Bowman remembered a legend about Caleb, a farmer who lived with his brother on a prosperous farm near Crazy Loon Cove. Passersby were used to seeing the pair farming the land, and were mystified when, eventually, only Caleb's brother could be seen in the fields. Had Caleb died? The brother was mum when queried by neighbors, and the locals set about searching the countryside. They found Caleb drowned in the family's well.

Neighbors knew that the brothers used to argue heatedly, but could old Caleb have been *murdered* so that the brother would have the farm's bounty to himself? No witness could be found to testify against the survivor and, even though the constable sifted through every bit of the scanty evidence, he could not prove foul play. And so, the brother gained the prize of owning the farm. But, the saga didn't end there.

Travelers and neighbors began to notice a strange glow around the farmhouse and a flickering light near the well where Caleb's body had been recovered. The brother also spotted the brilliance and did his best to drive the light away, but to no avail. Soon he was overwhelmed by fear, and many suspected it was a fear generated by his own deadly actions. The neighbors could often overhear the brother wailing, "He's out to get me!" and by the month's end the surviving brother no longer dared to sleep at night, hyper-vigilant lest the strange light attack him. Whatever phenomena were taking place inside the house, he wouldn't say. Driven to distraction, he could no longer manage the hard labor of the farm's upkeep. Fields went untilled and un-milked cows bawled in the barn. In the end, Caleb's brother just disappeared and was never seen again. The old farm sat untended and abandoned.

When squatters tried to live in the farmhouse and till the land, they, also, were driven off by ghostly phenomena, sounds and strange lights. In the end, no one tried to live there any longer.

Don Bowman and his labor crews arrived in 1930 and, by then, the house was falling in. "Even Old Caleb's spirit seemed to have deserted the farm by then, and gave us no trouble as we pulled down the house and barn to make way for the dam," he said.

Today, Crazy Loon Cove exists no longer, as it, along with Old Caleb's farm, lies beneath thirty feet of the Sacandaga's water.

The 'Almost Ghosts' of Ghost Cove

Glacier-polished boulders are a common site along the old Sacandaga River bed. The largest of these seemed to be in Beecher's Hollow on the north shore. Some of the early settlers commented that they looked like great globular ghosts when viewed in the moonlight. And the eerie shadows cast by these boulders led old timers to refer to the area as "Ghost Cove."

As the work of preparing the great lake bed began in the 1930s, and the labor gangs demolished old houses, Don Bowman's supervisor sent him and a worker named Lou to what was referred to as a "ghost house" near the cove. They heard and saw nothing out of the ordinary as they approached the abandoned building, so they searched inside to see if they might salvage anything useful. Having just discovered a few old pieces of serviceable furniture, they were suddenly startled by a creaking sound overhead. Soon the sound took on the suggestion of someone walking. But, looking upward, through the cracks in the first floor ceiling, they could see no one was upstairs. They began to rationalize that the house, sitting out in the hot sun, was undergoing alternate heating and cooling cycles, expanding and contracting the frame and wooden siding. At night, the structure would likely contract, with the shifting planks creating more strange noises. Having explained away the sound of footsteps, "we put *that* ghost to rest!" Don rejoiced.

Local businessman Bruce Brownell remembers a likewise humorous tale that took place during those demolition years in the valley. He worked among the demolition crews that cut and burned trees, brush and the dilapidated houses and barns that former owners didn't want to move. Small settlements disappeared under the axe, sledgehammer and flame. In the early months of 1930, the smell of wood smoke permeated the valley, with laborers torching old building after old building, many built of crude timber in the early 1800s. A large part of old Batchellerville and the entire community of Denton's Corners disappeared.

Bruce chuckles when remembering two local lads who decided to give a hand to the "barn burners." The pair decided to have their own conflagration and, taking kerosene and a box of matches, headed to an abandoned farmhouse by the light of the full moon. They drenched the building with kerosene and prepared to toss their lighted matches. Just then, there came a *thump, thump!* from somewhere in the building. Knowing the story of the valley's other old "ghost house," the boys scrambled away from the building and retreated to their homes. The next day, ashamed of their previous night's terror, they returned to the old house. Everything seemed normal and nobody could be seen. But again, when they reached the porch they heard a loud *thump, thump!* coming from a rear room. Again, they skeedaddled to a safe distance. But, again, nothing was seen to move—they weren't being pursued by anything or anyone. How could an empty house scare such brave lads?

Regaining their courage, they once more approached the building, but this time from the rear. This changed perspective showed them a shed just off the back porch. Again, louder now, they heard a *thump!* Gathering their courage, the lads pried open the shed door. Inside, they beheld an old workhorse tethered in the shed. Too old to work or pull wagons or plows, the departing family had abandoned the animal to the work gangs. All the poor creature could do was kick the wall and hope (if horses can hope) that he wouldn't become a roast equine. They untied the old steed and turned him loose to gallop freely off to some neighboring farm, thus liberating another "near ghost."

The Ring

One of the most poignant tales from those construction days involved a forbidden love. In *The Edinburg Newsletter* of October 1991, Don Bowman wrote of a tale he heard during his years of laboring and collecting stories throughout the Sacandaga Valley.

A major industry in the hamlet of Batchellerville was woodenware. The nearby forests offered abundant wood, and the local farm families, who couldn't work all year outdoors, found ready employment in a business that exported all over the world. Young men seldom finished high school in those days, so many began to make their living by the end of Eighth Grade. One such lad, whom we'll call Ted, hoping to get ahead in the world, found employment in a local mill, and fell in love with the owner's daughter, who often brought lunch to her father at noon.

Amorous looks soon turned to brief encounters as Marion returned Ted's affection. One day the father spied the two holding hands near the warehouse, and the next day the daughter was sent packing to a private girl's school far from Ted and any other poorly-educated worker. The father was an elitist and felt his daughter was too good for ordinary mill hands.

The father didn't know that Ted had secretly given Marion a ring as a token of their budding love, nor was he aware that she wore it secretly near her heart, on a gold chain inside her blouse. Away from her home, the girl pined for her Romeo and soon became afflicted with tuberculosis (often called "the white death" in those days). There was no cure for the disease and the sick girl was returned to her home in a coma to die.

After her death, as Marion's body was being prepared for burial by the undertaker, the ring was discovered, and the enraged father threw it into a woodstove in the family home, as if to obliterate the forbidden love and his daughter's disobedience. Marion was buried the next day, but the story does not end there.

Don Bowman remembered that, for years, the girl's ghost was said to roam Owl's Nest Farm, the family home, apparently seeking the ring as a connection to Ted, who had been dismissed from his job at the mill. Not finding the ring or her beau, Marion's spirit gradually faded from the building, and the house itself was demolished in the preparation for construction of the Sacandaga Reservoir.

Today, quiet waters flow over these sites of human tragedies and sorrows. Perhaps now, far above and beyond this earth, the spirits of Ted and Marion have found one another once more. Perhaps they also have found that factories and fortunes, *even a ring*, are but temporary illusions, but Love endures forever.

Harl, that you?

The Edwards family has lived on Tenantville Road for over 45 years. In fact, Priscilla and her husband, Jay, grew up in the neighborhood. The idea of ghosts in Edinburg didn't seem a possibility until a particular winter in the late 1960s. Their children returned one afternoon from happy play in the yard. Begging for hot cocoa and snacks, they shed their scarves, mittens and hats. A half hour later, fortified by Mom's food, they set about dressing again for the snowy weather. But there was a problem—one girl's scarf and mittens had vanished from where she had placed them only minutes before.

Priscilla and her girls, Andrea and Coleen, searched high and low, but the disappeared clothing was not to be found that day. Fortunately, there were spare mittens and scarves, so the girls were soon outside again, enjoying winter's fun. "Three days later," Priscilla told me, "while sorting through my basket of clothes to be ironed, I found the mittens and scarf, beneath clothes I'd put there *before* that incident. I know *we* weren't the pranksters, so Jay and I started wondering aloud just who the "Robbin Goodfellow" could be. Then, as we talked, we remembered a story told us by the old guy who did the electrical wiring in our home when it was built in 1961-1962. Working in the unfinished interior he had an experience that left him speechless. All he'd tell us was that *it was too scary to repeat*, and he never did, right up to the day he died."

This discussion led the family to wonder who the mischief-maker might be. "Then I remembered a merry elf named Harl Tenant, a distant relative by marriage, who lived across the road from where we now live. He was always doing something to bring smiles to peoples' faces. All we kids loved him and his dog Dewey. So, whenever anything mysterious and prankish happened throughout the 70s, 80s and 90s we always blamed Harl."

Priscilla recalled an incident from 1977 when daughter Andrea was in high school. The girl awoke in the night knowing that someone or something had just sat down on her bed. Her first thought was that it was the family cat, which used to sleep on the bed. Then, however, she snapped out of her drowsiness, recognizing that the cat was not that heavy; *this* was weighty! Too frightened to turn over and see, or even call out, Andrea lay there for some time listening, but finally fell asleep. As she shared this experience at breakfast, other family members realized that none of them had been near her room at the time of the incident, and couldn't have been the perpetrators. Andrea vividly remembers the event almost thirty years later.

"One Sunday evening in 1995, Jay sat watching television and our youngest daughter, Coleen, now grown, was visiting with two foster children she cared for. We sat in the dining room chatting. I should tell you that directly beneath us, in the cellar, we have an old piano. As we conversed, we began to hear single notes being picked out on the piano keys. We took a quick nose count: all of us humans were there. Then we looked for the most likely offenders—our cats. But they were both dozing in the next room. My daughter looked at me and the two of us hurried to the cellar door and went down. When we turned on the lights, there was nobody there. Now who, we wondered, would have so delicate a touch on the piano keys? We looked at one another, smiled, and said, 'Harl!'"

This most recent event at the Edwards house—nothing scary, was just another of those inexplicable events experienced so often by families around the world. When the prankster can't be found on Tenantville Road, Priscilla's family always knows who to blame first.

TOWN OF GALWAY

Tis o're! But never from my heart
Shall time thine image blot;
The dreams of other days depart
Thou shalt not be forgot

Shed not for her the bitter tear,
Nor give the heart to vain regret;
"Tis but the casket that lies here,
The gem that filled it sparkles yet.

S. Kelly 05

Town of Galway

T he town's earliest settlers came in a group from Galloway Shire in Scotland in 1774. No friends of the English king, George III, they sought the freedom to live and worship as they pleased, and came to America and the hills of western Saratoga County. After the Revolution, in 1792, the town's boundaries were drawn, and more sturdy Scots arrived to augment the small population. By the early 1800s a sizeable population lived at the major crossroads and near the natural beauty of Galway Lake.

Gussie

As one climbs into the hills west of the Village of Galway, an old house sitting near an intersection on Consaul Road cannot be missed. The builder obviously enjoyed the vistas to the east when the home was built after the Civil War. Many years later, in 1972, a woman came to town and was delighted to find the old house for sale. Within a short time after she purchased the structure she began to experience strange events. She continually saw an older woman peering at her from a doorway, but when she looked directly at the woman, the figure vanished. "I began to talk to my friends about buying a ghost with the house," she said.

The woman began to notice other "little things." She tried to keep an old bathtub brush on a hook behind the bathroom door, but no matter how securely it was hung on its hook, within a short time, she'd hear the brush clatter onto the bathroom floor. Then there was the wallpaper problem. She hoped to redecorate an upstairs room, but the intended roll of wallpaper kept moving its location. When she'd put it down, it wasn't in that spot a moment later. And when she found it, if she looked away, it wouldn't be *there* a minute later. By now, the owner figured the old lady was the culprit, and probably didn't like the pattern or color of the paper. In the end, the new owner gave up trying to use the paper.

It's not that the old ghost lady was shy, just mischievous. Within a few months, she granted the new owner a better look, appearing in a long white gown, wearing her long, dark hair done up. But the details of the elder's face were not clear enough to remember a minute later.

Two old sisters, the Caldwells, rapped at the door one day and asked the owner if they might come in and see the interior. They had once owned the house, they said, and were curious about the interior changes, if any. However, the owner suspected they'd been curious about something else. As the trio sat having tea after their house tour, the sisters reminisced about their good times in the old house, and shared a few photos of the old days. The owner asked, "Who was the woman dressed in the long white dress—the woman with long dark hair?"

"Oh my," exclaimed one of the sisters, "that *must* be Gussie!" The two gave each other a knowing look and nodded. "Earlier in this century, our 21 year-old cousin, Augusta, came to live with us. She was very pretty and caught the eye of a Mr. Cook, who lived in Charlton. Within a short time they were courting, and soon after, they became engaged. But then Gussie, that's what we called her, came down sick. And she got worse, and then shocked us all when she *died*, just before her wedding." The sisters recalled how their cousin had been buried in the long white gown that was to be her wedding dress. Pointing to the doorway where the new owner had first observed their mysterious housemate, they indicated the room where Gussie had drawn her last breath.

The owner smiled—that was now the TV room, so perhaps Gussie had become jaded by the quality of today's entertainment, and ceased visiting that room. "Now, most times, we hear her upstairs in the room above the TV room," the new owner commented. "My son has encountered her twice. The first time, he saw her slowly descending the stairs, and the second time, asleep in that room, he was awakened by someone tweaking his leg. Rousing himself, he turned to see a dark haired woman in white standing beside him. She then vanished after giving him a big grin!

"Of course, she has other tricks too. Though it is an old house, it is secure against the winter weather, but Gussie seems to specialize in making frigid breezes in other parts of the house, though the cold doesn't stay for long. One night, as our family sat watching television, we heard the front doorknob rattle. Was someone coming in? As I stood to answer the front door, I heard the back doorknob rattle. How'd they get out back so fast? I wondered. We switched on the outdoor floodlight and absolutely nobody was there. There were no footprints in the snow outside *either* door!"

The owner befriended a psychic and the new friend visited the old house once. She observed Gussie in the upstairs room where family frequently now sees her. The psychic indicated that Gussie was quite happy to "have a family again," and was just being active, living her life in her own time.

Now, the Caldwell sisters have also gone to meet their maker, and have been buried next to Gussie's body in the family plot at Galway Village Cemetery. They are apparently happy in their new abode, for they haven't yet returned to the old house on Consaul Road to visit Cousin Gussie.

Rachel's House

Her early married life had been an exciting time, but when her husband took sick in the early 1960s and then died, Rachel's life of frequent travel ended. Her home in Schenectady was filled with too many memories, so she sold the house and moved to a quieter community. She found that the Village of Galway, where she moved into a wonderful old 1800s farmhouse on the main street, was an ideal spot to raise her daughter, and it offered room in which to pursue her painting avocation.

At first, there was much renovation to do in the almost two hundred year-old house. Neighbors filled her in on the history, from the building's beginnings as a farm home to a later role as rooming house. Girls seeking a high school education at the village school in olden times, boarded there when deep winter snows made travel impossible. A friendly neighbor suggested that Rachel and her daughter again offer rooms to student teachers working in the village. Hoping to use rental income to restore the house and purchase art supplies, Rachel agreed.

Though the student teachers enjoyed the snug rooms and quiet of the neighborhood, some of them complained about the strange and inexplicable house noises they heard. One young woman told of hearing heavy footsteps on the stairs outside her room at 2 a.m. The sound always provoked Rachel's cat, which attempted to use the stair landing as a sleeping spot. It would jump up and hiss at an invisible something outside the door, awakening the young teacher. The young woman wanted to complain to Rachel about the noises, but whenever she opened her door to catch the noisemaker, the stairway outside was empty.

63

Eventually Rachel's daughter went to college, but at vacation times and during home visits, the girl often invited local friends for dinner. Several of the friends were amused to watch the iron latch on the dining room door raise itself and the door open, yet no one entered. "I never saw the latch do that, but I have many times seen doors in this house open of their own accord," Rachel said. "Some friends once brought a psychic man over here, and he stunned us with his vision of people sitting all around the dining room. Of course they were invisible to us! However, the man said he believed one of the people was my deceased husband watching over us. And that was comforting.

"This is a friendly house, but the ghost or ghosts love to play with electrical things here—especially if I leave the house for any length of time." She told of returning home after several days' absence and finding her electric toothbrush jumping up and down, vibrating in its holder. On another occasion, she returned home to hear her front doorbell ringing. Answering the door, she found nobody there, yet the bell button was depressed. Unable to turn the bell off, she called an electrician, but the man couldn't stop the ringing either, so he disconnected the device. When you visit Rachel, perhaps to purchase one of her special paintings, be sure you knock hard on the door because the bell no longer works.

A few years later Rachel remarried and once again had the chance to travel with her new husband. As they returned to the Village of Galway on Route 147 after a few weeks on the road, the couple speculated as to what the "voltage ghosts" might have in store for them once they reached home. Just as they reached the traffic light at the Four Corners in the village, it blew out, almost exploding above them as they passed underneath. Then all the street lights north of the intersection went out! Once in the house, they found a total power failure, and called the utility company, who sent a repair crew immediately. Upon examination, the service crew found that the blackout was caused by some force *within her house* overloading the transformer outside the house. When they called an electrician later, he found no flaws in the circuitry or other electrical devices in her house.

A friend once gifted Rachel with a small bottle of *My Sin* perfume, which she placed on top of her highboy dresser. The small bottle had a glass stopper. A few days later, when she decided to use the perfume, she was unable to open the bottle because the entire glass top of the stopper was now *gone*, neatly cut from the stopper bottom, leaving just the cork inside the bottle neck! In attempting to understand this strange happening, Rachel theorized that the mischief came from "an old rooming house headmistress or perhaps a puritanical former farmer owner. The spirit, objecting to the perfume's risqué name, showed displeasure by making the bottle unusable, because this was a *respectable* house for young women."

Rachel MacDonald still enjoys senior life in the Village of Galway, though she paints little these days. Her Golden Years are still brightened by the quiet companionship of former residents who have never moved on.

Top Notch Tavern

When the first settlers encountered the lower Adirondacks at the western boundary of Saratoga County, they noted a pass through the mountains that permitted a route of travel westward into what is now Fulton County. When the road was built through "the top notch" a small hamlet dubbed West Galway, grew there. Freight, mail and passengers moved to and from the lower Adirondacks through the small hamlet of West Galway, sitting astride the Fulton and Saratoga County boundary line. Soon, a stagecoach stop was created at a public house called "The West Galway House." This building served to lodge travelers, but also as a community center for political meetings, local trials, weddings and other public functions. Later, the building was renamed, "The Top Notch Tavern."

In seeking my first area ghost stories in 1971, I went to the legendary Top Notch, where spirits of both kinds were rumored to be found. Though I never observed a specter, I have discovered former and present employees who have had thrills aplenty. Upon entering the restaurant today, one comes to recognize that it is not the usual eating place. There is a tombstone in the foyer, inscribed with the name of *Lucinda Harris, daughter of Seriel and Phoebe Harris, aged 6 years and 4 months*, when she died in 1835. Local historians have found no record of the Harris family and nothing is known about Lucinda's manner of death. How the stone came to the interior of the Top Notch Tavern is another mystery. But some who have experienced the ghost phenomena there suspect that Lucinda, or "Lucy" as the staff calls her, may still be among those specters who reside in the old hotel.

A local repairman has been summoned to the Top Notch at times and always responds when called, "but I don't like it," he groused, "Every time I do a job something takes one of my tools." I asked if he'd ever asked the ghosts to return his tools, but he hadn't. Often a simple verbal request will resolve such issues, as many ghosts are just seeking validation of their presence. For those who lose something at their job, and suspect a ghost has purloined it, it is best to be sure you aren't overheard "asking" by the "normal" people around you.

One waitress in the restaurant felt the ghosts disliked her, and many nights she struggled to do her job with a smile on her face. For example, when she had to refill the salad dressing containers on the salad bar one evening, her metal service cart fell over, spilling its gooey contents. "Nobody was standing near my cart," she said, "so nobody could have pushed it—it was standing on a flat floor!" Stooping to begin cleaning up the mess, she was suddenly struck on the head by a plastic light shade falling from its lamp over the salad bar. She wasn't physically injured, but *was* embarrassed by the spectacle that she seemed to have created. As she tried to fit the plastic shade back into its holder, it wouldn't fit until she loosened the retaining screws, the very screws that were supposed to secure the shade from falling in the first place!

Another waitress, finishing her work one evening just before closing time, suddenly heard the faucet running in a downstairs bathroom sink. She knew she was alone in the building with only the bartender, and that no one else was there to enter or leave the bathroom, as she had a clear view of its open doorway. Though she knew the bartender hadn't been down to the room, when she entered and saw the hot water gushing, she yelled out, "Why'd you leave it that way?" The surprised man denied being near the lavatory and she believed him, but *somebody* had to take the blame, didn't they? And she didn't like the concept of ghosts. As she turned from the bartender, she heard the lavatory faucet turn on in two other bathrooms! She ran rapidly to one room and turned off its faucet, then exiting to the other bathroom to close that faucet, heard the faucet she had just turned off come on again!

The bartender also had his share of difficulties. When he arrived at the restaurant one day, he found the air conditioning unit broken and called the repairman. As he waited for the man to arrive, he was suddenly engulfed in a current of very cold air, as if some unseen presence were saying, "I'm still here." Then the chill vanished.

On another occasion a woman phoned Top Notch to inquire if they sold gift certificates. The waitress who answered the phone said "Yes, and please come around to the kitchen door where someone will greet you and provide the certificate." The waitress waited and waited, keeping an attentive ear tuned to the back kitchen door. But the woman never appeared at the door. So, it surprised the manager when the customer called a few days later to complain about the rude service. Dumbfounded, the manager asked what the woman was referring to. The caller said, "I came to the back door the way you told me, but the old man who greeted me, if you call it that, told me to go away, that I wasn't wanted around there!" Apologizing profusely and providing the woman with the desired certificate, the manager puzzled. There was no such old man on the staff. Was this a ghostly innkeeper from the past?

Another waitress had a stunning experience one evening after she finished serving a banquet in the upstairs dining room. After all guests departed she stripped the tables and took the soiled tablecloths downstairs after turning off the dining room lights. As she readied to go home, she remembered she had left her purse in the dining room. As she climbed the stairs she was puzzled to see a soft glow in the darkened room. When she reached the room she was startled to find all the tables reset with tablecloths and silverware, and on one table a single candle burned. "I began to realize the other staff members really *did* have some validity in their tales of ghost experiences," she said.

Waiters and waitresses sometimes smell cigar smoke in the smoking-prohibited dining room, usually upon arriving in the morning before meals are served. It is known that a former owner of the restaurant, a cigar smoker, died of a heart attack in that room.

A former waiter named Chuck told me a tale which has become my favorite—a story that hearkens back to the children who play in Scotch Church. Management of Top Notch gave Chuck a room upstairs, allowing him to serve as night watchman on the premises. Often times, hankering for some popcorn in the wee hours, he'd mosey down the stairs to the bar, where a popcorn machine was located. Sometimes, as he began his descent down the dark stairway to the bar, he would hear the happy voices of children laughing and playing in the bar room below. He could never quite make out what they were saying to one another, but their glee and enthusiasm were very evident. However, as soon as he'd reach the foot of the stairs, the voices would suddenly hush in the dark room. He never found any children, of course, and could find no other rational explanation for the sounds. Perhaps the happy laughter of children who lodged there in yesteryears has since permeated the old hotel's walls, and were "playing back" when the building was quiet at night.

67

Alice Gaudreau, a local craftswoman moved deeply by the thought of Lucinda Harris' unmarked grave, and hearing tales of ghostly activity involving children playing at the Top Notch, sewed an exquisite old fashioned little girl's doll, which sits now on a shelf in an unoccupied upstairs room where patrons never see it. But it is there, if a spirited little girl is seeking a comforting toy on dark nights in the old West Galway House.

TOWN OF GREENFIELD

THE YOUTH IS GONE, TO HEAVEN HE'S FLED.
HIS BODY RESTS AMONG THE DEAD;
NO MORE TO FEEL CONVULSIVE THROWS,
NOR MOURN HIS OWN OR OTHERS' WOES.
HIS SOUL INFLUENCED WITH LOVE DIVINE,
THE SPOTLESS ROBES HE MUST NOW SHINE.
AND WITH HARMONIOUS SOUNDS ACCORD
THE GLORIOUS TRIUMPHS OF THE LORD.
AE 23

Missed but not forgotten

Little Martha, daughter of L.D. & Ann B.,
5 yrs 2 months 9/18/1865

S. Kelly 05

Town of Greenfield

I n March 1793, the Town of Greenfield was created. Gentle hills and long stretches of fertile land made it ideal for farming. Many streams cross the town, also making a paradise for saw mills and grist mills. There was also a graphite mine, a glass factory in the hamlet of Middle Grove, and several small paper mills. Many beautiful old farms and residences have been preserved in Greenfield, testimony to the hard work of its early settlers.

Lake Desolation Road

One does not have to believe in ghosts to experience them. Here is one of my favorite tales, told by Gerry Ferris, a local businessman. On a cold winter afternoon in the 1980s, Gerry, not given to fantasies or supernatural beliefs, and his friend, Bill Quinn, drove slowly up Lake Desolation Road, seeking an open field in which to snowmobile. They found an ideal spot up toward the lake and backed their trailer into a pull-off. Hoping it was okay to leave the van and trailer there, Gerry went to the old farmhouse across the road and knocked, hoping to get permission.

He saw the overhead kitchen light illuminating the interior, indicating that someone was home. Then he saw an old man seated at the kitchen table and a dog wandering across the floor. Gerry knocked loudly. No response. He knocked even louder. The old man rose and went into another room. How could the elder have not heard him? Gerry figured the man was anti-social, shrugged his shoulders, and went to the van. He and Bill unloaded the snowmobiles and zoomed off to a late afternoon of thrills on newly-fallen snow.

Returning later after dark, the pair saw the farmhouse dark. That figures, thought Gerry, old folks go to bed early. So they reloaded their machines and drove quietly away. He couldn't know then that he'd seen his first ghosts.

Several years later he and his wife built a beautiful new home alongside the lake. By this time he had come to think of Lake Desolation with the mind of a resident rather than as a visitor. During his family's

71

vacation at the lake in 1988 he met a woman named Phyllis while dining with his wife at Tinney's Restaurant. In their conversation, Gerry referred to a rude old man who lived nearby. Phyllis was visibly puzzled—just which house did the old man live in? Gerry described the house and its location, and Phyllis recognized that it was *her house*!

"No old man lives there," she said. "I've lived there for twenty years, and we haven't even had an old man, much less a dog, visit during that time! And that was *my* house when you had your experience there in 1984." Gerry, somewhat apologetic, was beginning to doubt his experience. Phyllis then realized that he wasn't unfriendly, so she shared a tale of her own with the couple.

"My son and I often hear an animal's toenails hitting the floor as it walks through our kitchen, but we don't own a dog. It *really* puzzles us. Also, a few years ago I hired a roofing contractor to put on a new roof. When he finished he gave me a strange look, and asked, 'Lady, who was that old man?' I asked who he was referring to. 'The old guy that sat on a stump all day and watched me work—the guy with the dog that sat motionless all day?'" Phyllis had mumbled something to him about it being a neighbor, but she had also been puzzled and never told anyone else the tale.

Gerry Ferris had two confirmations of a ghost then—an old man, perhaps a long ago resident of the farm, and his dog. Perhaps "man's best friend" continues his friendship longer than dog lovers know.

The Wayside Inn

In the old days, as travelers journeyed from the hamlet of Greenfield Center to Wilton or vice-versa, The Wayside Inn was a popular stopping place. Town meetings and political speeches were made there, weddings were performed, and it was the center for sharing information in the town. In 1801, St. John's Lodge of the Masonic Order held its first meeting there. On the stairs, one may still see a "secret step" that quickly identified non-Masons, who stumbled there if they sought to intrude on meetings.

In the middle 1800s, as the struggle over slavery began to tear the Union apart, there were many ardent abolitionists in the town, and the stagecoach stop was frequently used as a "station" on the Underground

Railroad. A now-sealed underground tunnel was found in the Inn's cellar, a likely escape route if federal marshals tried to catch runaway slaves.

Dale and Karen Shook, who presently own the house and newer conference center next door, converted the old Harold Hall farmhouse property into The Wayside Inn Bed & Breakfast after 1970, restoring its original lodging function. As the Shooks have traveled widely throughout the world, their décor is a mix of Asian and North American *objets d'art*. Guests at the Inn often peruse the items, and one woman, after her house tour, asked Karen the identity of the old lady in black who was wearing an old-fashioned bonnet and sitting on the couch, quietly staring out the front window.

Karen insisted that the Inn had no such guest, or even visiting relative. From the guest's description, the strange visitor appeared to be in 1860s clothing. Perhaps the spirit of a long ago traveler chose to temporarily sojourn in the comfortable lodge. Ever since, visitors to The Wayside Inn have been on the lookout for this traveler's reappearance.

Locust Grove Corners

The northeast corner of Locust Grove Corners was once the location of a 93-acre farm, and the old house there dates back to the early 1800s. Old boundary lines are still demarcated by fancy iron gates. A Mr. Robinson once owned the property, having gained ownership under unusual circumstances. An old widow resided in the house, and it was a condition of sale that Robinson care for her until her last days. He agreed to do so and moved into her house. However, his pledge didn't require the woman to live *in* the house, so Robinson fixed up a small chicken coop at the side of the property and installed the elder there in a tiny cottage. Some years after the woman's death, Mr. Robinson sold the entire property. After many others, Mary, the present owner, concluded her purchase of the property and prepared to move in. The family moving out took one more stroll through the old house, ostensibly to "say goodbye to the ghost." Mary smiled. In whatever way they wished, she guessed, they were entitled to say farewell to the home they had enjoyed.

It wasn't too long, however, before Mary began to hear "Henry," as she calls him. The sounds of footsteps walking up the front stairs marked her first experience with ghosts. Not long afterward, she began to hear a frantic pounding on the house's front door at night. Her room overlooks the entry and Mary can easily see the front doorstep, so when the pounding begins, she can see there is no one at the downstairs door. She has come to believe that there is something seasonal about the phenomena. "At certain times of the year, things are sure to go haywire. Once I came downstairs and spotted two pictures that were supposed to hang on the wall, sitting side by side on the floor. They used to be on nail hangers and couldn't have slipped off. I really had to wonder how the ghost moved them so carefully!"

Mary simply loves peacocks, live or ornamental. Her home is filled with such mementos, and her favorite is a two foot-tall wire design in the shape of a peacock, which had always been securely affixed to her living room wall. In 1997, she found it *missing* from its accustomed location and only later discovered it leaning against the wall behind her piano. Who does her redecorating so carefully?

She remembers going upstairs to put clothing away in a bedroom one late afternoon in December, 1989. In the doorway she paused for a minute, deciding exactly where to place the clothing. At that pause, she felt a breeze, as if some invisible entity had just brushed past her. "And darned if I didn't hear a self-conscious giggle right then," she said. "It was almost as if someone just realized they had frightened or disturbed me and gave a tee-hee. Just to be safe, when I enter that bedroom nowadays, I always turn on the light first."

Over the years of her ownership the building has needed periodic repairs, and workmen in the cellar always comment on the building's age. These men have discovered three different styles of brick used in the different levels of the cellar walls. "Many owners have made their imprint on this house," she noted, "so I really wonder just who my ghost is. I call him 'Henry' because I can't be afraid of a ghost with a name."

In recent years, she said, there seems to be a strange, new activity taking place. As her son visited one winter day in the early 1990s, "He went into the garage to have a smoke and raised the big door. The ground outside was covered with newly-fallen snow and there were no footprints out there. In just a minute he hurried back into the kitchen, his face as white as the snow outside. He told me, 'I was leaning against the garage wall and saw a shovel on the opposite wall detach itself and come through the air right at me!' I took a photo of the garage interior with the door raised. In the prints you can see mysterious large dark orbs in the air, which I couldn't see with my eyes. Something new and strange is going on!"

As my own study of ghost phenomena has grown, this author has learned of a phenomenon that seems relatively new throughout the world, an apparition not commonly cited in ghost literature of the 1800s. This relates to orbs of light, stationary or moving, that appear at ghost sites, or in photographs taken there. Researchers aren't sure yet whether these are an encapsulated form of spirit energy, or not, but they do add a further level of mystery in Mary's old farmhouse.

Perhaps Mr. Robinson has returned from the next world to atone for his greedy mistreatment of the widow. Or perhaps she, herself, has returned, happy once more to enjoy Mary's house from the inside!

Little Girl

Another story involving orbs concerns a small house south of the corners in Greenfield Center on Route 9N. The young couple buying the building from the previous owner was ecstatic at the opportunity to have their own home. The previous owner had done quite a bit of renovation, but the floors and door frames were still in need of work. Lee, the husband, is a woodwork artisan and had a keen appreciation for the different periods of construction evidenced in the cellar timbers and foundation walls. Soon after they moved in, while he excavated along the foundation, he encountered a layer of charred wood and ash. Had there been a fire?

It was difficult to ascertain the precise age of the house. It seemed to be early 1900s in its above-ground construction, but the floor joists were planed trees, some of them retaining the original bark. These likely came from an earlier period. Also, the sills atop the foundation showed evidence of prior use in their old mortise and tenon joints, cuts and nail holes. Lee thinks these were timbers used in an old demolished barn and later re-used to frame the house after a long-ago fire.

The young couple worked very hard to strip and sand the floors, preparing to varnish and polish them to a final mirror finish. Exhausted by their labors, they would throw themselves into bed at night. One morning in November 2003, they found their kitchen door open when they arose. "We sometimes don't lock that door at night," said Lynn, "but it has a good catch, and how it popped itself open, we just don't know. In retrospect, that event was an indicator that something bigger was about to happen. After a hard day working at our jobs, we returned home and spent hours working on the floors again."

Lee stopped sanding, and looked around his work space at the top of the stairs. He had the distinct sensation that someone or something was observing his labors. Lynn joked about it and they resumed sanding. Another night, after hours of work, they stopped and, exhausted, fell into bed. Lynn, sleeping on the side of the bed nearest the doorway, suddenly became aware they weren't alone. She looked across the five feet separating the bed and doorway and was awestruck to see a little girl surrounded by an aura of orange and red light. "She stood there expressionless and motionless, holding a lit candle in her right hand. It was as if she was inspecting our bedroom. She was dressed in a pink shift. Maybe it was a dress or a nightie, as I remember a ruffle on the hem. But she didn't have any legs, which didn't strike me as odd until we talked about it later. I was a bit panicked and tried to turn over and nudge Lee, who was fast asleep. It was if I was paralyzed— at least I couldn't move." Then Lynn did what many others have done over the centuries when confronted by a spirit. She closed her eyes and pulled the blanket over her head. A minute later, when she dared to peek, the doorway was empty. Then, as from a far distance, she heard several voices in hushed conversation. "See? Everything's okay. They're good people," said one, as if reassuring another invisible entity. Lynn was unable to determine whether the voices emanated from upstairs or downstairs. The pair can now joke about the occasional phenomena because, fortunately for Lynn, Lee is perfectly willing to believe that invisible others inhabit their house from time to time. Lynn smiled and, casting a loving look at Lee, said, "It's nice to know your spouse doesn't think you're crazy!"

A few months later they were rudely awakened by their television turning on loudly downstairs in the den. They *know* that it was turned off. This is an example of the electronic mischief by which spirits communicate their presence in a house, something this author lived with for almost four years. "The television has turned on two more times, in February and July of 2004," said Lynn, "and it always comes on at 3:30 a.m. The second two times it wasn't as loud, as it turned on after the station was off the air. All we got was a hiss and the station's tone." Lynn and I agreed that it's unnerving to have a ghostly television addict in the house—one that keeps very different hours than do living working people. In the month following my interview,

Lynn later told me, and starting on the night of my visit, the television turned itself on four more times!

Because of the relative new-ness of this situation, we must consider the 9N house to be "a work in progress." The couple has been assiduous in efforts to determine past ownership, checking deeds and talking with old timers in town. There is much more yet to learn about past inhabitants of the house. This couple wants to assemble a complete "resident list" in their property's history, and especially the identity of a little girl who roams the house with a candle.

The Lombardi Farm

For many years Dr. Vincent Lombardi and his wife Kathy operated a distinctive bed and breakfast on Locust Grove Road. Travelers to Saratoga Springs always enjoyed Vince's New York Yankees décor and the restored elegance of an old farmhouse that had stood in ruins before the Lombardis came.

Benjamin Dyer built the old farmhouse in the early 1860s when he relocated from Vermont. Dyer, noted for his rousing anti-slavery speeches, was a rabid Abolitionist and permitted his house to be used often as a way-station on the Underground Railroad. The Lombardi's fully restored the old "gentleman farmer's home." Today, the Victorian "gingerbread" house, still sits near the fields and woods that once permitted escaped slaves to continue their journey north to Canada.

Dyer was as enthusiastic a Christian as he was an Abolitionist, and later opened The Vermont House in Saratoga Springs as a summer haven for temperance Christians visiting the city during summers of Saratoga's "Golden Age." Dyer and others felt that Saratoga's summer life, with wide-open, high-stakes gambling, rowdy drunkenness and horse racing, to name just the most profitable vices, was an immoral resort.

After his death, the Dyer home gradually became seedy, and then was abandoned by the late 1940s. One wonders what forces or energies took up residence there before the Lombardis came and brightened the old home again. As Vince and Kathy made it their home, Kathy was often troubled by a minor phenomenon on the stairs. Whenever she reached the third step going up, it was as if a small hand or energy tripped her or gave her a slight shove. "It was irritating," Kathy said, "as if someone invisible was trying to get my attention." She was interested in metaphysics and e.s.p., and attracted a small circle of friends of similar interests. They held a "circle" in the house from time to time, which was devoted to spiritual and psychic development. Several talented group members remarked at the sudden cold spots in the house, and believed these to be a residue of the fears of the escaped slaves who passed through a hundred years before. And a visiting psychic once declared the energy on the stairs had a poignant origin, as it arose from an escaped slave woman who had died there on her northward trip in the early 1860s. The psychic thought the cause of death was violent. She also believed the slave had a son, perhaps named Jesse, who had also died in some kind of struggle. The psychic declared that the mother and son's spirits had become separated after death, and the two were still seeking one another in the house. Perhaps the incidents on the third step of the stairs represented Jesse's childish pranks.

Group members assumed the story to be true and spoke to Jesse as if he were, in fact, still there. The child was urged to accept that his little body had died, and to step into the light that is visible to all those who have passed on. Interestingly, after this, there were no further cold spot incidents at Lombardi Farm, and it is likely that Jesse has rejoined his mother and entered whatever paradise awaits them.

This technique is a safe and easy procedure for anyone who feels a ghost is troubling and should be sent on its way. Talk to them—tell them they've died and you live there now, and that you will take very good care of the property. Many spirits don't know they have become separated from their body in death, and continue their normal routines. Others, in denial of their body death, continue attempting to force specific results on our plane, hoping their present confused state has some other explanation than that they're dead.

For years the old house sheltered at least two spirits along with the Lombardis and their two children, as well as numerous visitors who loved Kathy's cooking. Now, the Lombardis have moved on, leaving the old home to accumulate more new memories.

The Angel on Allen Road

Jim's family once occupied an old house on Allen Road, one of the countless back-country by-ways of the Town of Greenfield. Some former owner had christened it "Thunder Run Farm," though the soil was no longer worked during Jim's residence there. The house seemed to date from the early 1930s and neighbors told Jim's family that it had once been the home of a man who had a sickly daughter. One day the girl, perhaps rising from her sick bed, found her father's body at the foot of the stairs, where he had fallen and died several days earlier. Friends moved the girl to another house and buried the father.

Soon after Jim came to live there, he noticed a stocky older man shuffling from room to room upstairs, dressed in a brown suit and overcoat. The young man could see through the filmy form, so he had no doubt it was a ghost. From time to time he'd see the figure, which appeared more often in wintertime. Jim believed the spirit was unmindful of him and it always seemed preoccupied with its own affairs, so Jim had little fear of the apparition.

Before the family moved away a few years later, Jim had another experience, one that seems difficult to categorize. He's unsure if it relates to the elderly ghost or some other ambient energy in the old farmhouse. While seated in the dining room one day, Jim's attention was drawn to the wood grain pattern on the room's door. For a moment it seemed as if the lines shifted. Then he *did* see them move—quickly the pattern morphed into a human shape that pushed out from the door's surface. The figure took on the appearance of an angelic man who stood with eyes closed and arms spread wide, yet attached at his back to the door itself. Then, just as suddenly as it had come, the figure withdrew into the door and the surface was normal again. The young man sat astonished for some time, trying to make sense of the experience.

This event motivated Jim to begin a search for answers to life's most persistent question: what happens after death? He has researched the history of the house, attempting to discover the identity of the man and angel. He did turn up evidence about the dead man, but the angelic experience remains to this day one of the most powerful events of his young life.

A Haunted Automobile

Dr. Eileen Leary, a psychotherapist specializing in grief therapy, is chief counselor at New Insights at 105 Grange Road. Well-respected in her profession, she has helped many in the area to overcome the deep sadness that comes to survivors after the sudden death of a loved one. Here is one of the more humorous experiences from her career, which she shared in 1996 with members of The Compassionate Friends, a national grief support organization.

Christopher, a talented young man from the Capital District had died suddenly, leaving his father grief stricken. Seeking counseling therapy at New Insights, the man worked through many regrets and sorrows regarding his gifted child's life, too soon cut short. "One of the many little things that continue to plague me," the father told Eileen, "is that often, when I'm driving alone in my car, I smell gas! When he was growing up, young Chris often passed gas when we drove down the road. It used to drive me nuts, and I'd say to him 'Chris, how many time have I told you not to fart in the car?' But now he's dead. I know and accept that he died. But, from time to time, out of nowhere, I suddenly smell his gas."

Eileen asked what the father had done to remedy the situation when Chris was alive, and the father said he'd curtly admonish Chris. Eileen then instructed, "So, go back and drive the car. And if the flatulence comes again, just say what you always did. Chris may just be communicating with you to show you he is still there and okay."

Somewhat dubious, the father thanked Eileen and departed. He had been gone less than thirty minutes when he reappeared in the office. "What happened?" Eileen queried.

"Well, I had hardly gotten back on the road, than I smelled that gas smell again. So, I said out loud, 'Christopher, how many times have I told you *not* to fart in the car?' And the smell stopped instantly! Maybe that was his way of letting me know he was all right. And *I* let him know that I got his message!"

As Eileen Leary assures all her clients, death is not the end of life's journey. On many occasions her clients have experienced some special sound, word or smell, even a dream, which helps survivors remember a deceased loved one. There are those who suspect it is just a form of "wish fulfillment," of wanting the dead person returned. But others, especially you, reader, fascinated at the prospect of ghosts, must believe it is much more complex. Love continues beyond body death. Of that, you can be assured. And once the dead person has resolved his difficulty at arriving in the next world, they move on to greater prospects and vistas.

Zorro

Shortly after World War II a young Greenfield man named Teddy, driving on Route 9N, was unable to negotiate the turn on Splinterville Hill and smashed into an old stone wall bordering the road. His car flipped end-over-end on impact with the wall, and Teddy was killed.

Twenty years later, as dwellings increased in number along the road from Greenfield to Saratoga Springs, a young couple built a new brick house on the hill near the old stone wall. Shortly after taking up residence there, the housewife began to notice something strange. It was as if sometimes the dark shadow of a man walked through her house. In time, the "shadow man" became more distinctly visible, but he was always dressed in black. Often, when looking toward the master bedroom she would see him lounging in the doorway of the room. She felt the man was a figment of her imagination and tried to ignore him, but the shadow wouldn't go away. The woman didn't dare to tell her husband, as he'd think she was crazy. In her own mind, because of the man's black outfit, she dubbed him "Zorro," after the Mexican hero of stage and screen.

The housewife had come from California and thus had never heard of Teddy's death along that road. While growing up, however, she had experienced the spirit of a dead aunt who seemed to watch over her. She knew this ghost aunt had been a "teacher" of sorts, revealing unknown facts to her during her youth. Because of those childhood experiences, she wasn't scared of Zorro, and chose to think of him as just someone passing through the house.

At times she saw Zorro seated in the living room, and at other times standing with a hat on his head. He reminded her of the dead actor James Dean, as he often had a cigarette drooping from his lips. Nobody in her family smokes, yet she often smells a menthol cigarette smoke when Zorro is around. The ghost may be Teddy or some former resident of the area. "I don't know who he is. I only heard about Teddy years later, when I tried to make sense of the apparition. But, Zorro's no trouble to me, so he's welcome to stay as long as he needs to," the woman said.

The Ghost of Ballou Road

A few years ago, a friend of mine, a professional woman who often works late at her job, returned to her home on Ballou Road, high up above the hamlet of Porter Corners. She and her husband had renovated an old farmhouse and made a comfortable country estate of the surrounding land.

"Probably I was going a bit fast, but the traffic on Ormsbee Road over to Ballou Road is very light that time of night. I was tired out and wanted to get home and relax," she said. "All at once there was a man in the road—right in front of me! I never saw him coming. I jumped on the brake pedal, trying to stop, but I knew I couldn't stop in time, and braced myself for the impact. It never came. *I drove right through him!"* She stopped the car and quickly got out to inspect the road. "I felt funny, because I suspected nothing would be there, and there was nothing—nobody on the road. I just sat there for a long time, in the middle of Ormsbee Road, until I'd settled down. What did I remember? Not much except the man I hit was dressed in green."

That seemed to be the end of it, but five years later, while passing a cemetery near the site of that frightening event, she spotted the man again. This time he stood alongside the road and appeared to be carrying a large portfolio of some sort. Again, he was dressed in green. Was he real? She didn't dare stop to check.

The professional woman is an artist and uses color as her artistic tool. She is sensitive to shapes and sizes, as well as musical sounds. Therefore, she is a credible witness for the details of these sightings.

From time to time my friend hears the sounds of a flute emanating from the forest on Ballou Road, across from her house. Nobody lives in those woods that extend perhaps twenty miles to the north. What is the source of the music? All she can reason is that the sounds are a "leftover" from the musician who formerly occupied her old farmhouse. The main problem with that explanation is that the man was a pianist and not a flautist.

Sometimes, however, it is easier to soothe oneself with *some* explanation, even if it doesn't quite fit with the known facts. In conversations with neighbors, this woman has discovered that visitors to Ballou Road have twice seen a man, naked above the waist, standing among the trees, and who seems so much like an Indian brave, though Indians haven't occupied the area for at least two hundred years.

But the strange experiences are not limited to the outdoors. Inside the house, where she and her husband have done extensive renovation, she and her cats often observe shadows moving when there is no strong light source to cast the shadows. "It is more like shapes passing through thin air," she told me. "I see my cats watching them pass through the same area where I see these forms."

The Green Man continues his nocturnal visits. One night, exhausted by the hard restoration work downstairs, she went up to bed to sink into a deep sleep. An hour later, however, she was roused by the knowledge that she wasn't alone. Opening her eyes, she saw the green man standing in the doorway of her bedroom, less than three feet from her head. He vanished as soon as she saw him. She has no idea who he is or was, and even less understanding of why he has appeared to her three times.

The phenomena in her house are sometimes auditory. In the cellar there are large overhead wooden beams that she has decorated with heavy old cast iron frying pans, each hung on a stout nail driven into the beams at about a 45 degree angle. One day she heard a crash in the cellar and, rushing down, was sure she'd find a frying pan fallen to the floor. And indeed, there was a fallen pan, but it lay *fifteen feet from its nail*, across the room, against a wall. She wonders how such a heavy object can achieve a lateral motion when it weighs over two pounds.

Also in the cellar is a woodpile for the wood stove. The split staves of wood are piled to about six feet in height and the entire pile is angled back against the cellar wall to assure the pieces won't fall. One day she found the entire pile on the floor. Somehow it had fallen without a sound. Neither she nor her husband had ever heard a rumble from downstairs. Her cats never venture into the cellar and she and her husband are stumped as to what energy could noiselessly tumble that wood pile.

It is well known that attempts to renovate old houses or buildings often bring out the ghosts of olden times, spirits that haven't entirely crossed over to the next world. There are many artists living on upper Ballou Road, and the woman is intrigued that her house's spirits are also quite creative and versatile, taking an active part in the house's renovation. She wonders what these unseen forces of home and woods might be creating next.

TOWN OF
HADLEY

Hark from the Tomb,
a Doleful Sound.
Mine ears attend the cry.
Ye living Men come
view the ground
Where you must shortly lie.

Sleep on dear babe. Stake thy rose
God called thee home he thought
it best.

Delmore R., son of Ira & Permelia,
AE 1 yr. 2 ms. 6 ds.

S. Kelly

Town of Hadley

The towns of Greenfield and Northumberland both contributed some of their lands to the creation of Hadley in 1801. At first called Fairfield, it was later renamed Hadley after an early resident, and, in turn, supplied some acreage to form the towns of Corinth and Day. The natural resources of the town, especially the roaring power of the Hudson and Sacandaga Rivers in the springtime, drew early settlers and entrepreneurs. Tanneries, sawmills and gristmills quickly dotted the landscape and riversides. Among the early prominent politicians and business owners were the Rockwells.

Katherine's House

Crossing the bridge from Lake Luzerne into the Town of Hadley, one notices a "painted lady" Victorian house high on a hill to the left. It is the Saratoga Rose Inn and Restaurant, a building which provides not only captivating gourmet meals, but also a tantalizing ghost story.

Built by Judge Jeremy Rockwell in 1885, the house was a wedding gift from the Judge to his daughter Katherine and her husband, Meyer Van Zandt. The Judge was a prominent politician and civic leader in the rural hamlet, and always anxious to promote local commercial growth. Van Zandt had been lured to Hadley by Rockwell with the proposal to build a mill near the junction of the Sacandaga and Hudson Rivers. At their first meeting in Rockwell's home, Van Zandt became enamored of Katherine, agreed to stay and build his mill, and began to court the beautiful young woman. In celebration of their engagement, the Judge had a new house built for them on a hill across the road. On their wedding day, Meyer and Catherine announced plans to have a large family and fill the new house with children. But this never came to pass.

Within a few years, Meyer developed a virulent illness and quickly died. Katherine was grief stricken and, at the funeral, adopted the widow's black dress, which she wore until her death in 1918. One can imagine the grief that assailed her as the beautiful dreams for the future were dashed.

87

In 1919, the house was sold to The Hudson River Health Sanitarium, a business group that promoted the "Kellogg Diet," a vegetarian innovation that stressed whole grain consumption, and promised excellent health. The Sanitarium flourished, as it became a magnet for urbanites fleeing big city pollution and epidemics, such as the Spanish Flu that had just swept the nation. During the Depression, however, few were able to patronize the center and the business failed. In time the Rozell family purchased the property and maintained a funeral home there into the 1950s.

With the coming of the Interstate Highway System, however, tourists became diverted from the Adirondack foothills, and with the decline of small business and tourism in the area, Hadley's summer population slowly decreased.

Abandoned on the hill, the old Van Zandt house sat waiting. Jim and Margaret Mandigo, from Corinth, saw an opportunity to develop a unique restaurant, High Clere, and bought the old house, in spite of hearing tales from real estate agents and neighbors that all hadn't been quiet since the last occupants.

They were told that two city people, seeing the 'For Sale' sign in front of the house during the late 1950s, walked up the hill and onto the porch, while awaiting the real estate agent. As the house was reputedly empty, they were startled to see an old woman wearing a white dress sitting on a couch in the front room. Her face was turned away from them, so they rapped on the window glass. They reported that the woman spun to face them and "flew up to the ceiling." That was enough to quash the couple's plans, and they fled, leaving the real estate woman puzzled when she arrived. When the pair called her later, she discovered the real reason they were "no longer interested."

Additionally, just a few years later, another couple from downstate saw the listing sign and the still-magnificent building, with its Victorian architecture, as they passed by. They, likewise, contacted the real estate agent, made an appointment and waited for her arrival.

As they waited, they walked up the driveway and onto the porch. They were impressed with the beautiful hardwood floors that could be seen through the windows and, walking to the front door, were surprised to find that it opened easily. Entering, they began to tour the house. Outside, they heard the sound of wheels coming up the gravel drive...not an automobile, however, but iron-rim wheels such as those on wagons of long ago. Looking out the living room window, they were amazed to see an old coach pulling up out front, and a driver in frock coat and top hat stepping down from his seat. The man commenced walking up the long front stairway and onto the porch. As his hand turned the front doorknob, the couple was stunned to see a woman dressed in white lace coming from upstairs and descending the front stairway into the foyer. Then the driver and white gowned woman walked *right through* the city people!

At the foot of the hill, as the real estate saleslady pulled up, she was amazed to see the wide-eyed couple sprinting to their car, heedless of her hail, and zooming away. If this was a scene from Katherine Van Zandt's life, the down-staters wanted no part of it! But Jim and Margaret loved the old house and for several years had a successful bed & breakfast and restaurant operation there, working with Jim's cousin, Tom Gamache.

Their daughter, Cate Mandigo, famous Adirondack artist, worked with her husband at the restaurant when they were first married. Her spouse, bussing tables one evening, was taken aback by the sight of a lovely woman, wearing a long white lace gown descending the foyer stairway, probably about to enter the dining room. He didn't recall such an elegant woman lodging at the inn, and wondered at what table she was sitting. When he returned from the kitchen with an empty tray, he scanned the dining room. No such woman was dining there!

High Clere closed in 1983 and Tom agreed to stay on as caretaker until new owners could be found. But Jim warned him, "Tom, you're going to have to share the space with a ghost or two." Tom smiled; he didn't believe in ghosts, but, before long, he began to find his upstairs bedroom disturbed. Objects were mysteriously moved from where he knew he had placed them. His knick-knacks often unaccountably fell to the floor, and once he could have sworn that he saw one sail across the room. For Tom, the final proof of the ghosts' existence came one evening, as he began filling the tub in his room. As the water ran, he went to a nearby room to attend to some business. Hardly had he left his room, than he heard the faucets squeaking—someone or something was turning them off! As he went back to his room to find the culprit, he then heard the faucet in an adjoining room open and *that* tub begin to fill. "Well, Jimmy warned me!" was his wry commentary.

Eventually, Tony and Nancy Merlino bought the property and, before opening a new B & B, began a major effort to modernize the building without losing its Victorian flavor. In 1987, as they spruced up the interior, Tony sat atop a step ladder in the front room, repairing some cracked plaster near the ceiling. At midnight, their chime clock began to toll the hour. Instantly, all the lights in the house went out. Perched on his ladder, Tony listened to the next eleven chimes in total darkness. On the twelfth stroke the lights mysteriously turned on again, but Tony, naturally shaken, began to rationalize that he probably was "too tired," and descended from his ladder to call it a day. Though Cate Mandigo had forewarned them with baffling tales of her family's tenure, Tony still couldn't believe in ghosts. Consequently, because of his disbelief, he was hard-pressed to explain how or why his tools kept disappearing. He couldn't come up with a plausible explanation.

Another day, taking a break from painting, Tony sat on the front porch. A movement to his left startled him, and he turned just in time to see something (a woman in white?) disappear along the north side of the house. He sped down the steps and peered around the long side of the building. No one and no thing was in sight.

After their B & B had been open for a few years, a Vermont couple, water dowsers, lodged there. The pair knew nothing about the house's history, but sensed that it needed dowsing, and Nancy smilingly agreed. The pair turned up what they called "an energy field" near the fireplace in the foyer. Though Nancy didn't tell them, they were explaining their findings to her while standing next to Katherine's photo, which has stood on the mantle since the Merlinos became owners. Without telling the couple about the photo or Katherine's antics over the years, Nancy moved the picture into the Library, and then asked the Vermonters to dowse the house again. The second time, the pair was puzzled to find the energy field gone from the foyer, but now present in the Library.

When I first wrote this story in 1998, I visited with the Merlinos to get the details of their stewardship. Nancy sat with me in the dining room, providing some old photos and many stories. At the end of my interview I asked if I could see Katherine's photo, and Nancy escorted me to the foyer, reaching left around the doorway to get the picture. She frowned as we moved toward the fireplace. "Strange," she said, "it isn't there. But it's *always* there!" We searched the entire downstairs, though the photo was nowhere to be found. She showed me all the upstairs guest rooms, but Katherine's photo wasn't there either. Nancy apologized for Katherine's manners, but I hypothesized that the former owner just didn't want to meet me. Several days later, Nancy called to tell me that the photo had mysteriously turned up in the Library but, of course, nobody knew how it had gotten there.

The Merlinos and I have since become good friends and, several times a year I do "story dinners" there for the public's entertainment. A great dinner and two hours of ghost stories pleases the guests, who get an escorted tour of the house beforehand. Each time I've visited, I have tried to get in early to ask either Tony, Nancy or Ed, their chef, "What's new?" There always seemed to be some new and unaccountable activity. For some time in 2001, I'd hear about either the recurring sounds of breaking glass (when none could be found) or the actual breaking of glasses or bottles, often under strange circumstances. Of course, all these phenomena are attributed to Katherine Van Zandt.

In 2003, a new phenomenon came to light. Tony had a security video camera positioned to watch and tape any activities in the restaurant's interior after closing. One day, he noted that some movement had triggered the camera overnight, and he played back the tape, one frame at a time. There are frames where nothing moves, then suddenly, outside the office door, *there's a dog!* There is a malamute dog with its curly tail standing in the doorway—*just for one frame*, then he's gone. The Merlinos researched the house's history. Did the Mandigos or Tom Gamache have such a dog? No. Did any of the Rozells have such a dog? No, but a neighbor remembers that a *neighbor* of the Rozells did! So, one more chapter is added to the history of The Saratoga Rose. The tale elicits further questions, however: how does the ghost (if that is what it is) of a long ago neighbor's dog end up doing night patrol inside the building? What does a ghost pet have on its mind? Looking for scraps from the Prime Rib special? It has been difficult enough hypothesizing the intent and motivation of the ghostly humans there, but a canine spirit offers further areas for speculation.

In June 2004, the Merlinos decided to sell the Inn, and everything about the sale proceeded smoothly until, one day I got a phone call from Nancy. She had found the kitchen stoves unaccountably turned on when she came downstairs in the morning. Things were disappearing in an odd manner. Katherine was obviously upset! What to do? I suggested that Katherine had been "manager" of the estate for so long, that she had to be included in the negotiations, so I suggested they do a little ritual, old owners and new owners together. "Get the new owners and yourself and walk into each room of the house, inviting Katherine to meet you on the stairs. Then, after allowing her time to compose herself and arrive, address the (apparently empty) staircase and tell her you know she loves the house, as you and Tony have, and you've taken good care of it. If they'll go for it, the new owners might also tell that they, too, will enjoy making this old home a place of hospitality for others. That should do it," I said.

And apparently it did. The sale concluded without trouble and Richard and Claude assumed ownership. When I called one of them a month later, he said things were calm, "but, you know, there is this one light in the downstairs that is doing strange things...."

TOWN OF HALFMOON

Our hopes alas in the grave are crushed
And with thee buried in the dust
Yet still we would not dare complain
Our loss is thy eternal gain

Oh cease to drop the pensive tear
Tho death to dust lies mouldering here
My better part has winged its way
To regions of immortal day

S. Kelly 05

Town of Halfmoon

Halfmoon, drawing its name from Henry Hudson's discovery ship, was formed around the old Half Moon Fort in 1700. This place on the river was Hudson's northernmost penetration of the upriver wilderness in 1609. The town is bounded by the Hudson and Mohawk Rivers, as well as the Erie/Barge and Champlain Canals. Long a center of river and land commerce, Halfmoon today is a swelling suburban community.

The Brick House

Several ghost stories from southern Saratoga County are given in Dr. Louis Jones' folklore classic of 1959, *Things That Go Bump in the Night*. Here is a documented tale that is over a century old. On a hill just north of the Crescent Bridge on Route 9, stood an early 1800s brick house built and owned by P.S. Woodin, early businessman in the town. The home overlooked several Woodin holdings, including the old Dry Dock Basin on the Erie Canal.

A driving force in the town's early commercial development, Woodin had the finances and will power to compel others to agree with him. It was thus a frustration to him that at least one resident of his former family home would not obey his wishes for order. Someone's spirit inhabited the old brick home, which sat squarely on the old Indian warpath that ran along hilly slopes just north of the Mohawk River. Today, when all is said and done, we can only hypothesize that the ghost was a long-dead Indian brave or some long-ago Woodin ancestor that inhabited the structure.

In the 1920s, P.S. Woodin chose to rent the old house to the occasional tenant, though none ever remained there long. Sooner or later, giving a variety of excuses, the renters gave their notice and left. Eventually, the building became known publicly as a haunted house, and it became common knowledge that renters were being tormented by a mischievous ghost.

Woodin related the rumor to his cousin, who thought himself brave enough to face up to any wraith. The cousin agreed to move into the building and was astonished, on his first night there, to have the bedclothes forcibly snatched from the bed while he slept. Not willing to accept it as ghostly

95

activity, the man rationalized that the snatching had been caused by a strong breeze blowing through the window. Within an hour, the cousin found himself without covers again! He straightened the blankets once more and returned to sleep, but was rudely awakened in the same manner once more. This nighttime tug-of-war continued for weeks until the cousin could stand it no longer.

The cousin discovered another phenomenon: the bedroom door refused to stay shut. Secure it as he might, the cousin heard the door squeak open each night, as if some invisible resident were checking the house. In desperation, the man nailed the door shut when he retired to bed. In the middle of the night he heard the door squeak open and, lighting a lantern, found the door standing ajar. The fastening nail was never found. Eventually, the cousin threw in the towel and joined the list of those who had vacated the old house.

A few years later, when the house was again unoccupied, one of Woodin's workmen discovered the white bones of a human skeleton near a well or spring in the backyard of the house. Old Mr. Woodin gave the remains a decent burial in a nearby graveyard, hoping the structure would finally be habitable. But he hoped in vain.

For years afterward, even after old P.S. Woodin's death, tenants came and went. After 1950, there were several short-term owners, and neighbors became used to seeing the "For Sale" sign on the western side of Route 9, just above the Crescent Bridge.

In 2001, there was a mysterious fire in the house, leaving it too badly damaged to restore. Sometimes, when a fire occurs in a haunted house, the ghost takes the experience as an exit prompt. But, it might take more than a fire to send the ghost on its way here, because this long-term spirit tenant was tenacious, resisting all attempts to evict him.

Today, a commercial storage unit facility occupies the site. Without human inhabitants to frighten, perhaps the old ghost indeed has left, but there are so many stored contents to rummage through....

The Colonial Green House

From time to time, we hear tales of a ghost in a brand new house. How does that happen? Investigators of such phenomena must examine the previous structures, residents or activities on that site, hoping to gain deeper understanding of the energies that may remain at that location. Here is a tale that teases the historian.

In the early 1970s, the remnants of an old farm were bulldozed to create a development of modern apartment buildings and homes. Most of these apartments today house city workers who depart for urban jobs early in the morning and return in the evening. One such apartment building is a house on Cambridge Drive.

Chris and her husband, the owners, first became aware of their unseen resident(s) during Saturday morning bed making. He worked on his side of the bed and she worked on hers, stopping her sheet-tugging for a moment to align a small statue on the shelf over the bed. Her husband, irritated, asked, "Why do you *do* that? You know you can't keep it in one spot for two days straight." Irked at the derogatory comment, Chris became angry and words led to other words, and finally, to hurt feelings. The husband, who had a government job, was bound by fixed rules, and it irritated him that Chris couldn't get her knick-knacks in one fixed location that he could get used to. Every couple of days, the objects were moved. Chris always stated that *she* hadn't moved them and, in fact, had been oblivious to their movements. He was a fact-oriented guy, and he knew *he* wasn't moving them, so the culprit seemed obvious, hence his criticism of Chris. After observation for a few days, she reluctantly had to agree with her husband that *someone* was moving them!

Chris heard her daughters, seven and nine at the time, screaming in their bedroom one day. When she rushed to their room, she found the girls excitedly claiming that their radio wouldn't turn off, and it sat blaring away on the bedroom floor. "Just take the batteries out," Chris told them. "But Mom, we *did*!" She opened the battery door to find the children were telling the truth—no batteries. So, she gave the radio a few smart smacks on the floor and the noise stopped. She left the room scratching her head.

Just before Christmas in 1993, the girls invited some close friends to a sleepover. As she tucked the girls in, Chris checked all the decorative electric window candles, making sure that each was unplugged. Everyone

97

went to sleep, only to be roused around midnight by a loud banging in the unoccupied room at the end of the hallway. The girls stood frightened in their doorway as Chris approached the closed door of that room. She was puzzled at the light that shone beneath the door. Opening it, she found a candle glowing brightly in the window. This puzzled her, as she remembered her fastidious routine of pulling all the plugs from the wall sockets. And there was this cord, dangling alongside the socket—unplugged. *But the candle was lit!* She never figured how that could happen, as she couldn't also understand the electric toy that she saw spinning in the center of the room. Who or what had turned both objects on?

The following year, on New Year's Eve, Chris and her husband chose to spend the night quietly at home. Suddenly there came a sharp knocking sound on the front door. "Funny, I didn't hear the storm door outside open," the husband said. Chris got up and opened the door, only to find nobody there. And the outer storm door was both closed and locked. Her logical husband puzzled over who or what could get into the narrow space between the doors and knock?

As with most ghost stories, the events are seldom frightening, but those who live with ghosts can often do a lot of head scratching—Chris's family included. On many occasions she catches movement in her peripheral vision. Once she saw a transparent woman sitting in her wicker chair. When she turned to look directly, however, nobody was there. Many ghosts don't like scrutiny and vanish if you look directly at them.

On one occasion Chris visited a psychic to ask questions about her home. The woman told her, "The spirits want to come into your room with the gold chalice." The statement puzzled Chris, as she could remember no such object in the house, and she left the psychic, feeling that the statement was off the mark. She was happy to think that there probably was nothing extraordinary, and all the strange events could be logically explained.

The next day, she began to straighten the contents of her daughter's bedroom, and was startled to discover a needlepoint that the girl had been given for her First Communion. It was a beautiful fabric that had a gold chalice as its centerpiece. Now, Chris pondered—the psychic, who had never visited her home, *was* accurate, so perhaps, there was an influx of spirits in her home. She reasoned, "They couldn't be bad ones if they just wanted to see a communion chalice."

Bells

On April 29th, 1967, late at night, in a house just off Route 146, Marie Bell arose from bed and shot her husband Roy to death. Then she went downstairs and shot her son, whose body she carried to the upstairs. Going to her daughters' room she shot them both in their sleep. Then she left the house, traveling to a nearby supermarket, and bought several bags of groceries. She brought them home and placed them in the freezer, sat at the kitchen table to write a brief note, then took her own life. These events, which were for the most part impossible for neighbors to comprehend, produced such grief and outrage in the small community that the people I interviewed thirty years later are still suffering.

When the Sheriff's Department completed the investigation, relatives cleaned up all signs of the crime and put the house up for sale. Most local people, mindful of the house's tragic past, refused to even entertain making a purchase offer. Only an occasional outsider, ignorant of the carnage, cared to inspect the building. As the house seemed not about to sell quickly, the heirs rented the building. The tenants came, and then left, after only a short habitation. Perhaps some knew of the murders and some may have had overactive imaginations, but others reported disturbing phenomena.

Eric and his family lived there briefly and reported many strange events. He and his neighbor, Chris, preferred rock music and often turned the channel knob on Eric's radio to a popular station, only to watch in fascination as the knob turned itself to bring in a country music station, music they detested. Only later did other neighbors inform them that Roy Bell had been a country music fan. Many nights Eric's family heard footsteps echoing in the house when all were in bed. Normally warm rooms suddenly became frigid, as if to signal that an ethereal presence had just passed through, then warmed again. It wasn't long before Eric's family, like so many others, moved on.

Again, the For Sale sign was put up but, once more, few came to look at the property. Eventually, the sign was taken down and the house sat abandoned. During this period, a clairvoyant Schenectady woman, who used to commute along Route 146 daily in the 1970s, was surprised to often see a young girl around ten years of age "always standing forlornly in the same spot, next to the big tree in the front yard. Day after day, the little girl made no movement and had an expressionless face. She just sagged against the old willow tree in the front yard." Finally, the motorist stopped and questioned friends who live near the house. The friends could suggest no neighbor child of that age or appearance and, in any case, the neighbors were not likely to let their children play "at *that* house." The woman quickly recognized that the girl was in spirit, lost in a world of her own. As a spiritual clairvoyant, she urges passersby to pray for the spirits of departed loved ones, as *she* prays for the little girl when passing the former Bell house, so that the souls of the child and her family can be released into the Everlasting and find peace.

Today the house is inhabited by a long-term owner, but whatever experiences the new family has had are kept private. It is to be hoped that the souls of all the Bell family have now found release.

Old Jim

The Dater family came to Halfmoon in the 1700s and, around 1752, built an inn on what is now Meyer Road. The building was a place for local meetings and festive occasions at the time when the colony of New York was about to join in a struggle for independence. Stagecoaches traveling north, south and west often stopped there for a change of horses, and to permit travelers some refreshment in the tap or dining rooms, or to lodge overnight. But the tavern also had its local "regulars."

According to Dr. Louis Jones, in *Things That Go Bump in the Night*, the first rendition of this story in print, a local character named "Old Jim" was one who frequented the bar whenever he had a coin in his pocket. Most often, Jim was a beer drinker, but if his finances allowed, he'd spring for some "hard stuff." Even in the days of wide-open alcohol consumption, the prodigious amounts of alcohol that Jim quaffed on payday made him the object of the locals' criticism. In his defense, Jim usually responded, "Never a drop of water will pass *my* lips, or that will finish me!" And he made sure to consume enough liquid refreshment each night so as to be barely able to stumble home. When sober, he worked for a pittance, doing farm labor for the local agrarians, but on payday he always ended up at the Dater Tavern.

One day, a local farmer, needing help, sent to the Tavern to find Jim. Nobody remembered seeing him that day, and searchers went to his home. There, Jim was found in bed—dead. The Grim Reaper had finally come to take Old Jim "across the river," literally. Local people passed the hat and enough money was gathered to give Jim a decent burial on the hill *beyond the nearby creek.* One local farmer observed that, "We planted him close enough [to the Dater Tavern] so he can go down and get a drink if he wants one." And sure enough, from then on, strange noises were heard in the tavern's taproom on occasion, long after closing time, though nobody ever saw Jim arise from his grave and descend the hill.

In time, the Daters sold the tavern and it was converted into a farmhouse. During its years as a residence the new owners heard the occasional clink of drinking glasses in the former taproom and strange rustling sounds in unused upstairs rooms. One of that family's daughters is reputed to have walked uphill to Jim's gravesite one day, and kicked at what appeared to be a white stone. Dislodged, the object revealed itself as a human skull, which rolled down the hill and into the small stream at the bottom. Soon, creek water was rushing over the jawbone believed to have been Old Jim's. According to Dr. Jones' account, this surely finished off Old Jim.

Perhaps. But, when the building again reopened in the 1950s as The Olde Dater Tavern and Restaurant, strange goings on were again reported. Sherri, a former waitress who opened in the morning and closed again at night, was instructed by the former owners to leave a shot glass filled with whiskey on the bar before she left and locked up at night. They also had her leave that day's newspaper folded on the bar. She remembers, upon opening each morning, the shot glass was empty and the newspaper was unfolded and rumpled! Old Jim, again?

Waitresses in The Olde Dater Tavern recounted stories of the restaurant tables becoming unstable. Upon inspection, they discovered that one or two caps on the bottom of the table legs had been removed. No patron or employee was ever discovered doing this prank. Also, light bulbs were mysteriously unscrewed just to the point where they couldn't illuminate without being twisted in once more. Morning workers often found water faucets unaccountably opened and gushing.

The Olde Dater Tavern closed in 2000, and then reopened in 2003 as The Olde Dublin Inn, under the new ownership of Angie and Billy Byrne. Billy recalls helping with the interior renovations upstairs in the Galacia Room, which probably once served as sleeping quarters for the Inn's guests. "At quitting time each day that February we'd leave our tools on the floor

101

where we were working. Some of the tools were quite expensive. Then came the first triggering of the silent alarms on our security system, each exactly at 12:40 a.m. The Sheriff's deputies arrived with drawn pistols, expecting some bold burglars. But each time, they found nobody. We knew the legends of Old Jim, and one night, entirely frustrated at these events, I just called out, 'Okay, knock it off, will you, Jimmy?' There was no answer, but the alarms haven't rung since."

Billy took the author to the base of a large wall mirror and showed me some replaced floor planks that indicated that an old stairway had come upstairs at that spot. "One day I entered the Galacia Room, which was empty, and started walking toward that mirror," he remembered. "Suddenly I saw a man reflected behind me in the room. I spun around, but nobody was there. Since then, another of our staff has seen the guy, dressed in old fashioned clothing. None of us knows for sure his identity."

For the staff at the Inn, Old Jim is a reality, even if no one on the staff feels they have seen him clearly. The fourth light over the bar occasionally swings in large arcs, though no wind is blowing and no windows are open. Behind the bar is a brass 'tip bucket' fastened to the wall, and there seems no logical way for the bucket to move, though it is suspended on small link chains. Yet, from time to time, the cashier or bartender will see it swaying rapidly, seemingly in violation of gravity's forces.

One waitress went into the cellar to get an item and felt a woman's presence, though she saw no one. In the kitchen, the chefs occasionally see cooking pots sliding slowly across the shelf or range, untouched by any visible hand.

For those interested in good food and the opportunity to observe supernatural phenomena, it's hard to think of another dining spot in Saratoga County with such a variety of happenings. Do stop in and say hello to Old Jim. He may respond.

TOWN OF MALTA

I KNOW HIS FACE IS HID,
UNDER COFFIN LID;
CLOSED ARE HIS EYES;
COLD IS HIS FOREHEAD FAIR.
MY HAND THAT MARBLE FELT,
O'RE IT IN PRAYER I KNELT;
YET MY HEART WHISPERS THAT-
HE IS NOT HERE.

Death, thou art but another birth,
Freeing the spirit for the clogs of earth.

Town of Malta

Near the present day village of Round Lake, the first settlers put down roots in the 1760s, dubbing the settlement Maltaville. Early homes were also built along Dunning Street, which led westward toward Ballston Spa, and many of those early inhabitants are buried in the old Dunning Street Cemetery. Businesses were founded at the town's major crossroads, and these thrived as centers of commerce for the many local farms. At the town's center stood the Parade Ground, where local lads mustered and trained to fight in the 19th Century wars. Round Lake became a major summer campground for Methodist Church meetings, creating a quaint community of Victorian cottages. Saratoga Lake also became a major summer vacation spot with attractions such as White Sulphur Springs inviting health seekers.

The Weed House

In the early 1800s, David Weed built a frame house near the present Cramer Road. It was difficult ground to farm and Weed had to struggle. Only with the help of Louisa, his wife, and two sons could he make a go of the operation. One of the sons died in the 1830s, and then Louisa shortly thereafter. The loss of loved ones and helpers was too much for Weed. He deeded the property to his daughter-in-law, Fannie Brown, and moved to a new life near Oswego. He prospered there after remarrying and starting a new family, so he never returned to Saratoga County.

Fannie appreciated the inheritance but was unable to work the farm, and chose to put the property up for sale. At the time, women were legally unable to sell property in New York State, and the law stipulated that she have a man serve as her agent or guardian in legal matters, and the judge appointed a Mr. Thomas Anderson to fill that role.

Curiously, there seems to have been no ghostly phenomena in that house during the 1800s; perhaps Anderson was still alive. It has only been in the 20th Century that modern residents in the old Weed house have experienced the guiding hand of the ghost. In the early 1980s the present owners relaxed on the old house's sun porch. The day was warm and sunny and the breezes were gentle. The relaxing spell was suddenly broken by a resounding crash from inside the house. The family members scrambled inside to survey what must be great damage. They were astonished to find no disaster, no objects moved, and nobody else within the house. After that introduction, the ghost began to manifest more frequently. The daughter was puzzled on two occasions to hear a male voice call her name. In the first instance she believed it to be her father calling and, as is typical of teenagers, she did not respond. After the second, more insistent call, she responded, "What?" At first there was no response, then from another room, her live father said with shaking voice, "Did *you* hear that too?"

The son had an old car, which had broken down in the driveway and had not been drivable for a month or so. One day, the mother noticed that the car had moved some twenty-five feet along the level driveway. The vehicle was too heavy for the son to push, and she knew her husband and daughter weren't responsible. She stood stunned, holding wet clothes in her hands, and a clothespin in her mouth. How could that have happened, and *who did it?* She could only ponder the unthinkable—the ghost of Tom Anderson had been the culprit!

Many times it is the female members of the family who are the beneficiaries of Tom's assistance. One snowy evening, the daughter, Lillian, sat studying on her bed, having raised the window a bit to let fresh air into the room. When she completed her studies for the next day's test in school, she turned out the study light and dropped off to sleep hoping for a "snow day" on the morrow, and unmindful of the open window. She pulled the electric blanket around herself and dozed. A few hours later, her dream state was shattered by a loud noise. She awoke and realized that her window shade had suddenly and noisily zipped to the top of the window casing. She snapped on her study light and was stunned to note that snow had blown through the window and onto her electric blanket, which was now wet. She might have been electrocuted had she not been roused by the noise!

Tom seems to have taken special care of Lillian, awakening her one morning with a loud voice calling "Lillian, it's time to get up!" Figuring the voice was that of her father, she sleepily obeyed and headed for the bathroom. As she passed her father's bedroom she spotted him fast asleep in his bed. Who had awakened her?

It seems that Tom Anderson, having taken the oath to aid Fanny Brown over a century ago, is determined to remain on the job, helping all the women residents almost two hundred years later.

Marvin's Tavern

Along the Town of Malta's western border lies East Line Road, and though there are scant traces of it today, there was once a prosperous settlement called East Line there. Several churches and stores, plus at least one hotel served the neighboring farm families. Sometime in the 1830s, William Marvin came to the little community on East Line Road, and a few miles south of Dunning Street, built a small tavern. For many years the locals quaffed a variety of beverages, slaking a thirst built up over hours of hard physical labor. But farming was such very hard work, and as the 20th Century approached, more and more farmers sold their lands and moved to nearby cities to work for wages. Marvin's Tavern could no longer support its owner, and the building became a residence.

Through the years, the house had little upkeep and began to show its age. After being sold to its last family of residents, a young lad in the household invited a friend to spend the night while his parents were away. The two boys stayed up late chatting and finally fell asleep. Lawrence, the son, entered the borderland between waking and dreaming and soon heard the raucous laughter of a man. Something in his wakeful consciousness reminded him that he and his friend were the only occupants of the house—no man was present. He awoke and looked over at his friend sleeping—it couldn't have been him, so a puzzled Lawrence finally drifted back asleep.

The old house had an upright piano in the downstairs living room. It became a focus for the boys' good times. They sat for hours and played the only tune they both knew, "Chopsticks." Lawrence remembers, "The tip-off that someone else was there was the slight breeze and the change in the tone of our music, as if now bouncing off a surface very close behind us. We didn't know what else to do, and rather than give in to our fears, we just kept on playing. Have you ever been too scared *not* to move?" he asked. "At one point, the presence seemed to leave us, but when we started in on our next song, it returned. Our backs began to tingle as if someone or some *thing* was about to touch us. We turned to each other and said, 'There it is again! Did you feel *that*?' I asked him. 'Yeah, how about you?' he answered. And then we sprinted outdoors!"

The two boys never felt at ease in the house after that, and when Lawrence grew older he moved away. Today he lives a few miles south of Marvin's old tavern. In recent years it served as a storage building for farming operations on the property which had been willed to Lawrence. "Today, however, I never go in the place. I'm afraid old Marvin and some of his bar cronies are still there!"

East Line's Ghost House

It is always fascinating to find notations about ghosts in the newspapers of yesteryear. Folks had to deal with them back then too.

By the 1890s, the little hamlet of East Line was undergoing major changes. Some of its older buildings had been torn down and others had burned. What had begun as a thriving farm community in 1786 was rapidly disappearing.

In 1895, a major fire occurred in East Line, and the *Ballston Journal* of October 26th of that year recounted the details of the destruction of two buildings, a house and a store. The article told of very strong winds approaching forty-five miles an hour, and the conflagration, once begun, had engulfed the structures before the volunteer fire company could muster. John Oliver's wife and daughter, living in a nearby house, were forced to flee, fearing their own home would be consumed.

The newspaperman continued the story by noting with satisfaction that "The Haunted House" across the road (probably not the Olivers') had not caught fire, writing, "His ghost-ship was not disturbed." The article gave no speculation as to the ghostly identity. What the spirited manifestations might have been in the past, also, were not recorded. Suffice it to say that youngsters in the small village knew of the presence and avoided the house, especially on dark nights.

Years later, the old "Haunted House of East Line" was demolished, and nothing today indicates its precise location. New stores and a gas station are resurrecting the community of East Line, but few there know of its former ghostly denizens. Even today, the few scientists who are disposed to investigate such matters cannot say for sure what causes a ghostly manifestation to take place. Spiritual investigators, however, strongly suggest that it is unfinished soul business that keeps the entity earthbound.

Malta's Pit

Many of the old houses of Malta have secrets. Some are never to be revealed, and others come to light only by accident, and even then are imperfectly understood. On County Route 80 stands an old house dating from the 1800s. It was once the center of a grand farm, but modern times have ended the agricultural activity and changing economic conditions have created new challenges.

In 1981, the owner's husband died, leaving her with many expenses that needed resolution. She decided it might be nice to create a rental apartment on the side of the house where a small addition jutted out, to provide additional income and occasional company. She sought a contractor who could carry out her plans. The man she hired stripped off old clapboards and wall insulations, reducing the small addition to just framing timbers. It was decided to install a good floor, but first a new concrete footing for a support to hold up the center roof structure was needed.

By the time the excavation began for the footing, the chill early winter winds were blowing, and the work crew hurried to get the framework enclosed before snow came. As the workmen began to excavate a 4' x 4' hole, they noticed a strange phenomenon beginning. With each shovel-full of dirt removed, an additional shovel-full seemed to sift into the center of the hole and disappear. It was as if some unseen hand was aiding them *from below*. Soon the excavation was widened to one foot in diameter. Indeed, there was a cavity of some sort below the surface, into which the soil was disappearing. Having no light to drop into the hole, the boss picked up a long iron rod and plunged it into the abyss. The rod fell with a clunk onto some unseen object, and when the man withdrew it, pieces of oak wood were impaled on the tip. As the workmen studied the pieces of wood, it became clear that this was worked wood—one side of this sample had been planed smooth.

The work crew began to hem and haw: worked wood below ground level? It sure sounded like a coffin—could this be an unmarked grave, and if so, whose? The cold winds penetrated their coveralls and the men began to feel a chill of another kind. One of the men suggested that the wooden object below might be some long-buried treasure chest, but few reasoned that the farm family had ever been *that* prosperous. The boss called for the concrete truck to begin filling the hole. He figured it would take less than a cubic yard to do an excellent job, but when the truck driver settled his bill with them, the expense was great. Eleven cubic yards of pre-mix had disappeared down that hole. Strangely, none of the workmen really wanted to know where the concrete had gone, or why. The bill was paid.

The plywood sheathing and insulation board were soon secured to the wall studs and the building was completed before the snow came that evening, and before the owner returned from her employment. When she heard the details of the day's work she was horrified. But a lot of concrete and money had gone down that hole, and she judged it the better part of wisdom to accept what was done and look forward to the job's completion.

A month later, with wiring and inside finishing all completed, the apartment was ready to rent. But the first tenant didn't stay long, mumbling something about changed plans after just a few days residence. And the next tenant didn't stay much longer, either. Before leaving, one tenant told her that the apartment door would unaccountably fly open, making him too jittery to stay. Another departing renter told of a little old man walking slowly through the apartment and out the front door. To allay her fears, the woman had dubbed the ghost "Grandpa Henry," hoping to treat him as an ancestor of the widow's family. But the spirit's nocturnal wandering became just too much for her nerves.

Today, the owner has given up attempting to rent the small apartment. *She* gets along well enough with whoever or whatever remains in the house, so, "Why push my luck?" she asks.

Hair Raising?

A neat cottage stands at 123 Dunning Street today, offering the latest in hair-styling techniques. Over the last century, however, the building has passed through many owners since it was first built as a home for the pastor of the Malta Presbyterian Church across the street.

When Will and Cristina Connolly purchased the old house in May 2002, they found many problems in converting the former residence to a modern business structure. Some old walls had to be removed or altered; new windows were needed, as well as modern forms of insulation. The contractor's job was made difficult by an upstairs window that would not "stay in place" when installed. Each day, when the carpenter came to work, he found the window had fallen out of its framing and onto the floor, 4½ feet below, without breaking. Though he nailed it in place before leaving at night, the incident repeated itself over several nights before it finally stayed put. The man speculated that it was almost as if the building was resisting modernization.

An elderly neighbor informed the Connollys that a former resident of the house had died in a fire there. As they continued renovations, they did discover a burned section of floor in a rear room, but it looked as if the fire had been confined to a small spot. Golfing with strangers a year later, Will was surprised when one of the foursome, a retired State Trooper, told of carrying a burned man out of the building years ago. Apparently, the victim, identified as "Farmer Brown," had suffered a stroke in his chair, and his fallen cigarette ignited both man and chair.

The old kitchen at the rear of the house was too dilapidated and was removed. The new owners had the contractor build a new rear wing. One day, one of the workmen came to the Connolly's and asked, "What's with the old lady in the house?" He had seen an elderly woman's face looking out the window at them when they drove up. Cristina had to explain that there was no old woman presently in the house.

Hurrying to open on schedule, the Connollys worked to decorate the new interior. As Cristina painted a wall one day, she took a break and looked toward the back door. She was startled to see a man standing there. "Then, suddenly he was gone. He wore a hat, I remember, and I've never seen him since" she told me. On another day, she opened the door into the front hallway and briefly saw a woman in old-fashioned clothing, and wearing an apron, who quickly disappeared. "I remember that she didn't seem to have any real feet, and seemed to be floating above the floor," she said.

"Later, I began emptying the upstairs, as we had things to store up there. I had just finished cleaning out and sweeping a particular closet, and was moving to the center of the room, when a black plastic cap rolled out of what I *knew* to be an empty closet, and came to rest against my foot. There's something about that closet!" she told me, "I often hear knocking from up there when I'm working downstairs, but there is never anyone or anything up there when I check. And on a few occasions, I've felt knocking underneath the first floor, even though I *know* there is nobody in the cellar!"

The Beauty Society opened in July 2002 and immediately attracted customers. Soon after they opened, Cristina noted that a hand dryer on the counter kept turning itself on. Was this an electrical malfunction or a ghostly

111

hello? They checked the wiring and plugs but found nothing amiss.

In December of that year Cristina finished her hairstyling for a woman customer, who then left. Two hours later, however, the woman phoned and apologized for her question, but just had to ask, "Do you have a ghost?" She went on to relate how she had sat in the first chair and had heard a bell. The back door appeared to open and a man stood inside, doffing his hat. "I watched him look over into the styling room for a few minutes, staring at what you were doing, then, opening the door, he left. He wore a black hat and overcoat, and had a rather large mustache. When his hat was off I could see his hair was parted in the middle," the woman remembered. Cristina was at a loss for words because, though she was working assiduously, she knew that if another customer had entered, she would have noticed.

Bill Schwarting, noted area water dowser, believes he can also locate spirits as well as water. He has found it curious that his L-shaped locator rods work very well for water or objects in fields and outside peoples' houses, but almost never inside. Nevertheless, *in houses that have a spirit*, the rods become quite sensitive. He has slowly perfected his technique by visiting many of the known haunted sites in the Capital District. "I found my L-rods crossed only in the spot where the charred flooring was discovered by Will and Cristina," he told me. Bill notes that several other area dowsers use their Y-rods or L-rods to establish communication with ghostly entities.

It is difficult to ascertain who the man and woman ghosts might be. Their clothing styles indicate early 1900s, though the building was constructed about 1850, and the church in 1845. It doesn't appear that "Farmer Brown" is involved, though the site of his death agrees with Schwarting's sensitivity. My best guess is that the ghostly characters may be a former minister and his wife, still observing the home from which they did good work for others, and where they are now surprised or fascinated to find Will and Cristina, ministering more to peoples' outer, rather than inner, beauty as souls.

CITY OF MECHANICVILLE

Sleep on, sleep on
thou dearest one
To us thou wust
a treasure dear.
But god thought best
to take thee home
The dearest treasure
we have here.

Betsey A.,
Dau't of William and Elizabeth,
AE 14 years, 9 mos. & 16 das.

S. Kelly 05

City of Mechanicville

Mechanicville is situated on the Hudson River near the southern end of the Champlain Canal. After Saratoga Springs it is the County's second-largest city. Before the coming of the white man, it was already an important commercial location, situated on the Iroquois trading and war trails. The Europeans added to this network by extending rail lines of the Delaware & Hudson and the Boston & Maine railroads to the north, south, and east, locating a major switching yard here. Commercial and pleasure boats ply the canal, leaving the Hudson River and aiming for Lake Champlain, some sixty miles north. This city is the final resting place of Col. Elmer Ellsworth, Civil War hero and Lincoln's close friend.

The Methodist Church

In the Colonial times, a tavern stood on North Main Street and a small watering trough stood outside, offering refreshment to the tethered steeds while their owners quaffed ale inside. The proprietor of the tavern favored King George III but kept his sentiments to himself. However, once the Revolution began, he refused to permit Continental soldiers to water their horses there. As the following story unfolds, it is important to remember that there was friction and animosity among early residents of Mechanicville at that tavern site.

In 1885, the Troy Conference of the Methodist Church chose to erect a noble brick edifice at the former tavern location, and the congregation may have rejoiced at building a house of God where locals had once imbibed Demon Rum. Dedicated pastors and lay people created a firm spiritual community, but it is likely that at least one of them passed on with "unfinished business" and has remained in the building for some time.

In 1997, I met a member of the present congregation who apprised me of the church's ghost. He gave me a tour of the building, saying, "I love to take part in worship on Sundays, and even more, I love choir practice, although I don't like to be in here by myself. I pick up feelings and energies that other people are oblivious to." We walked the soft crimson carpet and enjoyed the afternoon hush while the sunlight streamed into the sanctuary, illuminating the wooden pews. There was nothing abnormal about the interior furnishings, so we continued on.

My guide related the experiences of an old friend, Robert, the church organist after World War II. He was a gifted man of great intelligence and love for his organ students. One afternoon, after the day's last student departed, Robert sat quietly for a moment, and then began to walk through the rear of the church, turning left toward swinging doors into the South Foyer. Strangely, the doors were moving slowly, as if some worshipper had just passed through, though Robert knew he was the only one present in the room. "Suddenly those doors opened out with a bang, and Robert was enveloped by a frigid gust of air that swirled around and around him for several minutes. Then, as quickly as it came, it ceased. The swinging doors closed and the organist was alone," he told me. Overwhelmed by the experience, Robert went into the foyer and crossed to the minister's office door. When the pastor heard Robert's tale he called Bishop Oxnam in Troy for guidance. Later, Robert learned that this was not the first call that the pastor had made to Troy. The bishop came to Mechanicville, did a blessing and exorcism of the building and departed. This appeared to be the end of the matter.

However, on a Thursday evening in the late 1980s, choir members assembled for weekly practice. It is traditional that singers enter the sanctuary from the Assembly Hall at the rear of the first floor. Members took their places in the choir stalls, opened their hymnals and prepared to sing. Suddenly, the pastor recognized that something out of the ordinary was unfolding. Then, other members observed a stranger coming down the aisle. A thin man dressed in black walked slowly down the aisle toward the choir and sat in a pew near the front. "He didn't look normal," my guide recalled. "He had a very sallow complexion, almost waxy, and seemed to stare rather than watch us. Our pastor knew every member of the congregation, but didn't know this man. He wondered how and why a complete stranger would be auditing weekly choir practice. Along with several other singers, our pastor was itching to make the stranger's acquaintance." But, as if sensing the choir members' curiosity, as soon as practice concluded, the interloper stood quickly and retreated back up the aisle and turned into the Assembly Hall doorway. The minister quickly pursued him, but when he entered the rather large room, nobody was there. It would have taken a minute for anyone to traverse the space to the outside door, which was shut. "We examined the small classrooms beside the hall, even searching upstairs, but all to no avail—nobody was there. How could he simply vanish? And why?" my guide asked.

For a few years, members of the choir debated as to the identity of the man in black, but no one could identify him. As years passed, the event dropped from their conversations. Some had theorized the figure was the shade of a dedicated former pastor. Others wondered if it might not be a former congregant who had died with an unsettled soul. And even others spoke in hushed tones of the possibility that an angel who loved heavenly music had been there to critique. Nonetheless, because the church is quiet today, the speculation has ceased.

The House on Second Avenue

"As far back as I can remember, my sisters and I had strange experiences in the house," said Marie, now in her thirties. "Most of the events happened upstairs where we most loved to play. I recall running through the hall one day, probably chasing my sister, and passing a bedroom. As I sped past, I noted a little girl sitting on the bed. A few seconds later I realized that couldn't have been one of my sisters, and I ducked back to see who it was. The room was empty. I was astonished by the experience, and my young mind puzzled as to just what or whom I had seen. It was a little girl with long hair who simply stared, as if observing our play. She had no expression. I kept these experiences to myself at first, but one day my sister, Ann, had been outdoors roller-skating and told me of looking up to a second floor bedroom window. A little girl stood in the window, and Ann was sure of one thing—it wasn't one of her sisters!"

Marie wasn't sure her parents knew of the phenomenon, but suspected her Dad, a professional man, didn't want to see or discuss such events even if he had seen the child. As the girls discussed the ghost girl's appearances, they discovered that they all had experienced someone invisible coming up behind them, though when each turned, nobody was there. "Dad retired when I was in Seventh Grade, and was now around the house more often, and we couldn't understand why he didn't see the girl. We asked him about it, but he told us not to discuss the matter, so we didn't do so in front of him. All through high school the events continued, but less often as we grew older," Marie related.

Eventually, she married and moved away for a time, and only returned to visit the house after she had her first child, a girl named Alana. "All of a sudden, with my little girl there, the frequency of sightings escalated. We started *hearing* the little ghost girl running through rooms upstairs, when we knew none of us was up there. One day, when Alana was teething, she felt miserable and was crying. I held her against my shoulder and was trying to soothe her when, suddenly, she stopped crying and began to chuckle. My Mom and sister, Theresa, could see Alana looking directly at a corner of the room and giggling though *we* saw nobody in the corner.

"On other occasions, as grownups, we've continued to have eerie experiences. I sat holding and rocking Alana a few years ago, when suddenly, from up on the shelf, we heard a music box begin to play. It had sat there, untouched for several months, and none of us had been near it that day. When it began to play, we all were concerned. Yet, music boxes are usually soothing for babies, and Alana *did* calm down and go to sleep. It's almost as if my sisters and I have an invisible nanny who wants to help us soothe our children."

In recent years, the grown sisters, not living full-time in the house, have begun hearing their names called in a flat, female voice when they return to their childhood home. They never have been able to discover any non-living source for the sounds, or any living person's trickery.

Taking our cue from the little girl ghost, we might speculate that a child living in what was once a duplex house, may have died. Perhaps a ghostly mother grieving the child's loss also frequents the house. Certainly, before the days of antibiotics and immunizations, many children died before reaching adulthood. In any case, this ghost child seems to enjoy Alana's company, as she appreciated the friendship of the girls of the previous generation, and is now trying to entertain them all.

Hanging Around

The freight yards at Mechanicville were a beehive of activity in the early 1900s. Many trains were "made up" there each day, and before the 1960s, when railroads were a major form of transportation, crews were reporting to their trains at all hours of day and night. Many of these workers stayed overnight in the old YMCA building near the corner of North 3rd Avenue and Elizabeth Street, just a short walk from the yards. Long hours and perhaps an unhappy domestic life led one of these train men to hang himself in that building's upstairs in the 1940s. For quite a while the man's spirit lingered, though today he seems departed.

For a few years the building was unused, and then the City of Mechanicville created a Community Center there, offering assistance to city residents with problems. John Volpe served as a counselor for teens in that building in the late '70s and early '80s, and remembers strange events upstairs when he worked the evening shift. "One of the first things I noticed was that we couldn't keep those upstairs windows closed," he said. "When we'd close up at night, I made sure to close and lock all of them, but in the morning, several or all of them would be open again. We never could determine who did it or why.

"Added to that, and maybe this is why people thought we had a ghost, were the noises we could hear from downstairs. When we'd have a discussion session with kids at night, or maybe a program, there would be the sound of slowly-pacing feet upstairs. Bob, who worked with me as a fellow counselor, heard unexplained sounds from the empty upstairs, which he shared with me, and I *knew* that nobody was up there. Soon, the kids began to notice the strange events also. Sometimes they would stop their conversations in mid-sentence, listen and look up to the ceiling. Probably they knew the legend as well as we did, but nobody ever ran up to look around, either."

John said that after four years the City closed the center and the building has other uses today. He has not heard of any further noises or phenomena, so perhaps, all the window opening was the action of the disconsolate trainman, trying to catch the wind of Spirit and fly from what had become an intolerable earth life.

TOWN OF
MILTON

121

Rest worthy sire, thy race is run
Thy toil is o're, thy work is done
Thy god propitious sits above
To bless thee with a Savior's love

She was but as a smile,
Which glistens in a tear,
Seen but a little while,
But oh! How loved, how dear!

S. Kelly 05

Town of Milton

Milton was formed from the Town of Ballston in 1792, and then gave up some of its original area to the Town of Greenfield the following year. Fast-flowing streams invited the development of grist mills and saw mills, and other small enterprises grew quickly, augmenting the town's reputation as a vacation spot because of mineral springs discovered there before the Revolutionary War. The Village of Ballston Spa occupies much of the town's southern area. Milton took its name from a contraction of its early description, "mill town." Two early manufacturing sites can still be viewed at Factory Village and Rock City Falls.

The Middlebrook Farm

Hezekiah Middlebrook, a courageous early settler, built a small farm on Middle Line Road near Gordon's Creek in 1773, as the Revolutionary War loomed on the horizon. Indian raids were frequent in the neighborhood and, coupled with raids by roving bands of Tories, made this frontier home a dangerous site. Middlebrook was a high priority target for British sympathizers because he was a member of the Town of Ballston Committee of Public Safety. Nevertheless, he and his family escaped royalist vengeance and the Middlebrooks held title to the farm until the early Twentieth Century.

In 1923, the farm was purchased by the Kingsley family, who employed a hired man named Bill. The last of the elderly Kingsley sisters promised to reward Bill's kindness and hard labors by deeding him the property when she died. But it was not to be. The woman, plagued by debt and the effects of the Depression, ran into financial difficulty and the farm was seized by creditors in satisfaction of the debt. The new owners permitted Bill to live in part of the house until he died. After his passing, the house was purchased by the Milanese family. Bill reappeared to help them as he'd helped the Kingsleys.

One day, Duke, an old friend of Bill, was delighted to see Bill again, peering in the window. He noted that the Milaneses were converting Bill's old bedroom to an expanded living room and wondered if Bill's consciousness had appeared to supervise the construction. Mark and Terry Milanese note

123

that it is in this new living room that Bill usually manifests his presence. They have an antique rocker that sometimes begins to rock of its own accord. And one of the Milanese nephews recalls that, when he came to visit from Ohio as a youngster, he sometimes saw a dark figure climbing the stairs when every other family member was accounted for. He related his story to the grandmother, who confirmed it was likely Bill, still active in "his" old house. To this day, though his appearances are decreasing in frequency, Bill is always polite, never frightening the family or its guests, and Terry notes that it is almost a pleasure to have his spirited company.

The Lost Jewel

In the late 1850s, Samuel L. Day came to Ballston Spa and opened a jeweler's shop. Day was innovative and inventive and loved the intricacies of machinery, especially small clocks and watches. In 1862, a daughter, Abbie, was born, delighting the Days. The joy was short-lived, however, when Mrs. Day died five years later. Raising the bright daughter was both a burden and a joy to Samuel, and Abbie repaid the love by remaining single and serving as her father's housekeeper until his death in 1892.

In 1904, following Abbie's death and burial in the Day plot at the village cemetery, the house was sold. For the next eighty years there was a succession of owners and tenants at 133 Milton Avenue. Then, in 1985, John and Heidi rented the house and began an adventure.

Just before Halloween of that year, the family was relaxed in front of the living room television. They were puzzled when a loud noise resounded from the upstairs front bedroom over their heads. All family members were watching television—who or what could be making the ruckus? As they pondered how to react to the person or thing that had broken into the upstairs, they heard the sound of an object moving—first into the upstairs hallway, then down the stairs. They began to panic, as do many people when confronted with the sudden appearance of The Unknown. Then, just outside the living room doorway, there was a scuffling sound, as if the intruder had blundered into some obstacle.

Heidi is involved in the antique business and prizes many old possessions, one of which was a unique floor lamp that she had placed upstairs. Suddenly she saw its lampshade quivering on the floor, just outside the living room door where the noise had abruptly stopped. "What's worse," she said, "the shade was moving—toward *me*! I jumped from my recliner chair and grabbed the lampshade from the floor and threw it out onto the porch, where it remained until the garbage man took it away the next day. I haven't shared this story with many people," she told me, "because who could believe the story of a lampshade moving under its own power?"

Her husband, John, joined her in front of the television on another late evening after the children had gone to bed. All at once, from the dining room, came the sound, "click-click." At first, neither one could fathom the origin of the noise, but then, John recognized the clatter as the metal drawer pulls on the buffet—suddenly clicking away, rising and falling onto their metal holders. He sprang to his feet, hastened to the dining room, and turned on the lights. He was astounded to see all the buffet drawer pulls rising and falling in unison, as if choreographed. "After that I was no longer objective about whether or not we had ghosts!" said John. Was someone or some thing trying to get their attention? And, if so, why?

He couldn't help but share some of the strange incidents with his co-workers. One of them, a woman named Maria, who believes she is psychic, told John of her previous night's dream, one in which she saw a man in a wheelchair peering from an upstairs window. The window's description sounded uncannily like that in John's upstairs. Then Maria disclosed her intuitive belief that the man seemed to be seeking a lost jewel or cameo, and she wondered if his search might be the source of John and Heidi's haunting. She didn't know what John and Heidi later learned—that Samuel Day had been a *jeweler*.

Up to that time, John and Heidi had referred to the ghostly presence as "George," a very common appellation for ghosts, by the way. Now they believe they have identified the spirit and loudly call him "Sam," whenever his activities become too rambunctious. Their landlord, an amateur historian, knows much about the early history of the village, but hadn't known the entire history of the house until the activities became raucous. Then, after two weeks of historical research, he produced the name and information about Samuel L. Day's family life. How could Maria, the psychic woman in Cohoes, stumble on a jeweler living in John's house a century ago? Likely, she is indeed psychic.

The house's ghostly activities flare up from time to time, though Sam has adapted pretty well to life with John, Heidi and their girls. One of the daughters sat doing homework on her bed a few years ago. Papers and books were strewn over the blankets as the girl rushed to complete her research on a school project due the next day. Suddenly, a heavy presence sat down on the opposite side of her bed. The girl called out loudly to her mother, "Mom, I'm trying very hard to get my homework done and Sam keeps turning my book pages!" Heidi counseled the daughter to speak nicely to the ghost and ask him to cease his interruptions. "Sam, please go away and bother someone else," was all the propriety that the girl could muster, but it seemed to do the trick. The opposite side of the bed rose and there was no more ghostly activity that night.

Whether the movements are caused by Sam alone, or Sam and his loyal daughter, it's hard to say. So dedicated to her housekeeping and care taking while alive, Abbie may well have stayed on the job in death. Many ghosts are the residue of a person extremely dedicated to an earthly task, and who cannot or will not recognize that death has intervened. Some need to feel needed, and remain in denial of the next step in their soul's journey.

Someone continues to move coffee cups about on Heidi's kitchen counter and, from time to time, a needed flashlight disappears. Sam, Abbie, (or whoever) seems to return the items within a matter of hours, however.

A wedding reception was held in the house during a warm summer, not long ago, and guests remarked at the frigid spot in the living room, which vanished the next day. Perhaps Abbie came, briefly, to witness a wedding that she never had. One hopes that Samuel Day is slowly getting the message that he no longer needs to cling to village life along the creek, and that he become aware of the river of time and life that continues to flow through eternity.

For several years the ghostly activity was less frequent, but there was a brief flare-up in 2002. The older children had moved on, and only the sixteen year-old daughter remained at home. At that time, Heidi met a woman with some psychic ability, with whom she discussed their many years of experiencing the phenomena. The woman informed her that when a child is in puberty, there are often strange events in the house, as hormonal energy flares up. Objects can seem to move under their own power, and many have called these phenomena "poltergeists." Shortly after this meeting, Heidi went upstairs to her bedroom to get a book. Her daughter and husband remained in the living room, watching television. As Heidi reached the stair top, she heard footsteps ascending behind her and assumed it was her

126

daughter, but when turning to speak to her, found nobody there. This corresponded with their hearing footsteps (Heidi assumes they are those of a man) walking through the upstairs hallway, pausing at each of the bedroom doors, as if carrying out a silent inspection, then moving on to the next. This may be a residue of Samuel Day, still looking for the cameo lost almost two hundred years ago.

"We're never afraid of these events," Heidi confided, "it's really a comfort to know that the house we love was, and *is*, loved by others."

Ben Franklin Comes to Ballston Spa

Few moderns are aware of the power of the religious pursuit called "Spiritualism" that swept America and Europe in the late 1800s. At that time, people interested in seeking information from the spirits, gathered in meetings, and eventually, churches, to receive "spirit messages" from or through mediums. Others privately used a device something like a modern Ouija board in their homes to make contact with The Other Side.

The Village of Ballston Spa was a hotbed of Spiritualist activity, especially at Centennial Hall on Bath Street, just south of the old leather mill on the creek. Now, long demolished, the hall was the weekly meeting place for dedicated seekers such as Samuel Hides, who farmed a piece of land on Malta Avenue near the present Hyde Boulevard. In later days, someone tried to name the thoroughfare after him, but did so ineptly.

Spiritualist mediums regularly claimed to access the spirits of Cleopatra, Julius Caesar, Abraham Lincoln and George Washington, as well as other historical notables and Native Americans.

Many people in Ballston Spa rued the day that horse racing and gambling had come to nearby Saratoga Springs, because these attractions had drawn summer vacationers and health seekers away from their small village's economy. Many hoped to regain the glory days of the Sans Souci Hotel, the Eagle Hotel, the Aldrich House (now Brookside Museum) and other spa resorts.

Samuel Hides literally became the instrument for renewed interest in American history and the Town of Milton's mineral resources. One evening while working his "spirit board," Hides noted that his planchette became suddenly invigorated. The spirit entity seeking communication identified itself as none other than Benjamin Franklin, who expressed an interest in the village and its springs. He promised to disclose the site of a new mineral spring, one "that will be for the healing of the nation." Fortunately, the spring was located on Hides' farm. He and other entrepreneurs began drilling and an artesian well burst forth, offering over three hundred gallons per hour of pleasant-tasting mineral water.

Hides incorporated his Artesian Well Company in 1869 and began bottling the fine waters. Many agreed that Franklin's description of "a spring of remarkable medicinal values," whose waters were now distributed almost worldwide, had been fulfilled. Until 1952, the Hides-Franklin Spring flowed, providing water used mainly in the production of local soft drinks in its last days. However, times and tastes changed, and the enterprise folded, with the spring capped off, and its old cobblestone building razed.

Today, Ballston Spa is again bustling and rebuilding, offering a National Bottle and Glass Museum, the Brookside Museum, and a re-drilled Sans Souci Spring. Perhaps it is time for the village elders to reacquire the spirit of Franklin and re-open The Hides-Franklin Spring. This inspiration can at least be for the better health of the Village's people, if not the nation's.

The Influence of George West

George West came to Saratoga County from Devonshire, England, in 1849, tantalized by the commercial possibilities in paper manufacture. He established several mills in the area, most notably at Rock City Falls, and became the inventor of the folding paper bag. West served in both the NY State Assembly and the US Congress, and as President of the First National Bank in Ballston Spa. His wealth permitted him to build a stately mansion in Rock City Falls and a sprawling factory in Ballston Spa, eventually the Union Camp Paper Bag Co., and later called Bischoff's Chocolate Factory.

Just west of West's Ballston Spa mill, on Prospect Street hill, were houses for his workmen and their families. A local woman grew up in one such house years after the Chocolate Factory closed. She recounted an incident in which a visitor to their home awoke during the night to see a small girl climbing the stairs to the attic. Later, in talking with old-timers on Prospect Street, she discovered that a child fitting that description had died of tuberculosis in the house years before.

This woman also remembered that a family member practiced sprinkling salt on the window sills at night because, according to family tradition, ghosts must pick up every grain of salt in the house before they can begin haunting. This tedious procedure must prevent much mischief. In any case, her home was demolished after World War II, and the haunting apparently ended.

My informant also remembers the tale of the "ghost bell" often heard on Prospect Street Hill at the stroke of midnight. No such bell existed when she was a child, but history records that the West Paper Bag Factory at the corner of Milton Avenue and Prospect Street did have a bell in the 1800s that sounded regularly, calling employees to their work shift. It was a common belief in the village during the first half of the 20th Century, she said, that it was old George West, himself, who sounded the bell, still calling workmen to their shifts in the empire he built.

Today, the main building of the factory has been rescued from the ravages of time, and converted into a variety of professional offices. There are no obvious ghostly phenomena, but many employees in the building testify to doors that mysteriously open and close, as well as unaccountable sounds. It may be that George West, or one of his old-time foremen, still prowls the factory. West apparently must divide his labors, however, as he also keeps busy overseeing his old Rock City Falls mansion.

During the years after World War II, West's Rock City Falls home fell into poor repair, even after local entrepreneurs converted it into a multi-dealer antique shop during the late 1960s and early 1970s. Along with the wear of constant foot traffic inside, the property declined outside. The first indicator of "something strange" occurred when one of the dealers encountered a Revolutionary War soldier in the upstairs front sitting alcove! He chose not to publicize the event because, historically, the house didn't exist until one hundred years *after* the Revolution, and such a sighting was surely "impossible." In the 1980s, other proprietors changed the old house into a bed and breakfast establishment.

None of these post-war efforts were financially successful until Jeff Wodicka and his partner, Neil Castro, bought the house and made a great effort to restore some of the West mansion's opulence. In December 2001, prior to The Mansion's grand opening, a painter named Jay was applying paint to an interior wall. Suddenly, all the lights in the house went out, frightening him. He walked to the open front door, saw the neighbors' houses still alight and, remembering the ghostly rumors, set down his paint bucket, and fled. As he did so, he swears, he heard a fiendish chuckle from the piano room doorway.

Jeff's daughter, Lori, now the manager, went on a European trip after The Mansion opened, so Jeff agreed to fill in as temporary manager. On the night that Lori left, and with a snug house full of summer guests, he went to bed in his favorite room, the small, former Servants' Dining Room. About 3 a.m. he was awakened by the screams of a small child emanating from a front downstairs bedroom. The crying continued for about ten minutes, leaving Jeff disturbed. He and Lori had agreed to a "no young children policy," and he wondered why she had let a room to a couple with a young child. In the morning, co-owner Neil asked Jeff if he had heard the child crying, and Jeff decided the incident *hadn't* been his imagination. He looked over the room reservation list, only to be stunned—there were no children in the building! At first, he didn't want to explore the implications—"Ghost Child in local B & B?" He could just *see* the headlines! Nevertheless, he soon had a confirmation. Early in the morning, shortly thereafter, he came into the Dining Room and found a hastily-scribbled note from a woman lodger who had departed during the night. She wrote that she had left because of having felt "watched" by some entity that she couldn't see. She loved her room, the service, and the food, but couldn't stand the suspense, and therefore had to leave. This puzzled Jeff, Neil and Lori, as they had restored The Mansion to its former elegance, and had spared no expense in creating, above all, a luxurious, but *restful*, atmosphere.

Lori has had her own experiences as manager. The Mansion is often used as a distinctive wedding site, and after giving an engaged couple a tour of the building one evening, Lori escorted them to the rear parking lot and saw them off. Returning to the house, she experienced the kitchen lights switching off as soon as she entered the room. Strange, she thought, that all the lights would go out just as she entered. She walked into the formal dining room and *those* lights also extinguished themselves as she entered! Then, the same event occurred as she crossed into the front parlor! "That was enough for me for one night. I gathered up my things and went to bed," she said with a smile. I didn't have the heart to ask if the ghost turned out her *bedroom* lights.

When I asked about ongoing problems, she expressed her frustration with the house sound system. A restful atmosphere pervades the house, aided by quiet music flowing through the downstairs. She has changed the location of the music system amplifier several times in order to stop the music from slowly decreasing its volume. Day after day, she has to return to restore the volume to an audible, though subdued, level. "It's as if there's someone here who wants absolute quiet, but I can't imagine who it is," she said with a smile. "Another incident that has us all puzzled was the experience of a Massachusetts woman who stayed here. Before she left, she took many photos of our parlor interior. Then, when the film was developed, she found an orb of light near the fireplace in one photo. We were together when the woman shot that picture, and I *know* there was no ball of light visible then." Readers who love ghosts and ghost stories will remember that light orbs are often thought to be visible emanations of spirit energy.

"Maybe my favorite story so far relates to another prospective bride, who also came to see The Mansion and interview us," Lori said. "She was so happy to finally see the interior of the house, as her grandfather had been one of the first chefs in the building's early bed & breakfast days in the 1980s and had often spoken about the house. Now she could see for herself the antique gas lamp chandeliers, the wonderful old paintings and the period furniture. As we walked and talked, the woman told me that her grandfather often spoke of 'The Lilac Woman,' a ghostly presence that used to announce herself with the fragrance of lilacs, though she was never seen. According to this granddaughter, it had been a delight for him to recount the story. I wondered aloud why *we* hadn't experienced the smell," Lori said. "The lady smiled and replied, 'Well, when Grandpa left his job here, he took some small item from the house as a memento. So, apparently, The Lilac Woman came along with that object when he came to live with us. We now get the scent in *our* house!'"

In August 2004, I received a phone call from co-owner Jeff Wodicka. A pragmatic and down-to-earth entrepreneur, Jeff nevertheless accepts that energies and entities *may be* an unseen dimension of The Mansion. He told me of a recent episode, in which a famous photographer from Saratoga requested the use of The Mansion to do a photo shoot involving a small ballerina in the Victorian décor. The man posed the little girl on the bed in front of a large mirror in the former Servants' Dining Room. The resulting print showed a wispy fog emanating from the mirror and completely surrounding his model. Was this a ghost, and if so, whose?

A month before this shoot, an employee brought her one and a half year-old daughter to work with her. The child amused herself by walking through the spacious rooms, then turned into the smaller room mentioned above. Quickly, the child emerged and stated to her mother, "Baby, ball!

Baby, ball!" When the grownups asked the child where the "baby" was, she took them to a corner of the Servants' Dining Room, where she pointed to an apparently empty space. A week later, again having brought her daughter to work, the mother lost track of the child and, searching the house, found her happily seated in the dry bathtub of *that* room, hugging an invisible being, who, she told her mother, was another baby.

Slowly, the evidence is building that The Mansion retains the spirit of a small child. Perhaps it is one of George West's family, who continues living on in the splendor of yesteryear.

Little Boy's House

Not far from the West home and Empire Mill in Rock City Falls, is a white frame house that once served as home to one of West's paper mill workers. Almost a hundred years later, in the 1970s and 1980s another family lived there, and one of the sons, whom I will dub "Tom," had some interesting ghostly experiences in the house.

As a youngster in 1975, he had an argument with his older brother, which continued on past bedtime. Much later, during the night, the older boy felt someone or something rub against his leg. He automatically brushed at the touch, as if swatting a bothersome fly, but felt no response. Ready to blame brother Tom for awakening him, he turned, only to find his sibling asleep. On several succeeding nights the same event occurred and the older brother was angered that his kid brother would persist in the mischief, but he couldn't catch the lad awake or moving. Resolving to catch the culprit, the next night he laid awake, feigning sleep. As quickly as his leg was touched, he sat upright. There stood a luminous little boy at the foot of his bed! In fright, he fell flat upon the sheets and covered his head with the blanket.

In the morning he related his tale to Tom, who now gleefully assumed the role of scoffer, refusing to believe his older brother's wild story. It was only a few years later, when the elder boy had left home, that Tom had his own confirmation of the experience.

Tom had moved his bed near the bedroom window, as he enjoyed looking out at the moon and stars before drifting off to sleep. One night he awoke and realized he could see no stars or moon outside—in fact, he couldn't see out the window! Some dark shape was blocking his view, and gradually he came to see its details. It was as if a man in black stood between him and the window, the man's head obscured in a black hood. Slowly, the figure's hands stretched out over Tom's prone body. His heart began to race and sweat dripped from him—what was coming next?

Suddenly the intruder turned and walked off, into a closet on the house's outside wall. How could he get out of there? He couldn't! White as a sheet, Tom leapt from his bed and ran to his parents' bedroom, where they greeted him with the question, "What's wrong, Tommy, did you see a ghost?" This incident provided plenty of dinnertime conversation for the next week. The family speculated—were there two ghosts, a child and a man? And if so, who were these entities? They never identified the man in black. A neighbor, however, was able to offer a clue as to the little boy ghost. He told of a six year-old boy that resided in the house years before. The child, who had gone out to play on the icy Kaydeross Creek behind the house one cold winter day, and fell through a patch of thin ice into the frigid waters. He drowned before rescuers could retrieve him. Apparently some part of the child's consciousness remains in the house that he called home.

Though these events happened almost thirty years ago, they awakened Tom's consciousness to other realities. They are still fresh in his mind today, and as he spoke to me about his experiences, he said, "This all caused me to think really deeply about life—how short it can be for some people, and the ultimate meaning of being alive."

140-142 Milton Avenue

A village parking lot stands on Milton Avenue today where a large white frame rooming house stood until the early 1980s. Before that time, Genny, living in a first-floor apartment, had a number of strange experiences.

She often sat in an easy chair just inside the apartment door to the left of the building's main entrance. Outside her door was the stairway to the second floor, and she could easily see other tenants coming and going.

One evening as she sat watching television, she heard footsteps ascending the stairs, though nobody had come onto the porch or opened the front door. Puzzled, she took one step, opened her apartment door, and looked at the stairs—nobody was there, though she continued to hear footsteps climbing the staircase.

Another day, her parents arrived to drive her to a medical appointment. She made one last trip to the bathroom and noted she had used up the last toilet tissue on the roll. Genny made a mental note to buy more tissue at the store before returning home. "I was expecting a baby and had a lot of things on my mind, but when we left the doctor's, I forgot to buy new paper. When I returned to the apartment there was a brand new roll of paper on the holder in the bathroom. It wasn't my parents or me—how do you figure *that*?" she asked me.

Genny admits to being intuitive, and therefore may hear and see more spectral things than the average person. Wherever she has lived, she has had ghostly experiences, or met other residents who have. One of Genny's neighbors at a previous apartment on Bath Street told her of a startling phenomenon. After supper one evening, the woman, whom I will call Mary, went to her kitchen and got a snack from the refrigerator, then returned to the living room to continue watching television. At the next commercial break, Mary returned to her kitchen and was startled to find all the kitchen cabinet doors standing open. There was no other explanation than that there was a resident ghost in that old early 1800s house.

Genny also met a neighbor named Sally while living in the old Lee House, a large stone apartment building on Bath Street. Sally told of setting prepared dishes of food on the kitchen counter as suppertime neared. Then, a ringing telephone interrupted her and she went to another room to answer. When the conversation ended, she returned to the kitchen to find that some mysterious force had pushed all the bowls and dishes to the far end of the countertop.

These three women lived alone in the old stone building. None could explain their experiences. What is known about the building is that Joel Lee, a local businessman, had built the house as a wedding present for one of his children almost two hundred years ago. Perhaps some of the love from that first pair of residents remains, with someone still trying to assist the present single residents in their daily tasks.

Apartment houses and hotels are often sites of ghostly events because of the vast number and variety of former residents. Each one has brought personal concerns, troubles, joys and sorrows. Just the act of leaving, of moving out, is often traumatic and perhaps there has been an accumulation of disturbed energies at this old house on Bath Street hill.

Elm Grove

John Howard and his wife built a grand farm near the intersection of Middle Line Road and Route 29. On a knoll overlooking Star Brook, in a grove of beautiful elm trees, they constructed a Federal Style home and many outbuildings. It was a prosperous farm for many years, and then passed into others' hands. Since the Howards' time, the property has had many functions. Once a hop farm, it produced large harvests of hops used in brewing. Later on, it was a sheep farm, and then in the early 1930s, it was converted into a quaint restaurant called "The Tavern on the Hill" that attracted well-to-do summer patrons after the horse races in Saratoga. In the 1950s, Bill Ashton raised beef cattle on the grounds. But none of these enterprises did well financially after the Howards.

When I first viewed the property in the early 1970s, The Saratoga Stud Farm operated there and the fields were filled with beautiful thoroughbreds. Shortly after that, a disastrous fire occurred, burning many buildings, one containing dozens of horses. The circumstances of the fire were suspicious but no arson was ever proved. Then the farm sat deserted for about ten years until veterinarian Mark Crootof and his wife Caren bought it in 1984.

Local people scoffed at the idea that this old farm could ever be beautiful and productive again, and criticized the Crootof's scheme for a veterinary hospital and clinic so far from Saratoga. One neighbor came by and told them of a ghost in the attic, where the window could never be closed and remain shut. Mark agrees that they, also, found it to be true—the window was forever open despite their best efforts to close it. That part of the house was old and structurally unsound, he said, so they tore it down, in effect solving two problems at once. The Crootofs not only established a thriving clinic on beautiful grounds, they also restored the old frame home to the beauty that the Howards had created.

135

Tearing down a haunted section of the house didn't solve the *other* spirit problems, however. On their first Christmas in the house, Caren was baking holiday cookies with the help of her three year-old in the kitchen. The little girl asked, "Mommy, who's that?" indicating someone in a nearby room. Caren told me, "First, I *knew* that my daughter and I were alone in the house. Secondly, I knew we had to finish those cookies that day. Thirdly, I knew if I looked and *did* see a ghost, *that* would be the end of baking that day! And I couldn't afford to look—I wasn't ready to meet a ghost!" But, mulling the matter later, Caren suspected the little girl had seen something or someone, and wondered who it could be. "When our cooking was finished, bedtime came early for the two of us *that* night," she concluded.

She recalled a favorite babysitter who worked for her. "The young woman was very helpful and trustworthy, but there was one room she just would not enter," Caren said, pointing to the dining room. When I visited the house I found that room not at all foreboding; it was big, bright and beautifully restored.

Some weeks later Caren heard the television playing in the downstairs after midnight, and she *knew* she had turned it off before going to bed. Nevertheless, she couldn't get to sleep without going back downstairs and turning it off once more. Yet, in the morning, when she descended for breakfast, the morning news was playing to an empty room. Perhaps the spirit, if it was one from olden times, was fascinated with the entertainment of today.

Then, a few years later, as another daughter readied to blow out the candles on her 8th birthday cake, the child inhaled, but was amazed when, what seemed a "sudden breeze," extinguished all the candles. Such a fortuitous gust has not occurred since. If the spirit was trying to be helpful, it gifted the girl with a never-to-be-forgotten experience.

Though no ghost opens attic windows today, something turns the attic light on from time to time. It is not uncommon to experience ghostly energies turning electrical circuits off and on. A psychic friend informed me that it is one of the easiest "tricks" for a spirit to learn when they no longer have a body, but want to communicate their presence to the living. Several such electrical incidents are recorded in the stories of this book.

One of the more exciting electrical "malfunctions" involved the dishwasher. Mark and Caren were expecting a relative to visit in the early 1990s. They wanted everything to flow smoothly as they hosted the visitor, but on the day the woman relative arrived, the dishwasher just quit. No amount of examination could reveal what had broken. However, on the day their guest left to return home, the dishwasher resumed its normal function, as if it had never been "on vacation."

One suspects that at least one of the spirits is female because of the sometimes domestic helpfulness that the Crootofs experience. One night several years ago, when the girls were young, one of them went to sleep covered only by a thin blanket. Nighttime temperatures crept lower and the girl soon realized she was cold. She was semi-awake at that point, and realized that a warm quilt lay folded in her closet, but she couldn't awaken enough to get out of bed to retrieve it. Slowly, she slipped back asleep. The next morning, the girl was astonished to awaken snuggled comfortably under the quilt. When she arose from bed she thanked her mother for being thoughtful and keeping her warm. Caren, however, said she hadn't gotten up in the night and had not covered her daughter. Is Mrs. Howard still attending to the comforts of the nicest family to occupy her home since she died?

When one interviews neighbors along Route 29, there are many memories of the horrible Stud Farm fire and the screams of the horses. Several people expressed their pleasure at seeing a busy animal hospital functioning there—now healing injured animals. Such a happy transformation of the old farm may be what keeps Mrs. Howard playing hostess to all the visitors who come to Elm Grove Farm.

Crandall's House

In the early 1880s, young Julia Stone from Troy fell hook, line and sinker for the smooth words of Sylvester Crandall from Ballston Spa. Despite her mother's cautions about Crandall being a con man and a no-good, the young widow married the tall, handsome man and moved north to the Town of Milton, where Crandall was in the process of constructing a fine Victorian mansion on the hill near the present day Milton Terrace School.

Exactly how Crandall amassed the money for such a nice house and grounds is not clear, as previous ventures as a stockbroker had been failures. At the dinner table each evening Sylvester hatched one get-rich scheme after another, but never succeeded at any. Julia's teenage daughter often looked at her mother and rolled her eyes as the step-father continued dreaming aloud. Neighbors often told of seeing him ensconced high up in the cupola at night, plotting and looking out over the village, as if it were his kingdom. Undoubtedly he was concerned over mounting bills and debts, as his financial intrigues were not sufficiently successful to keep the family from a bank foreclosure.

Finally, Julia's mother (also named Julia) talked some sense into her daughter, and came to Ballston Spa to rescue her daughter and grandchild and return them to the comfortable life they'd known in Troy. The train arrived at Ballston Spa station at 11 a.m. on December 19th, 1887, and Mrs. Stone hired a carriage to transport her up Shepherd's Hill to the house where young Julia and her daughter were waiting with bags packed. The southbound train was scheduled to pass through the village at 12:20 and all was in readiness for the party to escape. Unfortunately, just as the small group was about to leave the house, Sylvester appeared. He was wild-eyed and raving, and Julia wondered if he had been drinking. He waved a pistol and blocked the back door, beyond which, their carriage stood waiting.

Suddenly and without provocation, Sylvester shot the senior Mrs. Stone, the woman he believed had conspired to tear his family apart. Turning his pistol on his step-daughter, Crandall shot her through the heart. Then he turned the gun on Mrs. Stone's sister and traveling companion, Mrs. Ellis, who was too quick for Crandall, and lurched around the corner, locking herself in a nearby room. Seeing his dreams shattered, Crandall then turned his vituperation on his wife, finally shooting her in the chest. As she fell against a small table and slid to the floor, Sylvester began to realize the horror of his actions and knew his life was over. He moved swiftly to the cupola, and neighbors, attracted to the house by the gun shots, heard one final shot fired in that upstairs room. Then all was quiet.

Mrs. Ellis emerged from hiding and tried to comfort Julia Crandall, gravely wounded on the floor. Neighbors burst into the house and, discovering the mayhem, summoned the constable, who found Sylvester Crandall dead, with a bullet hole in his right temple.

This was perhaps the goriest murder in the Town of Milton in its history, and the double funeral attracted throngs of villagers. Julia Crandall, who survived the attempted murder, and her aunt, Mrs. Ellis, testified at the coroner's inquiry at the courthouse. The coroner concluded that Crandall was the perpetrator, and that Crandall was dead. There was no question about that fact—dead as a doornail. Yet, strange tales to the contrary were circulating.

One neighbor was astonished to pass the Crandall property months later, only to spot Sylvester Crandall working in the garden at dusk. The lanky shape was unmistakable—it was Crandall, sure enough. But, how? Then, in the winter of 1889, James Mann, a neighbor was negotiating Shepherd's Hill in a blizzard. His horse and sleigh were having a difficult time. They had just reached the crest of the hill when the sleigh's runner caught a rock along the road's edge, and the sleigh and Mann were overturned in a snowdrift.

As Mann sought to dis-entangle himself from the reins, and tried to avoid the horse's thrashing hooves, some great force *lifted* the sleigh off its occupant. The horse regained her feet, and the harness and traces all fell back into place. Mann was grateful for the stranger's help, and as the man passed the reins once more into Mann's hands, he was astounded to peer into the bearded, sallow complexioned face of Sylvester Crandall. For years afterward, when Mann recounted the event, nobody dared to question or disbelieve him. He was a church-goer, a pillar in the community, and a man well-known not to imbibe alcohol. But nobody could explain or understand the occasional mysterious sightings of Crandall either.

The old Crandall House has since passed through many hands and, in 1970, became the Dunton's house. Mindful of the legends, the new owner proclaimed "If I ever see a ghost around here, I'll put him to work in the garden!" And that threat seemed to forestall any sightings because, for a long time, there were no more stories. During Dunton's tenure, Universal Pictures Studio from Hollywood attempted to sign a contract to include the old mansion in the 1971 film, *Ghost Story*, but negotiations fell through.

When the house was deserted afterward, local people claimed to see a bluish light in the cupola, though there was no electric power in the house.

As the Ballston Spa Middle School and Milton Terrace Elementary Schools were constructed on the neighboring lot, hundreds of village children pass the old Crandall house each day. Many are drawn in fascination to take the shortcut through the rear lawn to their school. Others walk the entire distance around the Crandall property to get to school, lest a wraith or two ambush them.

The old house today is owned by a local publisher, who has divided the building into several apartments. He insists that all paranormal activities have ceased there, but on occasion I meet past or present tenants who tell of strange stains that will not vanish from floors or walls, while others relate

139

encounters with disembodied voices. So, perhaps the Crandall legacy remains in the energies and memories that occasionally take audible or visible form.

Murphy's Law

Sometimes a ghost will make but momentary contact with the living before passing forever out of this realm into The Great Beyond. Many times these brief appearances are just to pass on some bit of helpful information to the living. Such seems to be the case of a departed school principal.

Dr. Gerald Murphy became the new Principal at Malta Avenue Elementary School in September 1977, and was just settling into his new position. Some in the community felt that his new role at Malta Avenue was something of a demotion, for the man had previously been Principal at the Middle School. Irregardless, Gerry worked at creating a harmonious atmosphere in the old building, bringing teaching staff and pupils into a happy community.

In October, after another hard day's work, Murphy left his building a bit early. He'd been troubled throughout the day with a chest pain and figured to go home and rest. When he went to bed he suffered a ruptured aorta and died in his sleep. At the funeral, a few days later, one of his teachers wept at Murphy's situation, "I think it was a broken heart," she was heard to say. All the building's teachers were overwhelmed at the suddenness of the loss, and struggled to keep happy faces during daily instruction. One of the faculty veterans was Al Eisenhauer, a Fifth Grade teacher. For years after Murphy's funeral, Al recounted dreams of the man, and I believe one of these belongs in this book.

Eisenhauer told of a very vivid dream, one in which he sat reading a newspaper in the teachers' lounge in the old Malta Avenue School. He half-noticed the room's door opening, someone entering, and then sitting down beside him on the couch. He looked up and what he saw caused him to drop the paper. There sat Gerry Murphy, looking fit and happy. Al struggled for words, "Why, Dr. Murphy, I thought you were dead!"

"Yes, Al, I *am* dead, but *you* don't understand it all yet!" was Murphy's response, whereupon he suddenly disappeared from the couch, and Al Eisenhauer awoke. A devout man, Eisenhauer truly believes that

Gerry Murphy *did* come from the world of the dead, in love, to communicate a message of hope to the living.

The Banana

A Binghamton, NY, couple came to the Village of Ballston Spa in the early 1970s and fell in love with an old Victorian house on Bath Street. A real "fixer-upper," it was, at first, in too rough shape for them to move in, so they commuted from Binghamton on weekends while beginning the restoration. It was a wonderful old house, almost one hundred years old, and they looked forward to returning it to its original beauty. Almost immediately, however, they noticed something strange. On the weekends when they didn't show up to work on the building, some minor problem always seemed to erupt.

They found a broken water pipe had done some damage on one occasion, and another time, found the floor in one of the out-buildings had collapsed. Another time, they found a persistent leak had developed in the house. The couple looked at one another, but neither could verbalize the strange thought that "someone" there missed them when they didn't show up on weekends. A rational couple, neither one could conceive of an old abandoned house having a "personality" created by invisible occupants.

Nevertheless, they persevered with their restoration over many months, and were sometimes visited by Bath Street neighbors who were happy to see a re-vivified house, and who imparted some of its history. The locals gave accounts of the home's construction in the 1880s by a family of Irish immigrants. The family's two children, a boy and girl, grew up there, though neither ever married in adulthood. As a grown man, the son worked across the street at the old tannery after the parents died, and as a woman, the daughter did secretarial work at various businesses in the village. In the 1940s, the woman developed cancer and died soon after the diagnosis. Her brother continued on, living alone in the house and making his daily treks to work, then returning home to a lonely dinner at night.

A neighbor remembered that the brother continued to set a place for his deceased sister at the dinner table each night, and lived many more years in the house. Upon the old man's death, new owners rented the property to a succession of tenants before the Binghamton family bought it in 1969. When these new owners finally moved in fully and learned of the lifestyle of the tannery worker and of his compulsive table-setting, they discussed it at their dinner table one evening. Expressing compassion for the tannery worker's loneliness, and knowing that food often has a healing effect, the wife quipped, "Well, ghosts have to eat too!"

Later that evening, while watching television, she ventured into the kitchen in search of snacks. Remembering a banana in the refrigerator, she decided it would be the perfect item to munch on. Opening the refrigerator door, she was astonished to find the fruit gone. She returned to the living room and, hands on hips, confronted her husband. "You ate that banana!" she said. He replied that he was still stuffed from their pork chop dinner. "Oh no," she responded, "I just looked in the garbage and there was a banana peel on top of the pork chop bones!" Incredulous, he dashed to the kitchen and, seeing the evidence, found his wife had spoken the truth. But *he* hadn't eaten the fruit. And the two of them were alone in the house, *weren't they*? He just *couldn't* believe in ghosts. After all, he was an educated professional man!

But he was gradually persuaded that there was *some* force in his home, which manifested in irksome episodes. He remembered the time when they had stacked lumber in the front hallway during the early restoration process. A visitor had come to the front door and, as they discussed some matter, the person asked casually, "Do you have ghosts here?" Taken aback by the question, the owner paused for a moment and, as he did so, the pile of lumber began to shift, and then slide, quietly and slowly, until it was fully splayed on the floor. It was all very gentle, almost as if in slow motion— there had been no crash or other sound. It was as if some unseen hand simply moved to spread the wood to one level. With wide eyes, the visitor had his answer and departed soon after. The owner soothed his frazzled nerves by attempting to rationalize that this synchronicity was a fluke.

The incident with the banana was the culmination of all the "little things" the pair had experienced since purchasing the house. In the thirty years that have passed since the hectic flurry of unexplainable activity, the couple now accepts that one of the former owners of the house has, indeed, stayed on—a subdued and quiet presence now, to be sure, but still attentively caring for the old house.

TOWN OF MOREAU

Happy infant early blest
Rest in peaceful slumber rest.

"Her Candle Goeth Not Out By Night"

Nelly Gray,
wife of Charles-Civil War officer & physician 50 yrs.,
died 2/21/1934

S. Kelly 05

Town of Moreau

G en. Jean Victor Moreau, a participant in the French Revolution and, later, one of Napoleon's officers, visited Saratoga County in the early 1800s and found favor with the local residents. When it was learned later that he died in battle some years after his American trip, the newly-formed township was named in his honor. Settlers had been coming into the area since long before the Revolutionary War, building small settlements along the Hudson River near tumultuous waterfalls, along the placid waterside on West River Road, at Clark's Corners and in Fortsville. In a bit of irony—The American Temperance Society was founded at the old Mawney Tavern near Clark's Corners. Founded in 1805, the Town of Moreau quickly became the site of many small factories and mills and a burgeoning population seeking opportunities along the southern curve of the Hudson River.

Abigail Fort

Abraham Fort, an early Moreau entrepreneur, founded the hamlet of Fortsville, and with his wife Abigail, built another beautiful home near the ruins of Fort Edward in Washington County. Today, the house serves as a history museum and is run by a dedicated staff. Constructed near Rogers Island, base for Rogers Rangers during the French & Indian War, and built amid the post-molds of ancient Indian encampments, the Old Fort House seems haunted.

On one occasion, a local psychic visited the 1772 house and felt ice-cold spots and heard strange noises that could not be attributed to the day-to-day museum activities. The woman also sensed much disquiet in the upstairs, attributing these sensations to the spirit of Abigail Fort who, apparently, was not at rest. In the upstairs is a room not often shown to museum visitors—one in which an electric window candle sometimes glowed brightly, even when unplugged.

A staff member decided to check on the psychic information and sought out Abigail's grave, finding it in Saratoga County, on the river's west bank, in the Town of Moreau. When the man found her burial plot, he

145

noticed that a stone finial on the grave marker had fallen or been knocked to the ground. The grave had not been kept up and was overgrown with weeds. Filled with admiration for the town's early settlers, the man cleared broken branches from the site and cut the long grasses, restoring the finial to its socket on the gravestone and saying a quick prayer for Abigail's peace. The next day he returned to his duties at the Old Fort House.

When he arrived, he was greeted by other staff members, who demanded to know what miracle he'd done. "This place has been quiet as a church since yesterday," they told him. "The disruptive energies seem to be gone." Nevertheless, since that time in 1996, new events have occurred, and the museum staff wonders if the many Indian artifacts on display have brought with them long-dormant energies into play within Abraham and Abigail's old home.

The Olmstead House

There are few surviving "octagon houses" remaining in New York State, and even fewer "hexagonal (six-sided) houses." Far off Clark Road, the Olmstead family built a hexagonal structure in the 1820s. To the traveler, it might seem just another architectural curiosity on the County's back roads, but this house has a history a bit more complex than one might suspect. Some investigators, schooled in the Chinese discipline of *feng shui*, suspect that it is the reverberation of energies inside a six-sided structure that either attracts or holds the spirit energy from the past.

For over a century and a half, this was the domicile for farm families. Jennie, who grew up there, remembers many strange incidents that seemed forewarnings of death. Whether or not the manifestations were ghostly, we agreed that they belong in this book. She remembers a night in the 1920s when she was a girl and readying for bed. The entire family heard an unusual sound, the loud clanking of chains, outside the house. A search was unable to locate the source, whether above the roof or outside the second story windows, nobody could be sure. The adults went outside with flashlights but were unable to turn up any explanation for the sound on a windless night. However, the following day, the family received notification that an uncle had died about the same time as the ominous sound had occurred.

146

A second incident occurred one snowy morning in the late 1920s when the family was gathered in the living room. The daughter was surprised when, looking out the window, she spotted a police dog standing on hind legs and looking in. Nobody along Clark Road had such a dog, and everyone was puzzled as to whose pet it could be. Jennie, who was five at the time, ran to the door to see the animal more fully, but when she opened the front door, no dog was in sight—and there were no dog footprints in the snow! They all speculated that it might be a "ghost dog." Then, the next day, their mother was notified that her youngest sister had died in an accident along the railroad tracks.

In many world cultures, it is a well-established fact that there are recognized omens for impending disaster or deaths. One such omen or portent is the wailing *banshee*, famous in Irish folklore. Might these events have been communications from a relative who suddenly found him or herself outside the body, with no longer a normal way to communicate the distress? Believers in omens hold that coming events *do* cast a shadow before them. In any case, the old Olmstead House seems to be peaceful today.

The Speakeasy

For its entire length, Mott Road forms part of the southern boundary of the Town of Moreau. Along the eastern end of the road there are several houses that guard ghostly secrets. One of these, which often disturbed the neighborhood during the 1920s, was the Fish family's farmhouse. Prosperous farmers before World War I, the family encountered financial problems when the high agricultural demands of wartime lessened after 1918. Many rural families in the county also ran into financial problems, unable to sell their full harvest of grains, meat or milk. Most had to develop new sources of revenue or sell out and move.

After the Fish family sold out, the new owners also found bill-paying difficult at first, but then, as Prohibition had become the law of the land in 1919, discovered that illegal booze was being secretly transported south from Canada along a route that lay not far from Mott Road. All one needed to do was go west to Hogtown, near Route 9, and make a deal with the bootleggers. The old farmhouse soon became a "speak-easy," an illegal bar where moonshine, bathtub gin and hard liquors were available—for a price. The occupants were continually on guard against local constables, State Police, and revenue officials and permitted customers to enter only with a secret password.

All in all, they say it was a fun place to spend a Friday or Saturday night. I interviewed old time customers and some who may have been proprietors, though it isn't fashionable to admit to such activities today. "Yes, we had many good times there," one man told me. "We had a wonderful baby grand piano in the place, and many folks who came to drink knew how to play. So, we had quite a variety of music—jazz, classical and folksongs. They were tough times for those of us trying to make a living on farms, and our spirits were lifted by the music and easy comradeship of the booze. We usually headed home by midnight and the speakeasy was quiet again by 2 a.m."

The customer remembers, however, that it was only the *living* patrons that left each night. Apparently, there were some unseen, ghostly residents of the house that were drawn to the piano's ivories. "The people living there often told of the piano beginning to play after 2 a.m., when they were trying to catch a night's sleep. It wasn't a flowing playing, however, but deliberate—one note at a time, almost as if someone was trying to pick out a tune by ear. The owners would go downstairs, but when they got there, the house was dark and the piano silent."

This activity was repeated over and over during the next decade. "As far as ghosts go, that wasn't much of a spirit, because all it ever did was play the piano. And," he added, "the ghost never got any *good* at it either, so apparently practice *doesn't* pay off," he laughed.

One can only wonder if the ghost was trying to compose "Happy Days Are Here Again" on the keyboard before the good times did return. On into the Depression years of the 1930s, the piano spontaneously played during the night, never on a schedule, but only when the ghost felt inclined. "I can't remember now just when it happened, because so many people were moving in and out, but eventually the piano disappeared. Nothing ghostly, just that somebody took it, maybe sold it. I wonder what the new owner got along with the piano?" he mused with a smile. Eventually the speakeasy closed after booze became legal again, and today all one can see there is a home, exactly what the Fish family started with.

The hard times are over on Mott Road. New homes are gradually springing up, though few farms operate any more. Nevertheless, when old timers in the area gather to swap tales of long ago, they still tell of "the old Fish house" and smile.

TOWN OF NORTHUMBERLAND

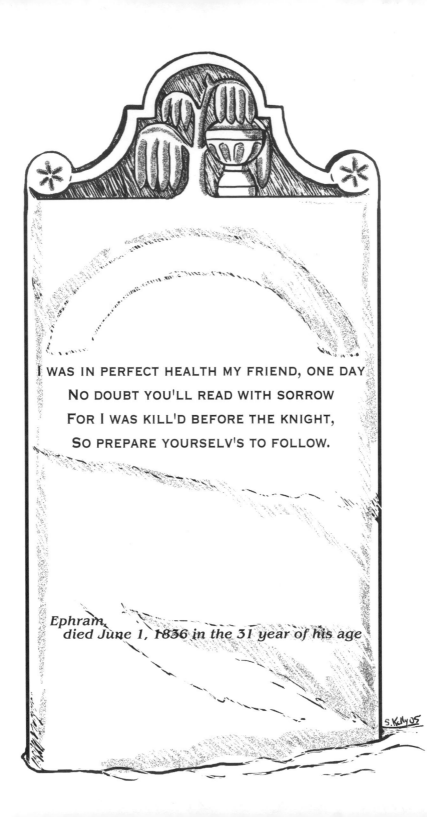

I WAS IN PERFECT HEALTH MY FRIEND, ONE DAY
NO DOUBT YOU'LL READ WITH SORROW
FOR I WAS KILL'D BEFORE THE KNIGHT,
SO PREPARE YOURSELV'S TO FOLLOW.

Ephram,
died June 1, 1836 in the 31 year of his age

Town of Northumberland

O ne of the early townships in the county, Northumberland gradually gave up land to the creation of new towns. In 1801, land went to Hadley, in 1805, some land was given to Moreau, and in 1818, more territory went to Wilton. West River Road still has many of the original settlers' homes, most now restored. In Bacon Hill more of the old homes are found, as also in the village of Gansevoort, named after a Revolutionary War hero. Northumberland, for many years, was prime rolling agricultural land, with deep, rich soils. In recent years the area has seen rapid growth and new homes appear like the cornstalks of old.

The Gansevoort Houses

As the Revolutionary battles wound down in the northern states, the government of New York State expressed its gratitude to Gen. Peter Gansevoort, heroic defender of Fort Stanwix, the Mohawk Valley "fort that wouldn't surrender" to St. Leger's British forces in 1777. Gansevoort may have been the first American general to see the "stars and stripes" unfurled in the face of the enemy, when the new flag flew from the fort's southwest bastion on August 3rd of that year. With the Tories gone to Canada, and with New York State having seized their lands, Gansevoort was granted much of the land holdings of the Loyalist, Mr. Munroe. As soon as practical, the General built small dams on the creeks and constructed what turned out to be very profitable grain mills and sawmills.

Gansevoort gained a reputation similar to that of his Dutch Patroon ancestors, acting almost as a feudal lord on his vast holdings. He had a small house near the crossroads of the village named after him, but his heart was among the gentry in Albany, with its prosperous and influential merchants and politicians. Today, his village home survives, appearing almost as a storybook house, with its high peaked roof and yellow siding. Behind the doors, however, there have been some strange events.

The owners of the house in 1998 had a baffling experience that seems explainable only if one believes in ghosts. In 1985, during his second year in the house, the man spent a tiring evening attempting to balance his

153

business accounts, working at his invoices into the wee hours, and finally falling asleep over his books. His wife awakened him to inform him that she had just written out all due checks, filling in dates and amounts, though he needed to sign one of these immediately and leave it on his desk for mailing. The man sleepily agreed to do so, but forgot, and was soon in bed, figuring that he could attend to it the next morning. However, by morning, the check had vanished. He wondered if his wife had taken the check to make him "more responsible" for a business on the edge of failing. Did she want him to "learn a lesson?"

He found her in the kitchen and raised the matter. She seemed truly astounded and went to the desk to be sure the check was, indeed, missing. It is a question which of them was the most upset, but after searching the entire house with his wife, the man took off to ski at West Mountain rather than resolve the matter. The irritated wife, feeling more responsible for the loss, remained at home doing more accounting work. As she opened her ledger to resume work, the dog, Emma, suddenly growled menacingly, as if a stranger had come into the room. Emma sped to the foot of the stairs, as she would in pursuit of a squirrel. She stared fixedly upward, suggesting an intruder that only *she* could see, had gone to the second floor.

The wife went past the animal and up the steps, sure that nobody had come in, and certain that nobody had climbed the stairs. To give Emma courage, she called downstairs, "Come on up, girl. See? There's nobody here." But Emma refused to budge, so the woman came down and let Emma outside. Weary and dispirited, the wife returned to her work table, and was startled to find the missing check propped up against the ledger that she had closed five minutes earlier! No other living person had been in the room—who could have returned the check?

Late that evening, her husband returned to hear the good news. He quickly signed the check and sealed it in its mailing envelope. They were totally baffled by the matter. It defied all logic. But, if Gen. Gansevoort was the spirit remaining on the premises, history records that *he* was a shrewd and fastidious businessman. *He* would have made sure that bills were paid promptly, and would not have gone on a leisurely skiing trip!

Near the center of the village is the large grey house of the General's son, Herman Gansevoort. Until recently, a large sign in the front yard advertised "The Gansevoort Mansion," because the old frame building is larger than the General's modest farmhouse. Throughout the early 1800s, Herman held many local political posts, including Justice of the Peace, Town Clerk, and Assemblyman in the NY State Legislature. After his death, the building came into the possession of a Mrs. Patterson, and later, a Mrs. Miller. Though little is remembered today about these women, they must be considered when one contemplates the ghostly events in Herman's house.

In the late 1800s, the big old home became the village's Masonic Lodge, with secret meetings held in the upstairs. Even at that time, however, rumors circulated in the village that the house was haunted. Housekeepers told of icy drafts, especially noticeable during hot summers. In the early 1900s, the Masons rented the downstairs to the local Boy Scout troop, as it offered abundant meeting and activity space.

In the 1960s, Bill Bayard was the scoutmaster, and when I caught up with him years later, he still chuckled about the strange goings-on that seemed a part of every Scout meeting. "I had the only key to the downstairs— I know that for sure," he told me. "Yet, during almost every Scout meeting, we'd hear voices and footsteps echoing in the upstairs. A few of us were courageous enough to look up the stairs but, because it was pitch black up there, we decided we really didn't *want* to know the cause of the noises *that* badly! We could clearly hear that the upstairs voices were human, and we knew it wasn't the wind or any other common sound. Yet, we could never quite make out any of the individual words."

During the 1960s, the Masonic membership declined, and the Lodge eventually sold the building. For a while, a section of the house was a beauty parlor, but when I interviewed its proprietor, a woman who had lived with ghosts elsewhere, she expressed her frustration, "I really wish I had a ghost here, but I just haven't heard or seen anything." So, perhaps the spirits are resting peacefully, waiting for new occupants to raise their energies once again. And, there is always the chance that the ghostly presences have finally seen The Light and moved into higher realms.

The Rescue

Many times it seems certain that ghostly presences are a residue of failures or grief in our ancestors' lives. To free those spirits, spiritual "rescuers" or genuinely loving people can help the trapped spirits to move on by using prayers or other ceremonies. Such an approach is illustrated in another old Gansevoort village home, one dating from the General's time.

Gen. Peter Gansevoort hired competent people as mechanics and technicians to keep his profitable mills and farmlands operating. One such individual, an English immigrant drawn to employment there, built a house not far from the crossroads. The happiness that the Englishman and his wife sought in Gansevoort Mills was short-lived, however, as their young son died soon after the house was completed. Brokenhearted, the mother died soon after. The fate of the Englishman was not recorded, but he surely grieved for the loss of his wife and son, interred in the local cemetery. In such graveyards, all over the eastern United States, we can appreciate the difficulties faced by our ancestors, when we see entire families buried within just one year.

In 1963, the home was purchased by the current owners, and the wife was immediately struck by the "spooky appearance" of the house. She inquired of the seller, "Do we get a ghost too?" At first the man responded, "No." Then, scuffing the ground with his foot, he thought a bit and said, "Well, maybe." He seemed tentative, but gave no details.

The new owners were ecstatic to own a two hundred year-old house, and on the night they moved in, the wife prepared a light supper before putting her five year-old son to bed. That night, and for several successive nights, the parents heard a boy's footsteps scampering throughout the upstairs. Tired at day's end, the mother preferred not to climb the stairs, and instead, shouted upstairs for the little boy to get back into bed. There never was a verbal response from their child, and when the parents, themselves, retired, their son was always fast asleep. One night, however, the scampering had gone on far too long, and the parents snuck on tiptoes up the stairs to catch the mischievous boy "in the act"—only to find him sound asleep.

One morning at breakfast, his mother asked the child why he trotted through the upstairs at night. The tot scowled, not understanding his mother's question. He claimed he always went right off to dreamland. After a minute's pause, however, the boy told his mother about awakening some nights and finding his toy rocking chair rocking away with nobody in it! The mother then realized that they probably *did* get a ghost with the house, as she had suspected at the outset.

She wrote to Dr. Hans Holzer, the famous author of ghost stories, explaining her apprehension for her child's safety. Dr. Holzer advised her to stand outside the building and call the ghost (which they assumed was a child because of the light footsteps) outside, and then send the spirit on its way into The Light, by gently explaining to the child where to go and what to look for. Well aware of her neighbor's judgmental attitudes toward such unorthodox behavior, the mother did as advised after her neighbors left on vacation. However, this remedy didn't work.

The mother's cousin, who seemed to know about ghost-laying techniques, advised her to use a Ouija Board to contact the child. Setting up the board in her living room one evening, the two women were startled to see the pointer move rapidly on the board's surface. They received the spelling of a woman's name and the date on which she died. Assuming this was at least one of the spirit entities inhabiting her home, the owner went to the County Clerk's Office in Ballston Spa, where she researched property deeds in her village. She was startled to find that, indeed, a woman by that name had lived in her home during the time period indicated in the spirit message.

The village priest heard of her predicament and offered to bless the house for the family. Yet, after his ceremony, the footsteps continued upstairs. To make matters worse, their babysitting teens began to spread the word that "their house is haunted!" One girl was brave enough to remain in their employ, however, agreeing to baby-sit the toddler and, eventually, his two younger siblings. When she grew up, Eileen, the babysitter, later worked in the Fort House in Ft. Edward, and experienced Abigail Fort's ghost there.

As the mother worked making beds in her upstairs one day, she heard footsteps come up behind her. She knew she was alone in the house and was frightened. Nevertheless, she turned and, bravely facing the apparently empty room, said, "Don't scare my children!" She hoped that the ghost got the message, though there was no audible reply. Then it dawned on her…ghost mother and ghost child in her house! They must be looking for one another. Leaving home, she went in search of the long-ago mother's gravestone in the village cemetery. With some difficulty she finally found the old Colonial grave marker partially hidden by a pine tree trunk.

Returning home, she called to the little boy, "Little boy, come out of my house." And after allowing time for the child to come to her, she softly said, "Your mother has died and is no longer here. Go to the cemetery, and there you will find her gravestone, and you can now move on into The Light." That night, and from then on, no one heard the child's footsteps upstairs, yet, intuitively, she felt that a quiet third entity was still present in the old house.

She called her cousin once more, and the two conducted a second Ouija session, at which they received a communication from an entity claiming to be the ghost boy's father. He said he had returned from The Light and was in search of his child so that he could reunite the family "on

157

the other side." The owner told the father's spirit that the mother and son were now reunited.

After that, the cousin made numerous attempts to operate the board by herself, but began to receive scary and confused messages and, fearing that dishonest spirits were trying to inflict discord in her life, she wisely threw it away. Many times, unless the operators of such boards are selflessly or spiritually motivated in their quest, troubling or demonic sounding messages can result, causing turmoil as to whether the seeker wants to serve The Light or Darkness. So the cousin did the right thing in breaking off the messages.

All the children who grew up in the house are now adults with their own children. One adult daughter is still frightened to go up to the old bedroom in the attic, however, as she isn't quite sure the ghosts have left. The old couple's grandchildren, nevertheless, delight in the old home, now well over two hundred years old. As they grow up they are hearing the tale of how their grandparents once helped a dead little Colonial boy find his way home at last.

The Manse

Ghosts seem to inhabit all kinds of buildings. As most ghosts are not really evil entities, but more likely confused, addicted or obsessed earthbound spirits who were once alive just as you or I, they can continue to cling to their association with office buildings, schools, churches and even rectories or manses that were important during their life.

One of the earliest houses of worship in the Village of Gansevoort was the old Dutch Reformed Church. Next door to it stood the manse, or pastor's residence, which was occupied by a minister until the congregation dwindled in the 1950s. As oldsters died off, and other members of the congregation slowly dispersed to larger population centers, the church was abandoned and the manse was rented to a succession of tenants. One of those, Bill Bayard, lived in the old house for about ten years, and was continually delighted by the antics of a ghost.

"Many times we'd hear footsteps climbing the stairs to the second floor, but whenever we looked to see who it was, we found the stairway empty. Way upstairs in the attic, we had a light that just didn't want to turn off," he said, "even though we'd be sure to turn it off before leaving. At the foot of the stairs, I'd look back up, and see the light turned on again. I can't tell you how many times we had that frustrating experience. If I could get it to stay off after just three trips, I'd consider it a good day," he smiled.

"Another prank that ghost had was opening the closet door at the end of the upstairs hall. We'd close it, hear its locking click, walk away, then turn back to see it standing ajar!" Bill was continually amused by the antics of the spirit until he moved to South Glens Falls in 1972.

One should not be surprised to find religious leaders, ministers, rabbis, imams, priests, nuns, or the like, remaining after death in a more "subtle body." They likely came to their avocation with high idealism and strong values, and these are not easy to lay aside when the body is discarded. Of course, religious people are as imperfect as everyday people, just perhaps a bit more open to enlightenment as to the earthly illusions that shackle us all. Being fully human requires us to confront our powerful outer and *inner* conflicts, which so often center in the emotions. Many who remain among us as ghosts are individuals who have either avoided the necessity for this spiritual struggle, or only worked half-heartedly at understanding their individual natures. For that reason, houses of worship can also be sites replete with ghostly activity. Religious residences of all types, including monasteries, convents, ashrams, etc. are also places where the battle against imperfection is not easily won.

All ghosts seem obsessed or possessed by some need, or else entrapped by the failure to relinquish guilt or some unfinished earthly business, which then immobilizes their spirit in the land between Life and Death—*a real Purgatory*, until they can perceive The Light. Edgar Cayce, a wonderful spiritual teacher, wrote that, immediately after death, we are the same as we were in life—no wiser and no more ignorant. We are simply without bodies. Severed from expressive physical bodies, we can no longer communicate to the living or act on our desires in a physical way, except perhaps to ring doorbells, stomp up stairs, rattle pots, pans or chains, or interrupt electric circuits to get attention.

What we hold onto in life, what consumes us (positively or negatively), we cannot shake after death. Best then, that we work to gain a higher vision throughout life, understand that a physical end comes for us all, and not die coveting piles of gold, Grandma's vase or Uncle Harold's sports car.

TOWN OF PROVIDENCE

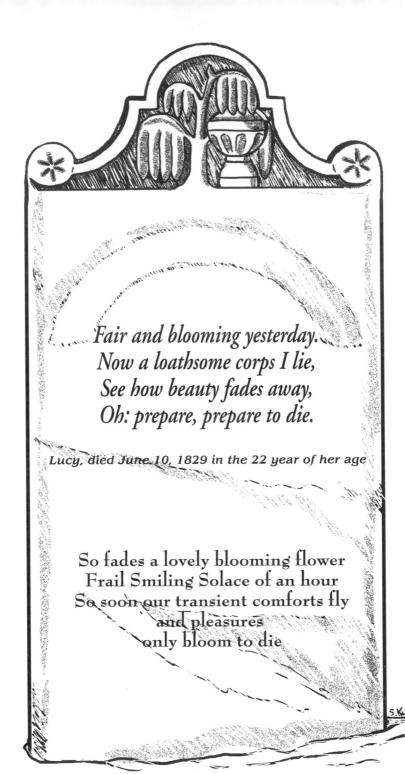

Fair and blooming yesterday.
Now a loathsome corps I lie,
See how beauty fades away,
Oh: prepare, prepare to die.

Lucy, died June 10, 1829 in the 22 year of her age

So fades a lovely blooming flower
Frail Smiling Solace of an hour
So soon our transient comforts fly
and pleasures
only bloom to die

Town of Providence

The rich soils of the Sacandaga Valley attracted farmers to Providence before the Revolutionary War, but none could stay at their homesteads because of constant Indian raids by England's Indian allies. By 1796, however, many settlers had returned and the township was formed. Twenty years later there were numerous farms, sawmills, gristmills and a Quaker Meeting House. Hagedorn Mills was a bustling crossroads where grain was milled into flour. The town's biggest employer eventually became the Tuberculosis Sanitarium, now abandoned, in Barkersville.

The Watcher

One of the town's oldest farms stands not far off South Line Road, and it has been in the family for over three generations. When the present generation began to experience ghostly activity, they were pretty sure it had to be a relative.

I visited the farmhouse seeking information about former owners of a neighboring home, not suspecting *this* was also a ghost haunt. Knocking at the door, I identified myself and asked if I was speaking to the owner. The woman who answered my knock said yes, she and her husband owned the house, and she knew of my ghost search from a newspaper ad I'd placed. To my delight, she continued, "Well, I suppose you've come about *our* ghost." I was surprised, but before I could say I hadn't known of their ghost, the husband appeared and kindly invited me in.

"Well, do you want to tell me *your* story?" I asked, after they had helped me with details about the neighboring haunted house. The pair struggled within themselves, as do so many of my informants. It's not easy to tell a story that neighbors are liable to ridicule, and especially, if the person confiding is prominent in the town and may have a reputation at stake. Nevertheless, they declared that they knew darned well what they'd experienced and were going to tell the truth, and *let* unbelievers scoff and shake their heads! I often wish I could show such reluctant witnesses how *numerous* ghosts and valid ghost stories are, a factor that motivates me to write books such as this.

163

They said the old patriarch of the family had died in 1982 after a long bout with cancer. His family had lovingly cared for him in his ancestral home as long as they could, but in the end he had to go to the hospital, where he died soon after. During his dad's confinement at home, the adult son had begun modernizing the old downstairs bathroom and installing a shower. The renovation was incomplete at the time of the elder's death.

As the husband resumed his modernizations after his father's funeral, the wife noted shadows moving in and out of the bathroom. Was it a ghost? she wondered, and if so, was the ghost inspecting her husband's handiwork? Then, at night, the couple began hearing the tread of slow footsteps upstairs. "It was hard to accept the fact that those sounded just like Dad's footsteps, yet we knew he was gone. And if those *were* his steps, what could we do…what *should* we do?" she said. Many families experience reoccurring sounds of a deceased family member's former routines after a funeral, and need to understand that the sounds are just the conscious energy of the dead person "tidying up a bit" in the affairs of the just-ended life. Many families feel or suspect that a deceased loved one is hovering around to say a final goodbye. More often than not, such noises cease within a few days or weeks.

"When we'd return home at day's end, we often found our living room pole lamp with a single light on, as if someone was welcoming us, but we *knew* the light hadn't been on in the morning when we left. We both miss Dad," she told me, "and we figure he's still hanging around to watch us living our daily lives. Whenever I catch a movement out of the corner of my eye, I say, 'Come out where I can see you, Dad.' So far, he hasn't done so."

The wife has learned to live with the shadows and sudden, slight movements, but still becomes frustrated when objects turn up missing. Many times she has had a problem that is shared by others who cohabit with ghosts—setting an object down, then reaching for it a few moments later, only to find it gone. Not just moved, but *gone*! Often times she will find the item is returned in some other corner of the house, where *she* didn't put it.

There is both comfort and distress when families of the deceased realize that some part of their loved one has continued on. This family has realized that, in St. Paul's words, "love *is* eternal."

The House at Stoney Lonesome

Don Bowman, who shared with me many stories in this book, came to the Sacandaga Valley in the 1920s from his roots on Long Island, and initially owned a farm between South Corinth and Porter Corners. The proposed great dam at Conklingville on the Sacandaga River offered good wages and hard work for those seeking the same in 1927 and, as a youthful adventurer, Don reported to the Black River Regulating Commission for work. Unique among his fellow laborers, Don often wrote down his conversations with co-workers and those displaced by the building of the Conklingville Dam. Residents of the area to be cleared could choose to sell their property to the Commission or move the buildings. Here is one tale that impressed him.

An old house called "Stoney Lonesome," located on the river's south bank, had to be demolished, and as often was the case, the owners couldn't afford to move it. They took their buy-out payment and moved away. Don learned that the house had a long history of being "haunted." An Albany man, Cabe Craven, had first rented the old house before 1900 and fell in love with the fine fishing on the river. He soon found work at a tannery in the hamlet of Fish House in nearby Fulton County. Deciding to stay in Providence, Craven got a private loan from a Mr. Hollister and purchased the old house he was renting. Money was hard to come by, much less borrow, in rural western Saratoga County in the early 1900s, but Hollister supplied the funds through a no-longer-legal instrument called a "land contract." The process called for the purchaser of the house to make a payment of a fixed amount to the lender at noontime on a certain day of the year. If a payment was late or not made, the lender could immediately foreclose on the property.

Craven was happy to get his loan and bring his wife from Albany to the small community. He secured a second job at a nearby sawmill. The better part of each paycheck was invested in rehabilitating the old house, but Craven wasn't worried; he still had plenty of energy, time and opportunity to set aside money for his annual payment. Then, in a macabre turn of events, his daughter suddenly became ill and died. Reeling from this death, Mrs. Craven was soon diagnosed with tuberculosis. Having no money for hospitals, Craven worked his two jobs and attempted all the while to care for his ailing wife at home. Finally, he had to let the sawmill job go, as his wife's care was demanding. Despite his valiant labors, Mrs. Craven died.

165

Many believe that bad luck comes in threes, and not long after Mrs. Craven's funeral, Cabe accidentally gave himself a severe cut with his axe, and the wound became infected. The doctor was called, but could only offer amputation as a remedy. Mustering his last reserve of courage, Cabe Craven submitted to the surgery, but was unable afterward to do the required work at his tannery job. The foreman fired him for not keeping up with the other workers. Now, without a paycheck, Craven had to dip into his remaining savings just to put food on his table. Eventually, the fund he had set aside to pay Hollister was gone.

Providence folks were feeling the effects of the post-World War I recession, and Hollister not only wanted, but needed, his loan payment. And, as the loan contract stipulated, he demanded it on time. When the fateful day arrived, Craven, penniless, couldn't comply. Hollister's agent came by the house and ordered Craven to be out of the building before midnight. Having had one dream after another dashed, Craven took up his shotgun and committed suicide. At midnight, when the agent came to evict the debtor, he found instead a lifeless body on the floor. The agent heard strange moaning sounds resonating throughout the house—physical life had departed but something invisible and sad remained.

After Craven's pauper's funeral, Hollister found new renters, but they would not stay long in a house where sobbing was heard, and where objects moved or disappeared. One tenant family, hurriedly packing up their belongings, told Hollister they "refused to abide in a house where the limping ghost of a one-legged man prowled each night after dark." Realizing that *he* also had bills overdue, Hollister decided to "lay Craven's ghost," sending it on its way into Eternity, thus permitting the shaky Hollister fortune to increase once more.

Leaving home at dusk, carrying a Bible and a candle, Hollister informed his wife that he'd stay overnight at Stoney Lonesome, perform an exorcism, and return at dawn. But, when he hadn't returned by noon the next day, Mrs. Hollister, now deeply concerned, asked friends to visit the old house and discover her husband's whereabouts.

Entering the gloomy old house, searchers found Hollister hanging from the ceiling supports on the first floor. No one could ever fully explain this ironic twist of fate. Some speculated that Hollister, upon encountering Craven's ghost, was suddenly struck with remorse for his greedy acts and committed suicide. Others believed that Craven's ghost itself, in a rage, had entangled the landlord's body in a rope and hanged him. Whatever the cause, the inexplicable problems at Stoney Lonesome then became even more mysterious. After Hollister's funeral, the agent that Mrs. Hollister sent to inspect the property sped back to her house, excitedly recounting having met up with *two* ghosts in the old house—one looking just like old Hollister himself! None of the neighboring folk would ever enter the home again and, abandoned, it rapidly deteriorated.

By the time Don Bowman's "Barn Burners" showed up to demolish the house in 1927, it lay in ruins, overgrown by vines and with a section of the roof caved in. Nobody missed Stoney Lonesome when the steam shovel tore it down and the work gangs set the broken timbers afire. The old house had long ago "died," a victim of two men over-reaching their resources.

Blaine

Recent studies of potential contacts with the dead indicate a fifty percent probability that some family member will have a contact with a deceased family member. Many readers who contact me, more often than not, report the ghost of a family member, rather than a stranger. Here is a typical story that took place some years ago in the hamlet of Barkersville in the Town of Providence.

His ancestors had opened the Barkersville General Store in the late 1800s, and Blaine worked hard there all his life. Before the days of mini-marts and convenience stores, general stores in small hamlets were gathering places to buy essential foodstuffs, fill up the gas tank, see neighbors, and catch up on news. It was a busy store, especially during the years of the Sanitarium's operation.

Suddenly, in the late 1970s, Blaine was stricken and died, leaving his widow, Mary, the full responsibility for running the store and her home. Throughout it all, she had little time to grieve, as she needed to keep the store open for long hours. She missed her husband greatly and was often unsure if she could bear the burden of the work all by herself. Several months after Blaine's death she was near collapse with depression and the inability to fully grieve her life partner's loss.

On a beautiful spring day she walked through her yard, only half-noticing the beauty of the apple tree blossoms and the blue sky overhead. As she sat in a lawn chair, she found herself embraced by a strong but invisible arm. She knew it was not her imagination because her dress wrinkled with the caress and she *felt* the strength of the individual. She turned to see who had silently come up behind her, and was startled to see Blaine. He looked healthy and fit and she immediately knew it was her husband. He was smiling and wore his old fedora. Audibly he said, "Mary, you'll be all right." Then he disappeared into the sunshine.

Stunned for a minute, she contemplated how *real* it had all been. Her grief lifted and she felt empowered by his love and strength from beyond the grave. *He* had somehow survived, and she knew *she* would too. She composed herself, straightened, and returned to work with a lighter heart.

How seldom do the fear-mongers of Hollywood provide us with such positive stories, preferring to fill young minds instead with fear of ghosts. Tales similar to this take place all over the world every day, as dear departed ones make a last contact with those they leave behind, assuring them that love *is* ongoing, and that they *will* one day see loved ones again.

Ethel

An old house on South Line Road had sheltered several families in its life before becoming a speak-easy during Prohibition. A local hangout and "watering hole," it burned to the ground in 1929, leaving just a scorched foundation. A few years later a new house was constructed upon the old stones, and its owner became a pioneer in the Christmas Tree farming business in Saratoga County. The man and his wife labored long to clear surrounding forest and fields, planting and cultivating the seedlings, nurturing them over the years until their harvest as a cash crop. Cutting his trees, late one autumn, the farmer disappeared, only to be discovered later, dead among his trees. Apparently he had suffered a heart attack, leaving his wife to do an impossible job by herself. Overcome with grief and hard work, and after a short illness, she also died. The couple's heirs then sold the house to the present owners.

The new family had children, and soon laughter and pranks marked the formerly sad site. But, the newcomers soon recognized that there was a "someone else" living there too. First, the housewife walked into her kitchen to discover her dinner plates, fallen from the kitchen counter onto the floor, yet unbroken—how was that possible? Eventually, while working in the kitchen one day, she watched as a plate, lying on the counter, flipped off and landed on the floor in what might be called "a controlled landing." Like the others, it didn't break. Perhaps invisible hands were juggling her plates.

"We had a woodstove here," her husband told me, "and the ghost or ghosts helped us keep it going. Everyone in the house either attended school or worked, so the house was vacant during the daytime. In the morning before we left, we loaded the stove with wood, then dampered it down until there was very little draft, just enough for minimal combustion. So, usually, when we got home at night, the house would be toasty warm and the fire in need of tending. Yet, so many times we'd come home and find the stove hot—not just warm and ready to be filled, but *red hot!*" he told me. "We'd open the stove door and find it crammed with wood. Now, either none of the wood had burned since morning, which was impossible, or...someone had just reloaded the firewood before we came home—and *that* was equally impossible!"

Apparently, they had an invisible benefactor and felt impelled to give the entity, who seemed so at home, a name. Stoking the fire seemed a task that the former housewife might perform, so someone intuited "Ethel," and that became the ghost's name. Perhaps, the former housewife reached some type of recovery in the spirit world, and was now ready to carry on working as she had been unable to after her husband's fatal attack. "We're one big happy, and need I say *warm* family today?" the present owners conclude.

Sara Ann

In the early 1900s, Sara Ann and her husband, Joseph, came to the town of Providence and, finding a rundown farm for sale at a reduced price, bought the place. It was never an easy life because the land was not very fertile and farming costs were high. Nevertheless, they struggled to be independent of charity. Sara Ann had a puritanical streak and forbid the use of alcohol and tobacco in her spic-and-span house. Visitors to the home had to smoke outside or in the woodshed, or forego their puffing until they left. The couple lived a happy life, though they had little money and had accumulated few possessions when they died.

The clean and unpretentious house then passed to a younger couple who were more liberal in their use of addictive substances. This couple's out-of-town friends were also materialistic, often filling the house with cigarette smoke and imbibing alcoholic drinks during their visits.

One day, as the housewife was preparing for a picnic, to which friends who smoked had been invited, she was unable to find any ashtrays. She asked her husband if he'd disposed of them, but he assured her that a smoker never would. It took a long time for her to discover their whereabouts, usually in some bizarre or illogical hiding place.

She knew that *she* had not put the ashtrays away—she *never* put ashtrays away! And, in any case, s*he* wasn't in the habit of emptying the butts and ashes and, especially, *washing* ashtrays. Yet, whenever she finally did locate an ashtray, always in an out-of-the-way spot, it was immaculately clean. When I first heard the story from the homeowner in 1997, the phenomenon—Sara Ann?—still continued to frustrate the housewife, even after fifty years.

CITY OF
SARATOGA SPRINGS

No pain those happy regions know,
Forever bright and fair
For sin the source of mortal woe,
Shall never enter there.

Grant J., died 11/13/1824 in the 54 year of his age

"Waiting Beyond The River"

Mary, wife of W.C.
29 yrs., died 6/5/1881

S.Kelly

The City of Saratoga Springs

The first gathering of Native Americans in the area took place near a fabled mineral spring, which the Iroquois dubbed, "The Healing Spring of the Great Spirit," located in what is now Congress Park. As white settlers came into the area, new springs were discovered in most nearby valleys and along stream beds. By 1800, a small village had grown near the famous Congress Spring, and a summertime health resort developed and flourished after the building of the Putnam Tavern and Congress Hall. In less than twenty years the village incorporated, and within another twenty years, small gambling establishments gave health seekers an alternative activity, if not lifestyle. In 1863, thoroughbred horse racing came to town, attracting notables from all over the world. Saratoga's summertime social life was often viewed as scandalous by proper Americans. In 1915, the village was incorporated as a city, but the "Golden Age" was slowly slipping away as American lifestyles changed again. Later, in the 1970s, began an upsurge of interest in the city's historic buildings, springs, harness racing, equestrian and thoroughbred events, as well as numerous cultural attractions.

Olde Bryan Inn

Alexander Bryan, former Revolutionary War Army scout, moved from Waterford to the bluff overlooking the Healing Spring in 1787. Though still a wilderness, the site had begun to attract a steady flow of notables, such as Gen. George Washington and his friends, the Schuyler family. Bryan understood that offering tourists an alcoholic alternative to the strange tasting mineral waters might generate a fortune, so he erected a log cabin tavern on the rocky hilltop. Building a wooden stairway from the spring, up the face of the hill, he enticed travelers to sample his offerings and he *did* prosper.

In the early 1800s, the log structure was replaced by the present stone building. In time, the tavern closed and the building became a commercial laundry, and then, for years, a private home. By the 150th anniversary of its construction, the building, one of the oldest in the city, was known to harbor at least one ghost.

173

A Saratoga Springs woman, Nancy, grew up there in the 1950s when it was a residence, and helped me understand what life was like in a haunted house. She remembers awakening during the night when she was eleven years old, hearing someone calling her name. She sat up in bed, right next to an elderly woman in a high-neck Victorian era dress, sitting beside her on the bed. "I felt almost as if I were under a spell," she said, "and it was very difficult to move. The lady then dissipated, leaving me to wonder if it had all been a dream. I looked down and saw the depression of another person's body in the blanket beside me."

On another evening, Nancy and her sister heard water running in the bathroom. Certain that all faucets had been turned off at bedtime, she arose and turned off a running lavatory faucet. The attic door, in the bathroom wall, stood open—was someone or something from *up there* responsible? She didn't dare look. A year or so later, on another nighttime trip to the bathroom, she came face to face with a soldier in a tricorn hat, riding on a white horse. The man seemed to carry a lance of some sort. She was frightened enough to run back into the bedroom and cover her head with the blankets! However, seeing a Colonial soldier and large horse in the bathroom caused her to become more interested in the house's origin.

Nancy wasn't the only occupant who experienced a ghost in the Maple Avenue building. Her brother, Kevin, often found the shower running when nobody had used it. Also, as he readied for school each morning, he would stand before a large downstairs mirror to comb his hair. On occasion he saw an old woman standing behind him in the reflection. He spun around each time, but found the room behind him empty.

In time, the family bought a new home and Nancy, before leaving, decided to make her long-feared trip to the attic. Hesitantly, she ascended the stairs in the daytime, prepared for anything. But there was little to see. One of the few items she found was a box that fascinated her. Opening it, she discovered a green, high neck, Victorian dress—the very one she had seen on the ghost woman years before! She decided it was best left where it was. When she questioned family members about it later, she discovered that the dress had belonged to her dead grandmother, Beatrice. Eventually, the building became a restaurant, and when she spoke with the manager some years later, she discovered that the old dress still reposed in its box in the attic, perhaps giving Beatrice's spirit something to still cling to. Over the years, there have been several sightings of an older woman wearing the green dress.

Corky Dorr worked in the kitchen during the 1980s, and remembers a large potted palm tree that stood in a large brass planter in a rear corner of the bar. "In the morning, on many occasions the cleaner found the tub, which must have weighed two hundred pounds, in the center of the room! Around Christmas one year, and near closing time, I sat at the bar and noted, in my peripheral vision, a whitish man walking into the dining room. Thinking it was the manager, I called out to him, but got no response. Later the manager came downstairs into the tavern room, and I realized it couldn't have been *him*. The three windows on the Rock Street side of the building and all our tables had small oil lamps. It was our custom to extinguish them before we closed the building at night. Yet, after seeing the white figure, I noticed the three lamps in the window were already out. I remembered from history that families used to keep a light lit in the window when a family member was away, then extinguish it when they'd returned. Was the figure I'd seen someone from the past who'd just come home?"

Nate York, a chef at the O.B.I. (as hip Saratogians call the Olde Bryan Inn), has collected many current stories about the restaurant and is astonished at how often "the dress" is mentioned by those who visit the restaurant unaware. Tina, a waitress, encountered an elderly patron trying to escort her granddaughter up the stairs to the restrooms. The child would not budge because she told her grandmother there was a lady in a green dress looking downstairs at her. Though the ghost woman may indeed be Beatrice, she is customarily known to the restaurant staff as "Eleanor."

A lunchtime patron came into the bar one day in the summer of 2001, and asked bartender Jill if the inn had a ghost. When Jill answered in the affirmative, the woman then asked, "Is it a woman?" Jill concurred. The woman then related her experience of seeing a ghost woman on the stairs. The ghost communicated her name as "Ida," and projected a scent of lavender sachet. Hearing this story, those who remember the stories of Beatrice smile. They know she was an actress of sorts, and possessed a wonderful sense of humor. Perhaps she is re-inventing herself, as she has a wonderful "house" to play to.

Nancy, the woman mentioned previously as having grown up in the house, took one of her sons to dinner at the Old Bryan Inn in 1993, and Tommy went to the restroom before the meal arrived. She sat reflecting that she hadn't told her children much about growing up in the old building, which had undergone a radical interior transformation since her girlhood there. She wasn't sure if the children would care about her stories, but when Tommy returned he was ready to listen. "Mom, you won't believe what I just saw," he said. "When I was coming downstairs from the restroom, I looked over into the dining room and saw an old woman coming down from upstairs through the air!" *Now*, she decided, he was ready to listen to her stories of childhood there. She told him about Beatrice, and that there *used to be* a stairway at that spot, but that building renovations had removed it.

Every time I visit the OBI, there seems to be a new incident. Chef Nate York remembers finishing his shift in January 2004. Around midnight, after changing into his street clothes in the break room, he went downstairs to find Robin and another employee standing transfixed underneath a swinging chandelier in the dining room. The restaurant had been closed for an hour, and these three employees were the only occupants of the building. The only way anyone could have started the chandelier moving would have been to strike it with a long stick or broom. But Nate had been upstairs, and the manager and other employee had been within sight of one another downstairs.

AnneMarie took a break from her kitchen duties in 2003, walking upstairs to the third floor office to chat with another employee. As she conversed with the woman, the desk calculator suddenly sprang to life, spewing out a long paper list of meaningless numbers. Yet, each woman was two feet from the machine. Perhaps the digits had some hidden meaning to "Eleanor." On another occasion, Maryann sat working at her office computer. It had been a long day and her back was tired. As she stared at her screen she suddenly felt a pair of warm hands slowly caressing her back. She sank into it and enjoyed the touch, until suddenly, she realized that she was alone in the office, and spun around to see who was massaging her. Nobody was there.

Others have been "touched" by the ghost or ghosts at the OBI. Michelle, a waitress, was brushing her hair in the bathroom during a rest break, and all at once, an invisible hand brushed her cheek. She could even make out the pressure exerted by a particular finger. "That was the quickest comb-through I ever did!" she said. Another employee, Andy, a prep cook, felt someone brush his arm when he was gathering up fresh towels in the basement. Assuming it was his friend Pete, trying to scare him, Andy whirled around, only to find himself alone in the room.

And so it goes. It is fortunate that the staff at The Olde Bryan Inn lives and works as a big "family." I found no employee who admitted to being scared. Instead, they return to work eagerly each day, expecting that another bit of Saratoga's long history most assuredly will re-emerge to teach, if not "reach," them.

The Witch of Saratoga

Many ghost experiences can easily be traced to an historic event or personage. One such tale, perhaps the most famous one in the city, is that of Angeline Tubbs. As an old woman, Angeline recounted tales of her early life, claiming to have been the sixteen year-old mistress of a highly-placed British officer (a few have suggested Gen. Burgoyne himself) during the invasion of Saratoga County in 1777. After the British defeat in October of that year, many camp followers had to fend for themselves, as the British soldiers were sent into captivity down south. Angeline migrated to a hill that she dubbed "Mt. Vista," on the southern end of the Palmertown Mountain chain, which lies just west of Route 9 north of the city. There, she built a rough cabin of logs and scrap lumber and lived the solitary life of a hermit frontier woman, hunting wild animals for food. Her only companions were her cats. Early settlers in the small village of Saratoga found not the cast-off beauty of British army days, but instead, a terribly disfigured woman. Her deformed appearance, fondness for cats, coupled with her many idiosyncrasies, caused many to label her a witch.

To a trusted few, Angeline Tubbs confided a tragic tale of not only being cast off by her British lover, but of his bungled attempt to murder her! Bitterly, she told of his attempt to strangle her by hanging, and thus be rid of "unfinished business." With her former lover confined to an American prison camp, Angeline survived to prowl the forests north of Saratoga Springs as it rapidly became a famous American resort.

Angeline found a photographer among the summer people, a man happy to photograph such a repulsive visage, and she sold small photo souvenir cards to summer visitors as a way of supporting herself. Angeline also learned to cast horoscopes and perhaps to cast spells, enhancing her witch reputation. In 1865, as the Civil War was ending in the South, she died at the age of 101. And that should be the end of a sad story. However, in the early 1950s, the people of Saratoga had cause to resurrect her memory.

Famous American author and historian, Carl Carmer, wrote a book in 1952, in which he recalled a puzzling episode from the summer of 1932, when he had been in residence at Yaddo, the artist's retreat, along with another artist named Ben Carradine. Carmer had all but forgotten Carradine until, passing through Saratoga Springs in the early 1950s, Carmer's car broke down. While it was in the repair shop, Carmer lodged at the Gideon Putnam

Hotel, and while dining, was approached by a tall stranger who greeted him by name. It was Ben Carradine, and Carmer invited him to sit and renew their acquaintance. Carradine had never become an author, but had found success and happiness in business. He then told Carmer of a strange event from that summer of 1932.

Carradine told of having gone for a drive north of the city, up Route 9 and, seeing a field of wild flowers, stopped to pick a bouquet. Gradually, he wandered far from the highway, when a sudden thunder and lightning storm erupted. Unable to quickly reach the shelter of his automobile, Carradine sprinted to the shelter of a rocky cliff overhang, all the time being pelted with rain and hail. He remembered the sky turning black and the strong wind howling. Then, above the howling of the wind, he heard a piercing scream. Amazed that anyone would be outside in the storm's fury, Carradine left his shelter temporarily, and looking up to the top of the cliff, beheld a most awesome sight.

Atop a nearby hill, he sighted a woman whose hair streamed in the wind. With outstretched arms, the figure shrilly invited the elements to do their worst to her. And, though the lightning flashed about her, she remained untouched. Unable to fathom such dangerous behavior, Carradine quickly returned to the shelter of the ledge, wondering if he hadn't imagined the scene. After a while, the wind slackened and the rain subsided as the storm moved eastward. Carradine stepped out to search the neighboring hilltop again, but the woman was gone. Suddenly his mind was filled with images of red-coated soldiers and a tall pole from which a rope or noose was suspended. Abruptly, the vision vanished. Stunned, he hurried back to the car.

Afterward, upon his return to Yaddo, Ben Carradine wanted badly to share his anomalous experience with another artist, and had gone to Carmer's door to knock. Then he got cold feet, he told the author, and dismissed the urge. Now, in a fortuitous meeting twenty years later, Ben wanted to air the mystery. "What do you make of it all?" he questioned Carl. The historian had accumulated tales from many parts of America by that time in his life, but didn't immediately have an answer or reference. "I'll have to get back to you Ben," Carmer responded, "but you *have* jogged my memory. Somewhere in this area's history, there's something that rings a bell."

Four years later, after research, Carmer assembled the information and published *The Screaming Ghost and Other Stories*, composed after consulting William L. Stone's *History of Saratoga*, wherein Stone recounted the life of Angeline Tubbs. It was Carmer's contention that Carradine had encountered, perhaps on the single occasion of her manifestation, the distraught spirit of Angeline, standing atop Mt. Vista and taunting the forces of Nature to destroy the life that her British lover had been unable to take. Today, Mt. Vista is still a rural patch of land to the east of the Skidmore College grounds, an entrancing place for quiet walks to say a prayer for Angeline Tubbs.

A few years ago, Donna and Michael Wilcox of Saratoga Springs offered me an opportunity to see and hold a small five inch tall china doll that was once owned by Angeline Tubbs. The object has been passed down in the Wilcox family for a hundred years. Contemplating the delicate features of the doll, one is immediately struck with the fact that no dark witch could ever have treasured the small and beautiful object. Perhaps Angeline Tubbs valued it during her life as a memory of her own girlhood which had been stolen away, a theft that on at least one occasion anguished her spirit enough to reappear on Mt. Vista.

Shadows

Wall Street stockbroker and financier Spencer Trask brought his wife Katrina and three children to Saratoga Springs, where he'd purchased the old Dr. Childs estate east of the village in 1881. At the time, the Trasks were still in mourning over the death of their five year-old son, Alanson, who died in Brooklyn the previous year. The parents had summered in the Saratoga area for some years and were attracted by the influx of artists and musicians that were drawn to the spa. Their four year-old daughter, Christina, when asked what to name their summer home, responded in a childish voice, "Yaddo." Hoping to one day become a poet like her mother, the child loved words and often created her own. She liked "Yaddo," as it rhymed with the word, "shadow," though she foresaw no shadows in the house's future.

Yet, shadows of another kind *did* come. While restoring the old estate, the family once more experienced tragedy. In 1888, Mrs. Trask contracted diphtheria and was expected to die. Because the disease was thought not to be contagious, their now eleven year-old daughter, Christina, and baby Spencer, Jr., less than a year old, were allowed to kiss their mother

179

goodbye. The children quickly became infected and died within 24 hours, while their mother survived. The following year, baby Katrina was born, but died within twelve days.

In 1891, their Queen Anne villa burned and, though heartbroken at the loss of all their children, the Trasks considered selling their shadowed estate to spend more and more time in their New York City mansion or abroad in Italy. But the lure of Saratoga was strong and the Trasks, pulling themselves up from grief, designed a marvelous, fifty-five room Victorian Gothic mansion to stand where their villa had stood. They took up residence there in 1893, in time to throw an elegant Christmas party, which became an annual event for the hundred or so servants, employees and their families that were necessary to run the five hundred acre estate.

In 1899, the Trasks recognized that they had no heirs. To prevent their beloved estate falling into less harmonious hands after their deaths, the Trasks were inspired to formulate a great plan for the estate. Because the site was a place of harmony and beauty, Katrina and Spencer planned a haven for artists after they, themselves, died. Spencer designed a gravity-fed water pipe system to feed an Italian style fountain with an imported Italian statue at its center, on the great lawn, planted different species of trees along its edges, and created a Japanese garden at the top of the hill near the estate's greenhouses. He created an Italian Renaissance rose garden south of the great lawn and presented it to Katrina on their anniversary. More fountains, steps and bird baths, as well as a stately pergola, were constructed amid the many varieties of rose bushes.

Whenever they were in the city, Spencer and Katrina made it a point to invite whatever performers, writers and artists were sojourning in the village to dine at their home, and frequently, these artists shared their talents and gifts with the family and guests, making the house a cultural Mecca.

Then came another crisis. In 1907, Wall Street underwent another of its periodic panics, and a sizeable part of the Trask fortune vanished. Desperate to diminish his losses, Spencer spent more and more time at work in New York City. Two years later came the final tragedy for the ill-fated Trask family. Leaving the Croton-on-Hudson Station for a return trip to Saratoga, Trask's train was rear-ended and he was killed.

Katrina was desolated by her final loved one's death. Perhaps her determination to create and fund the artists' retreat gave her strength to persevere amid so many sorrowful memories. She closed the mansion, scrimped and saved, dismissed many servants and coachmen, and lived a penurious life in West House, a large cottage on the grounds. She took an active interest in affairs in the small city of Saratoga Springs, and a horticultural club there bears her name today. She also chose Daniel Chester French to sculpt a bronze memorial to her husband. A symbol for the city, "The Spirit of Life" statue stands today, overlooking a reflecting pool on the west side of Congress Park. In 1921, Katrina Trask surrendered to the entreaties of her former suitor, George Foster Peabody, who was the family lawyer and Spencer's business partner, and married him. She died less than a year later, in January 1922.

A corporation to run the Yaddo retreat was established and the first artists arrived for a summer's work in 1926. Since that time, each summer between Memorial Day and Labor Day, up to thirty-five artists, who work in all media, can be found in private studios within buildings that used to house cows, horses, carriages and the like. And some of these creative people, perhaps more open than many to subtle universal influences, claim that there are genteel ghosts at Yaddo.

Speculation as to the wraiths' identities has focused on two women: Mrs. Ames and Katrina Trask herself.

In 1926, Elizabeth Ames was hired by the Corporation as Executive Director of the facility, and some say that during her lengthy tenure she ruled the house with an iron hand, to ensure Katrina's vision of beauty, and to encourage each artist to take maximum advantage of the free room and board and studio space in an artistic community.

Among those who have shared their ghostly experiences is composer Daron Hagen. In September 1992, having just completed his *Walt Whitman Requiem*, he relaxed, reading near the main fireplace, as the clock ticked toward midnight. He glanced up from the book and was taken aback to see a woman wearing an old-fashioned white dress, coming down the main staircase. Quickly, it came to mind that this was the same dress Katrina Trask wore in her life-sized portrait hanging just outside the dining room. The descending apparition had her right hand raised, as if she held some significant but invisible object. Not completely familiar with the distinguishing features of Mrs. Trask's visage, he felt an inner certainty that the spirit could only be the former grand lady of the house.

Simultaneously, a sudden cry from upstairs pierced the quiet, and Hagen looked up to see writer Doug Unger, who had just emerged from working in his second floor room. Hagen asked Unger what he'd seen, and the shocked man responded, "It was Katrina!" Prior to that, neither man had professed a belief in ghosts.

181

At breakfast the next morning the pair related their shared vision with the other assembled artists before they began their day's creative work. Several knew of the specter, having heard first-hand of other past artist-in-residence experiences with the woman ghost. One recounted his personal experiences in the second floor bedroom opposite the stairs, where an unseen entity opens the windows if something less than "pure artistry" is taking place within the room. Following discussion of the Katrina-sighting, one visiting artist volunteered a reminder of the ironclad rules in force when Mrs. Ames directed the building's activities. The suspicion is common that a ghostly Elizabeth Ames still scrutinizes the residents' activities. Others joined in the discussion to hypothesize that this was the same being said to slam the closet door in what was once Katrina's bedroom when the resident artist there was taking too much leisure time away from contracted creative work.

From time to time a strange whistling is heard near the tower at the rear of the estate. I was told by a retired city police detective that, during the 1950s and 1960s, rookie policemen were stationed near the Yaddo tower during the non-resident season of autumn and winter, to do a night watch. Each of these rookies had an unforgettable "pseudo-ghostly experience," humorously created by senior comrades on the police force. I was not given the details of these pranks, but such scares were fun for all those involved, and took the form of an initiation. Nevertheless, the whistling takes place there in-season too, whether or not an artist is nearby to hear it.

Two local photographers, unknown to one another, have at different times taken photos of the area beneath the evergreens on the southwest corner of the rose garden. Both photographers have shown me the images of a ball of light, visible only to the camera lens, hovering about two feet above the ground at that spot. Traditionally, such lights or orbs are said to represent a spirit. On the day *I* tried to replicate the phenomenon, my camera malfunctioned and rewound itself after I snapped my eighth photo on a 24-picture roll. It may be worth mentioning that I had just silently invited any spirits present to make themselves known through my camera. Perhaps I should have been more specific. None of my photos showed anything strange, in any case.

Katrina Trask, who helped establish the Wiawaka Holiday House for working women in Lake George, was deeply moved by the spirituality of the Native Americans who inhabited this region long ago. When she first arrived in Saratoga, she experienced an "exquisite loveliness" in wilderness, and developed a sensitivity to the energies wafting from lakes, ponds and rivers and, with Spencer, chose to leave a material legacy to creative people of all talents, while cradled in the bosom of nature.

Daron Hagen summarized this energy field of Yaddo as "a place where a sane and humble person can see ghosts and believe in them. It's a place where we can be transformed by our talent and the magic of being a guest here into heightened creatures—we're made better than we were."

254 Church Street

The area around Saratoga Hospital has undergone a number of changes in appearance over the past quarter century. At one time an early 1800s brick house stood at 254 Church Street, and was demolished in the late 1990s. While it stood, the old house was an exciting place for its residents. Among the last inhabitants was a woman named Mary, who had no unusual experiences *until* her husband's aunt died.

One evening, as she watched television, Mary became distracted by furtive movements to her left. At first, when she looked, she saw nothing. But as the interruptions continued, all of a sudden she discerned a hand slowly making its way up the banister. There was no arm or body to accompany the vision—just a hand slowly ascending the railing! She tried to make herself believe it was only imagination and looked away. But when she looked again, the hand was still there, moving upward. A few minutes later it dissolved into thin air. Over the next few weeks the ghostly hand appeared on an irregular basis. Then, as suddenly as it first manifested, it ceased.

A few days later, Mary's grandson, Chris, ran excitedly into her living room, breathlessly telling of a strange woman in the upstairs bathroom. That room was fairly large and had doors at both ends. Unable to understand who had come into her house, Mary hurried upstairs and, just as she entered one door of the bathroom, the silhouette of another woman vanished through the other door. After a complete search of the house, Mary and Chris found themselves alone.

Many people, having such outlandish experiences, tend to repress the incidents because they aren't logical. American society does not raise its young to expect encounters with the dead, so such episodes are not "sensible" to those whose education has been narrowly focused. Unfortunately, the mass of modern society seems not yet ready to understand how profound "eternity" really is. Mary attempted to dismiss the event, as many people do, but just a few weeks later, the old ghost woman reappeared, this time in her kitchen.

Mary was seated at her table, quietly conversing with friends, when a sharp metallic sound interrupted them. Turning toward the cellar door, she watched as the door's dead bolt slowly slid back and the door opened. The awed group then heard footsteps descend the cellar stairs. After the last footstep at the bottom, all was quiet. Each individual stared at the others, but nobody dared venture a comment.

Reasoning that the one person who could potentially visit her house in spirit was her recently deceased mother-in-law, Mary later concluded that the ghostly activity represented her mother-in-law's taking leave of the old house and the earth plane. This explanation sounded credible when I first heard it. It would have been interesting to examine Mary's cellar, to see if some object had attracted the ghost woman's spirit downward, or if the ghost was trying to show the family something. However, by the time I heard this story, the old house was demolished.

When I first wrote of the incident, I surmised that Mary had been correct, but as I pondered the issue, there was a nagging contradiction. Ghosts aren't known to leave the earth by burrowing deeper into it. A ghost vanishing into a cellar indicated to me that there was more to come. A few months later, the old brick pile, that had been a house, was cleared away and new construction started. Oh good, I thought to myself, some new building is coming and I just *know* that ghost is still around. Probably it will show up in the new cellar.

When construction finished, a signboard was erected on Church Street, announcing the new building would house medical offices. Doctors and ghosts! I wondered how they would get along. It was some time before I found out.

In 2001, I had my first appointment with a doctor at 254 Church Street. A traditional man, I thought he'd not likely tell me what he knew, if anything. But when I passed the front desk after my exam, I asked the secretary and receptionist, "Okay, who's going to tell me about the ghost?" The two women shot glances at one another, as if to inquire, "Who told?" Then one smiled. She recognized me and felt safe relating her experiences to a "ghost guy."

184

"Well, the ghost is in the elevator now," she explained. "This has been going on since the building opened. About once a month, the brand new elevator simply stops. It won't budge. So we call the elevator repairman. He comes and examines the inside of the unit. 'Nothing wrong here, it seems just fine!' he always says, and pushes the start button. The elevator always starts right up. That's the way it's been for several years. Recently, however, there has been a change." The two women again shot looks at one another, and then both grinned. "Now, when the repairman's truck pulls into the parking lot, the elevator just resumes its operation. The repairman doesn't have to come upstairs or charge us for a service call, and our elevator is back in business as soon as the truck arrives!" All three of us laughed.

I think the old lady ghost has the right idea. Immediately after her death, she signaled her desire to go "upward," ostensibly to Heaven, by ascending the stairs. Then she showed her desire for purification from her earthly attachments by appearing in the bathroom. Now, apparently impatient to find a way to Heaven, she believes the elevator is a faster vehicle for ascent. Should you visit a doctor at this address, please use your waiting room time to silently wish the woman well and send your prayers to help her, but also be sure to note the location of the stairs.

The Walworth House

Many visitors to Saratoga Springs have dropped in at The Casino in Congress Park, which houses the city historical society offices and two fascinating museums of local history, one devoted to the Walworth Family. One of the city's best ghost stories took place in the old Walworth home, Pine Grove, which once stood on North Broadway across from the Prime Hotel, and next to the old firehouse. A gas station occupies Pine Grove's former location, leaving no evidence of the building's former grandeur.

Judge Henry Walton had originally built the structure at 525-527 Broadway, a huge 55 room mansion where some of America's most famous personages came to call. Many ghosts arise from circumstances of tragedy, so, even in Walton's time there was the making of a good ghost story there. One of Judge Walton's daughters was engaged to marry a bright and successful businessman who had a final business deal to conclude in Europe before they could marry. Late one night, the woman awakened from a nightmare-filled sleep. In her dream she had experienced moans and groans and agonized cries, accompanied by the crashing of waves on a rockbound shore. At breakfast, the entire family pressed for an explanation of what appeared to be a bad omen.

The meaning was quick in presenting itself. A messenger arrived the next day, bearing the sad news that the fiancée had perished at sea. The time of his death coincided with the nightmare. It is said that the daughter became inconsolable and was troubled by that recurrent nightmare, usually at midnight, for the rest of her life. Gradually the woman devolved into insanity, further grieving the Judge who, brokenhearted, sold his house and moved further up Broadway to a wooded estate, now the grounds of Skidmore College.

Judge Ruben Hyde Walworth became the new owner of Pine Grove in 1823, when Saratoga Springs was still a small village. In time, Walworth was designated as Chancellor of New York State, a judicial position that ceased after his death in 1846. The judge, seated at a large slant-top desk, held court each morning in the mansion's large, first floor room. His home was also a social center for the famous individuals who visited Saratoga Springs in the summers. Washington Irving, Henry Clay and Ralph Waldo Emerson were among the notables entertained there.

One by one, the Walworth children went off to their destinies in the world. One became a member of the Catholic Church, much to the scandal of the righteous Protestant Walworths. Another, in time, was found guilty of murder. A daughter, Reubena, redeemed the family name by courageously enlisting in the Army Nurse Corps during the Spanish-American War, only to die heroically nursing suffering men. Her burial with full military honors was a major event in Saratoga Springs in 1899.

In the end, only Clara Grant Walworth remained in the Saratoga house as the world moved into a new century. Though aged, she strove to uphold the Walworth family honor, grace and social station in the city during the early 1900s. Near the finish of her life, no longer able to climb the stairs, she had the old courtroom converted into a bedroom from which she conducted the family affairs. As Clara became more sickly, Bessie Lewis, a local nurse, was hired to oversee her daily medical care which would, in the end, have but one outcome. Georgianna Slattery (an ancestor of the Wilcox family, who now own the Angeline Tubbs doll) was hired to assist Bessie during the nights.

In her book, *Chronicles of Saratoga (2nd Edition)*, Evelyn Britten, Saratoga's historian during the mid-1900s, told of sitting with Clara during her last night on earth. Mrs. Slattery had just come on duty and entered Clara's candlelit bedroom to help keep the deathwatch. Entering the dim room, Mrs. Slattery looked at Mrs. Britten with a puzzled look and inquired, "Mrs. B., you hired *another* nurse?" Baffled, Evelyn Britten, looked at Mrs. Slattery, who stood wide-eyed and pointing at a suddenly-visible third nurse in the room. The new nurse wore a no-longer-fashionable long style nurse's uniform and cap, and bent over the comatose Clara. The golden-haired woman smiled at the pair and once more bent over the bed, letting her tresses fall upon Clara's cheek. Suddenly Georgianna and Evelyn saw the new nurse vanish as Clara drew a last breath and expired. The pair stared at one another for a moment, and then Georgianna Slattery fled from the room and into the hallway.

Outside, she came to a halt before the portrait of Reubena Walworth, the heroic Spanish-American War nurse. Mrs. Slattery had been sure it was her, but *now* she was certain. For the remainder of their lives both Georgianna Slattery and Evelyn Britten vowed that they had encountered Reubena Walworth's ghost in a final act of mercy, escorting the last of her family to Paradise.

Not too many years later, the house was razed and some of the furniture was donated to the historical society, to establish the Walworth Exhibit in The Casino.

The Batcheller Mansion

The most photographed building in Saratoga Springs is undoubtedly the striking mansion at the corner of Circular Street and Whitney Place. In an architectural style suggesting a French Castle or Moorish minaret, the building at 20 Circular Street has attracted visitors and sightseers for over a century, though the house itself almost became a ghost.

General George Batcheller from the hamlet of Batchellerville, returned from the Civil War famous and well-acquainted with the rich and powerful politicians who ran America. His old friend, President Ulysses S. Grant appointed him to the position of Judge Advocate on the International

Tribunal, which oversaw the trials of foreigners in Egypt. Before leaving for his post, Batcheller began construction of the unique house in 1873, copyrighting the design so a duplicate cannot be built. During vacations in Europe, he and his family developed a cosmopolitan outlook on world affairs, which they transferred to their home and social life whenever they returned to Saratoga Springs.

In 1885, President Benjamin Harrison appointed him Acting Secretary of the Treasury, a post he left a few years later in order to serve as U.S. Ambassador to Portugal. Then under President McKinley, he returned to the International Tribunal in Egypt, later being promoted to a judgeship on the Supreme Court of Appeals there. After his death in 1908, the home passed to his daughter, who was able to enjoy the house for a few years more before having to sell it in 1916.

New owners found the mansion to be a goldmine for summer tourist rentals until 1937. It slowly deteriorated into a seedy boarding house until, dilapidated, it finally was abandoned in 1968. The stately entrance was boarded up, as were the shattered windows. Some passersby were sure they saw bats flying from the chimneys after dark. By 1971 there was serious talk of demolition, as the land seemed worth more than the derelict building.

Then, a local attorney purchased the building in 1972 and found historic grant money available to aid in the house's restoration. For a while the building served as office space, and then, once fully restored to its Victorian elegance, became a luxury bed and breakfast retreat, which status it enjoys today. During the years of its abandonment, perhaps because of the bats and boarded windows or the Victorian look that Hollywood stipulates for haunted houses, the Batcheller Mansion acquired a reputation as Saratoga's most scenic haunt.

If there are ghosts at 20 Circular Street, they are quietly busy ones. Visitors over the past thirty years have shared stories of watching newspapers rippling in a non-existent wind in the library at the rear of the first floor. Once in a while, a page turns, as if deliberately moved by an unseen reader. In the large doorway adjacent to the dining room, others have experienced bursts of air, as if an invisible passerby has just dashed through the hallway to the cellar stairs. Interviews with chambermaids, past and present, have confirmed tales of "feeling watched" though not threatened in any malicious way—almost as if a ghostly chief housekeeper is observing their work.

In the Whitney Room upstairs, a chambermaid was making the bed and tidying the room one morning. The heavy door to the room stood open. The woman smoothed the sheet once more, then became aware that the door was closing itself while a phantom hand depressed the door handle. Stunned by the door's abrupt slamming, the woman curtailed her work and fled. She later found that other staff members had experienced the same phenomenon. They told her that similar activities have taken place in the Putnam Room nearby. For many staff members who are just trying to do their job, these are unwelcome distractions.

In 1996, when I worked for Saratoga Travel and Tours, I led a group of visitors on what was billed as a "High Adventure Tour" through the city. Our itinerary called for us to visit several old mansions, and keeping to the time schedule was important. As soon as I stepped off the tour bus at Whitney Place, I sped up the steps and into the front hallway, to ensure that our tour and refreshments would go as scheduled. There were supposed to be no guests inside at that time of day. I looked ahead through the hallway and then proceeded into the music room on the left—good, nobody there. From my position in the center of the music room I looked straight through into the dining room at the rear of the building, where refreshments awaited our group. A man in old-fashioned dress (dark slacks, vest, string tie and holding a cheroot cigar) stood with his left elbow resting on the dining room fireplace mantel, looking back at me. Darn! A guest must have slept in and decided to spend the day in house, I thought.

I quickly scanned the front foyer again and observed my tour group just entering. Feeling that I should say something tactful to the man near the fireplace, I turned back, but he had vanished! And the only way he could have left the dining room that day was to come past me. And he hadn't! So that was my own experience of a Batcheller Mansion guest or ghost. From his clothing style, he was from the early 1900s, though I can't ascertain if he was a Batcheller or simply a later lodger. The man had looked quite alive. This personal experience certainly was some "high adventure" for *me*.

To seek your own "high adventure," perhaps you would enjoy a weekend stay in this landmark, restored to the beauty of Saratoga's Gilded Age.

Mayor Butler

Walter Prentiss Butler, Saratoga Springs' first mayor, lived for years in the beautiful house at 22 Greenfield Avenue. It was originally the home of architect Gifford Slocum, a disciple of famed architect Henry Hobson Richardson. Slocum designed many famous structures in the city (the Bracket Mansion on North Broadway, the Algonquin Building at 510 Broadway, and the old firehouse at 543 Broadway). Strangely, his home, behind the Bracketts, was the one structure for which Slocum didn't use brick as a construction material. Neither did he live there long.

Butler came to Greenfield Avenue in 1890 and made the old Slocum house his home until he died there in January 1942. He had been one of the reformers who, early in the 1900s, attempted and succeeded in ending wide-open gambling in the then village of Saratoga Springs. In 1915, Saratoga incorporated as a city and Butler was chosen as its first mayor. He amassed his fortune as president of the old Saratoga National Bank. A shrewd "money man," Butler also capitalized on the shortage of posh residential rentals during the summer thoroughbred racing season, and for years rented his home to the legendary Diamond Jim Brady and his lady love, the famed actress, Lillian Russell.

Speculation as to the identity of the house's ghost always points to Butler, as he was the only individual known to have died there. Retired celebrity photographer "Smoky" Bair lived there between 1975 and 1984, and has had perhaps the most active relationship with the ghost. Soon after moving in, Bair sat one winter evening in the library of the large house, and suddenly felt a cold draft of air. Scanning the room to identify its source, he was drawn to the turning of the large brass key in the room's door. "I tell you, that sure was better than nighttime television," he said. As he later attempted to understand the phenomenon, Bair reflected that his experience had come in January, the month of Butler's death, and he later found that Butler died in the room that became Bair's library.

"I knew for sure that I was dealing with a ghost, and no ghost was going to lock or unlock *my* door! So I put the big key in a vase inside the china cabinet and locked the door. When I came into the room later, I found candles that had been in a deep-socket candelabra on top of the cabinet smashed on the floor. How old Walter lifted them out, I don't know. After that, I just left that key in the door and let Walter have his way," he laughed.

190

Bair testified to hearing footsteps echoing throughout the house, though he knew he was alone. In the November 1980 issue of *The Chronicle*, Bair recounted his numerous experiences, saying that he didn't mind sharing the house with Butler. One strange event involved the disappearance of the four canaries that he kept in a cage in the kitchen. They simply vanished and no trace of them was found for months, until, entering the kitchen one morning, he discovered two of the birds dead in the cage. He never learned what had happened to the other two birds.

Bair eventually sold the house to local attorney Keith Ferrara and his family. Just before Halloween in 1997, I interviewed Keith outside the pumpkin and ghostly sheet-decorated house. He good-naturedly assured me that life at 22 Greenfield Avenue was interesting, though not scary. He told of returning from shopping one evening with a heavy grocery bag in each arm. "As I climbed the step onto the porch, I mulled which bag to put down in order to open the porch screen door. When I got to that door, it suddenly opened for me, even though it requires a strong pull and has to move 'uphill' to open."

"Wow, I'll bet that was scary," I responded.

"No, I just said, 'Thank you very much' and walked in," he smiled. Later he told of hearing the echoing footsteps that Bair had heard, and he pointed to a large oak door that opens onto the porch. "That door opens when it wants to do so, it doesn't need a wind or even a breeze as an excuse," he said, grinning again. At first his family tried to investigate the strange noises emanating from the stairway to the second floor, but they gave up responding, as there was never anyone there and no rational explanation for the unpredictable sounds.

At the time of my interview with the owner, the family was beginning to ponder a phenomenon that they hadn't encountered before. Asleep in their second floor bedroom, they were sometimes awakened by a stooped man wearing a brown suit and derby hat, walking through the bedroom, then out the second floor window! This phenomenon needs study because, as far as anyone knows, there never was a stairs or walkway outside that window. Is Butler signaling his desire to be "out of it all" and on his eternal way?

1 Phila Street

For many years, Saratogians knew this store as "The George Bolster Studio." Bolster chronicled much of Saratoga's 20th Century life with his camera before dying in 1989. He also helped preserve the works of earlier photographers, and these now reside along with his archives in the George Bolster Collection at the Historical Society. I only had one discussion with George about ghosts, and it was inconclusive, but somewhere in his archives, he said there is a wedding photo taken with flash at night, in which the bride and groom stood in front of a large tree. One negative was never printed because, in the tree, it showed a face looming over the bridal couple's heads. Perhaps coincidentally, one of the two spouses perished not long after the wedding.

When I began work on my first book about ghosts in Saratoga County after George's death, I interviewed George's longtime assistant, Mike Noonan, who had taken over the studio. Seeking information about a house in Saratoga, I dropped in on Mike in 1997, and during our discussion he asked, "Do you know about *this* place?"

"One night when I was working at the enlarger in the back of this cellar studio, I turned and there *he* stood," Mike began. "The man wore a turn-of-the-century suit with dark brown vest and pants, along with sleeve garters. I jumped back startled, and said, 'Who *are* you? And what do you *want?*' The guy just turned quietly and left through the wall." I examined the wall at the spot Mike indicated, and saw it to be composed of brick. The two of us chuckled that brick or stone seldom impede dedicated spirits.

Mike told of another occasion in which he worked in the dark developing room. Something brushed his leg and at first he thought it was his dog. He looked down and, in the dim red developing bulb's light, was startled to see a cat, which he did not own; then the animal vanished. Such eerie incidents became common in that back room. Mike sometimes looked up from his work to see a woman staring at him from the doorway. "When I worked in that darkroom, I often encountered her. She didn't move much— just appeared and disappeared." he told me. Because he and his wife, Maeve, often worked long hours there, Mike was prompted to research this cellar workspace.

Hardly had his study begun, than he discovered the cause of charred timbers that he had found behind a wall panel. This wall had once been part of the original structure at that address, The Arcade Building, which burned in June of 1902. Press reports of the time indicated that three women's bodies were pulled from the ashes, though only one of them was a building resident. It took another day for firemen to extricate the burned corpses of David and Anna Howland, whose bodies were found in a deathly embrace. Mrs. Howland, an Irish immigrant, still clutched the rosary that she carried into death.

"It was a sad story," Mike told me. "Howland had just lost his janitorial job at the G.A.R. lodge rooms (a Civil War veterans' organization) in the Arcade cellar, *which became my studio.* They were preparing to move out to an uncertain future, and neighbors said he was depressed. I'm pretty sure my visitors there were David and Anna Howland, who have been unwilling or unable to release themselves from the scene of their deaths. Maybe David is still trying to tidy up the old lodge rooms, which were incinerated along with the city post office, the Western Union offices, doctors' offices, and other businesses on that June night so long ago. Old timers I talked to believe the Howlands had several pet cats, so we probably have a cat ghost there too."

When I asked about George Bolster's experiences there, Mike said George had never experienced contact with ghosts, as far as he knew. As George had passed on less than ten years before our interview, I asked Mike if George, himself, had ever "returned." With an impish smile on his face, Mike said, "You know, it's funny that you should ask. We've had things that just disappeared or seemed to move of their own accord. Maeve and I just joked and said, 'Okay, George, bring it back!' and we always found the object again."

Two years later, Mike moved his business to George West's old factory in Ballston Spa. From there, he still keeps an eye on, and photographs, the passing history of Saratoga Springs. Stuart Armstrong established his popular "Reruns" store at the 1 Phila Street space that Mike vacated. "Reruns" specializes in the sale of objects from days gone by. Ghostly phenomena have been scarce, but Stuart remembered that in the summer of 2003 an unexplained event occurred. One evening, two antique dealers, entranced by the shop's charm, sat and talked with Stuart and a friend. "Suddenly, we all heard a loud explosive sound from one side of the store. It was as if someone had dropped a flash bulb or a light bulb had exploded. It took us all by surprise, and the woman visitor was really shaken. I searched all over and couldn't find any cause for it. Three days later, while doing some rearranging, I picked up a stack of Depression glass plates, and to my surprise, I found that one in the middle of the stack had split evenly down the middle. How this happened, I have no idea, since nothing was sitting on the plates."

There may be a new chapter about to be written in this old space.

57 Phila Street

The structure at #57 Phila Street has had many names over the years. Now restored, the 1875 Second Empire building was once known as the Hotel Mazor, then the Gould Family Hotel, catering exclusively to New York City Jews who found Saratoga irresistible in the summertime. Orthodox Jews needed a kosher diet and thus preferred to lodge together. Also, there was a distinct anti-Semitism among some who visited Saratoga during the summers. Many visitors to this part of Phila Street were first and second generation Jews of European ancestry, and it was a tradition in Judaism to "be well," meaning, to avoid illness in the first place. So, many rode or walked out to the Spa Reservation to partake of the various mineral waters that were reputed to restore health. Others simply sampled the several dozens of waters available within the city limits.

During the 1940s, a restaurant, now a beauty parlor, was built onto the east side of the main structure, but this addition seems to harbor no ghosts. This knowledge aids in determining the period from which the ghost or ghosts emerged.

The Boghosian Brothers purchased the building in 1987 and renovated the top two floors creating modern office space for their company. The first floor became a bright office space for Dr. Carpenter, a dentist. After the Boghosian Company began working in the building, an employee working alone and late at night on the top floor was startled to hear voices in the reception area outside his office. Curious as to the source of the several voices, the man peered out his door. The conversation ended. He knew he was alone, but when he withdrew once more into his office, the jovial, if indistinct, voices resumed their merriment. Again, he got up from his desk and peered out. The conversation again ceased and, clearly, nobody was there.

"Many times when some of our staff enter this office space, we smell a musty scent which vanishes just a few minutes later. Those of us who work at night often hear a door closing noisily, but nobody comes into the offices. I'd have to see them if they did," the employee told me.

"Another phenomenon is 'The Green Man.' I may be working alone late at night and I'll hear someone slowly, heavily trudging up the wooden stairs between second and third floors. Often, it doesn't immediately occur to me that we removed the old wooden stairs years ago. Now there is a spiral metal stairs connecting the second and third story," he said. "And, consider this—you can only get to the second floor today by coming up to the third floor and walking down, so I knew nobody was down there after hours. If I look out and down the hallway, sometimes I've seen an indistinct man glowing phosphorescent green. He crosses from the stairway opening and through a wall into what is now an office. Before renovation, however, there actually was a lodging room at that spot. The guy, who wears a hat, is actually walking through a doorway *from another time!*"

One might ascribe this man's experiences to fatigue because of his long working hours. For that reason, he himself was suspicious of this repeating phenomenon until he couldn't contain himself any longer. He told a co-worker what he'd been seeing, but the man replied, "Oh, the guy in the hat? I've seen him *lots of times!*"

These office workers on the top floor at first preferred not to disclose their experiences to the dental office employees on the ground floor, but eventually, they learned that the women downstairs were trying to keep *their* secret too. In Dr. Carpenter's dental office, Fran took her job seriously. Often she was called upon to go to the storeroom to re-supply the dentist with some item. "Generally, I rushed down, got what I needed and returned, so there was no slowdown. One day I entered the storeroom and was taken aback by a moving shadow that definitely was not mine. It was moving on the side wall, while *my* shadow was cast on the back wall. I beat it out of there as quickly as I got what I needed," she told me.

The receptionist in the outer office often heard a heavy wooden door slam on the Phila Street entrance, but she remembered that as long as the dentist's office had been there, there was only a metal door. In any case, she usually waited for whoever had entered to come around the corner to her reception desk. But on some occasions, when the wooden door slammed, nobody would appear. Instead, she would then hear footsteps ascending to the second floor, but the old stairway had been removed, and the stairway space walled up long before the dentist moved in! It was impossible to climb a no-longer-there-stairs. Today the dental office has moved and a business office occupies the first floor. The secretary there told me that the office is so busy that she has never noticed anything ghostly.

I account for the Green Man phenomenon by hypothesizing that in the old hotel days, a resident of the building suffered a stroke or heart attack as he ascended the stairs. Many times, the deceased don't sufficiently understand that the body has died, so their consciousness continues and their spirit body seems to move onward, permitting the individual to remain in denial of their death. This problem appears to cause many ghost appearances—a failure to understand or accept that the body has died. Often, those who encounter such ghosts may do the entity a service by explaining to the spirit (even though it may not be visible) that its body has died and they need to move on.

Here is another story from nearby Warren County, which is the most evidential tale of consciousness surviving death that I've collected in my years of research.

A good friend, psychic Gail Putnam from Glens Falls, NY, led a meditation and psychic development group at her home during the 1980s. On a Saturday evening in October 1983, the individuals were once again gathered for their 7 p.m. class. After everyone relaxed into a receptive state, Gail was suddenly interrupted by the sight of four soldiers walking through the wall of her cellar recreation room. "Who are you soldiers and why are you here?" she asked the leader. The man responded, "We're not soldiers, ma'am. We're Marines on patrol and we're lost. And we saw the light that your group is giving off, so we came here." Putnam realized there was no war going on, and was puzzled as to the Marines' identity, but she knew for sure they were dead.

First, she explained to them that they were dead, that their bodies had died. Secondly, she told them that they could find everyone and everything that they loved if they would just turn, look over their shoulder, and see a bright, white light, then walk into it. This is a common technique for freeing the spirit of the deceased from its limbo. She noted that the men, all carrying weapons, exited through another cellar wall and were gone. "So, we just continued with the class, which ended at 9 p.m., and everyone went home."

The following morning, when she awoke she turned on the Sunday morning television news, and was startled to see reporters covering a disaster. Terrorists had bombed the U.S. Marine Barracks in Beiruit, Lebanon during the night and over 200 American Marines had died in their sleep. Apparently, these men never knew what happened. Suddenly they were without bodies and lost. They regained consciousness in the world of spirit, as apparently many or most of the 9/11 dead did. "What really clinched it for me later," said Gail, "is that I translated the time of the Marines' coming to my house into Beirut time. It was exactly the same—they were dying in Lebanon, and at least some of them instantly appeared in Glens Falls, seeking understanding and guidance."

Of course, this anecdote leaves many questions unanswered. Where did the other dead Marines go for solace and understanding, if they have thus far found it? We can probably never know. It is in our nature to speculate on this point, and hope that all those servicemen and women are now free of this violent world and are at peace in a higher realm. Recently, at a speaking engagement, I met two local parents of one of these young Marines. Hearing this tale of contact and survival, their grief was greatly lessened, and they accept their loss as only temporary.

Another positive point in this story is that it affirms what people in religious or prayer groups have often believed—that a dedicated group gathered for a greater good can send a resonance of light and help into the world far beyond ours.

The Cottage Place Carriage House

Most of the old buildings and cottages on Saratoga's east and west sides have their stories and memories, and perhaps even their ghosts. Joe, one of my former students, lived for awhile on Cottage Place. My research suggests that the building was once a carriage house attached to the old A.S. Bushnell estate during the 1870s. In intervening years, the second story was converted to an apartment.

During a period of renovation in the 1970s, the Cushing family discovered an old pistol and bloody cloth secreted behind a wall. Older neighbors told the Cushings about an ill-fated love affair that ended there long ago.

During the 1880s, the legend goes, a married couple lived over the carriage house, and a caretaker on the estate became enamored of the wife, lusting after her when the husband was out of town on business. The husband allegedly returned earlier than expected, and found his wife in the arms of the caretaker. Seizing his pistol, the husband is said to have shot the pair and disposed of the bodies in a secret place. Apparently the man, famous for his rage, intimidated the neighbors into silence, so the crime of passion was never reported to police. I interviewed an older city resident in that part of the city as to the details of this story. It was her opinion that Saratoga Lake was the place of burial, a location favored by many miscreants over the years, those who wished to cover up crimes.

The young man I interviewed was a tenant in the carriage house after the Cushings moved on. He swore that he sometimes heard a man and woman in subdued conversation within the apartment, and wonders if the lovers' tryst continues in time, if not in space. Popular neighborhood belief is that the two clandestine lovers still meet in the cottage on the anniversary of their murder. "If it's only once a year, that's enough for me," Joe told me, wiping his brow.

108 Circular Street

The restoration of this stately old house to its former elegance began about 25 years ago, and its present summertime residents tell me that all the old negative vibrations have ceased, but what a circus of phenomena took place there over the years!.

Originally built in 1843 as a residence for businessman James Savage and his wife, the former Eunice Barnum from Ballston Spa, the house had many happy days during Savage's prosperous ownership of a hardware store on Broadway. The soaring Corinthian columned porch was the height of fashion in the Greek Revival style before the Civil War. By 1868, his fortunes diminished, Savage was forced to sell the grand house. For almost one hundred years, the building was a boarding house catering to both year-round and transient lodgers. In 1922, the rear of the house was extended and more rooms were added. Old photographs of the period show a beautifully maintained flower garden along the front and south sides of the house. For much of the 1930s and 1940s it was known as The Ro-Ed Mansion, an appellation comprising the two owners' names. By the 1950s, the building began to show its age, maintenance was sporadic, and the quality of the tenants seems to have declined. In 1956, it was called The Hil-Win, and by that time the building seems to have acquired several specters.

Helen Hathaway, in the fall of 1986, wrote an article in *EYE on Saratoga* about an Elisha Isbell, a lodger in the old mansion around the time of World War I. Apparently at one time, this man had a vaudeville or circus act, and kept about one hundred birds—all red—caged in his room. According to Hathaway, Isbell returned to his room one day and found all his birds fluttering about in the room, liberated from confinement by an unseen hand. During the days of The Hil-Win, a woman resident claimed she could hear the ghostly Isbell and his daughters still bouncing about the room, trying to recapture the birds.

Then there was the jockey who found cheap accommodation there during The Hil-Win days. For just one too many times, he awoke in the night to find his bolted door standing ajar. He had conscientiously secured the door at bedtime and knew its unlocking was not his fault. The jockey swore that invisible people were entering and leaving his room all night long. Spooked by the apparent ghost activities, he moved out. Other residents also claimed to hear doors slamming on the second floor during the night, though it was never ascertained just whose doors these were. On one occasion, a man who owned a German Shepherd guard dog, rented a second floor room, only to find his pet cowering and whining, refusing to climb the stairs. He had to give up his room. Many residents, by that time, referred to the ghostly presence as "Egbert."

When the Hil-Win closed, the building was briefly incarnated as an "art center," where many of the residents apparently achieved their artistic vision aided by *cannabis*. After a year, the building stood dilapidated and abandoned. Some city residents feared that the demolition men would be next on the scene. Instead, a visionary couple from Putnam County, owners of thoroughbreds, purchased the house and began its restoration.

A construction man named Rich was the general contractor and provided many of the following incidents. "I'd always been curious about that old place, and it was enjoyable to get in there and try to restore some of

199

its former function and beauty. Local people often stopped by and asked us if we knew the rumors about the ornamental black wrought-iron fence out front. We said no, and they told us that the fence mysteriously became red-hot at times, even during wintertime. We never found it so, but it is still a common legend on Circular Street, even today." Every time I pass by the house, I, also, grab hold of the fence, hoping one day to find it hot, but so far have been unrewarded.

His work crew began operations about 7 each morning, then took a coffee break about 9:30 a.m. "During our break one day, with the guys sitting outside and the house wide open, I walked through the downstairs. Suddenly, overhead I heard something very heavy—almost certainly the cast iron bathtub—being dragged across the floor. Who's up there? I asked myself. All my men were accounted for, so I ran upstairs, worried about damage to the floors. Nothing was out of place; the bathtub was exactly where it had always been. So what made that noise?" he asked.

It was dark out when work finished on one winter work day, and Rich went to turn off all the building lights at the breaker panel in the attic, then locked up the house and prepared to drive away. From his pickup truck at the curb, however, he spotted the attic light still on. Scratching his head, he returned to the house, unlocked it and trudged to the top floor. There was still quite a bit of sawdust on the floor, and only his footprints over to the electric breaker box were visible. These were footprints he'd made just five minutes earlier, when he'd gone to the box, thrown the breaker and left. There were no other footprints there, yet the breaker was now on. Scratching his head, he once more turned the breaker off and left. This time, the light stayed off, so he went home.

When the house was 99% finished, Rich stood looking with satisfaction at all the good work done to restore the entryway and foyer. Suddenly a slight noise caused him to look upward in the two-story stairwell. An electric light bulb, somehow unscrewed from the chandelier, was falling directly toward his head. Reaching quickly upward, he snared the bulb before it hit him. He stood for a moment, stunned. The only way anyone could reach that light fixture was by using a long ladder, which was *not* there. Were the ghost stories true, then? Was there, in fact, a phantom on Circular Street? Well, maybe, just maybe, Rich concluded.

About quitting time soon afterward, he heard soft footsteps upstairs. Knowing his men had already left, and alarmed that he might finally come face to face with the ghost, he cautiously made his way upstairs. At the stair top, he found the neighbor's collie, which had somehow let itself in and was taking a tour of the restored grandeur! Chuckling to himself, he corralled the dog and left.

Helen Hathaway also claimed to have uncovered a legend of a man murdering his wife's lover in the house, but evidence about this claim was difficult to find. Neighbors of 108 Circular Street at the time claimed that the murdered woman's ghost still stomped up the stairs and around the house at night, but Rich never encountered the wraith.

When I first wrote this story I spoke with the gracious woman who, with her husband, owns the house. She was anxious to help me with my research and books, but was almost apologetic that she had had no experiences since moving in; the house is peaceful and has apparently been so since Rich finished the extensive restoration. "In any case," she said, "I hope there are no ghosts. I wouldn't want them to scare my grandchildren!"

The Case House

The frame house near the intersection of York and East Avenues was built in 1865 by businessman George Case. His heirs sold it 101 years later to the parents of the present owner when she was sixteen. "I lived here for almost nine more years, but it never felt like home; in fact I was scared sometimes, but couldn't explain why. There was always something sinister about having to come downstairs at night when I was a teen." Many times, the fear created a mental image of being stabbed by an intruder, though she knew no one to whom such a thing had ever happened. "When I finally left, I never thought I'd come back," she told me.

In 1980, her parents decided to move and offered the house to the young woman, now a wife, who surprised herself by accepting the offer. "So, at age 27, my husband and baby boy and I came to live here on York Avenue. Upon returning to live here, what surprised me most was that I no longer feared being murdered. But we sure ran into some other surprises," she said.

One day while working at the kitchen sink, the woman caught a slight movement in her peripheral vision. The image seemed to be another woman wearing a long-sleeved, floor-length black dress, crossing the kitchen. "For a moment I thought it was my neighbor, Pat, who'd come to visit. I turned to look directly at the woman and saw that it wasn't Pat, and that the stranger was wearing a bonnet. I realized that I'd seen a ghost when the woman, who continued to cross the kitchen, just vanished near the back door. I remembered that, when I was a kid, there used to be an old shed that's now-demolished, outside that door. Apparently, the ghost lady was still walking out to that shed. Sometime afterward, I began to see an apparition of a two or three year-old boy out of the corner of my eye. If I looked directly at him, he'd quickly vanish. Another ghost! I wondered who the boy was, and from what period in the house's history he came."

Together with Pat, she began to research the history of the old house, tracking down the initial information about the Cases, who built it. An elderly neighborhood woman told them that long ago, a mother and son had died of diphtheria there, perhaps about 1919. After finding the identities of the woman and boy, she never saw them again. It was almost as if they appeared just to say, "*We* once lived and died here."

"A few years later I had a second son," she continued, "and when I changed his diaper on the living room floor he'd often laugh. 'Funny man,' he'd say in his baby talk, and point through the doorway into the dining room, telling me about how the man made him laugh." Although she couldn't see the man, she humored her son rather than reprimand him for claiming something that Mommy couldn't see. Still, she had to admit, from the boy's description, the figure sure sounded like her deceased grandfather.

The boys are adults today and seldom remember the ghosts of childhood. The mother, however, retains vivid memories of the former residents who proved an untraditional "neighborhood welcoming committee."

The Casino

Irish immigrant John Morrissey came to Saratoga Springs from Troy, NY in the 1850s to try his hand at a business he'd learned in New York City—gambling. From his arrival in America, he'd been a scrapper. New York's street gangs seasoned him for real fight work. He became the bare-knuckle heavyweight champion in the U.S., then, turned from physical fights to political ones, joining the Democrat Tammany Hall organization.

Tammany promoted his political career to Congress, where he served two terms as Congressman from the "silk stocking district" of New York City. All the while, however, he had watched and learned about human weaknesses in the gambling dens of New York City. After retiring from politics, he moved to Troy where he continued to fight the upper classes of society.

From Troy it was only a short hop to the resort village of Saratoga Springs, where he opened a small, exclusive gambling house on Matilda Street in the early 1850s. To avoid trouble with local people, he devised a strict policy of permitting no local people to gamble in his clubs (avoiding citizens losing their shirts and resenting his operation). Thus, he avoided difficulties in the early years of his business, while employing many people and making generous gifts to city charities.

In 1863, in the midst of the Civil War, he joined other wealthy patrons of thoroughbred horse racing in holding the first stakes races on the village's east side, a move that was so successful that a racecourse was built on Union Avenue the following year. This venture added to Morrissey's coffers, and he planned the building of a grand gambling Club House in what is now Congress Park. Completed in 1870, "The Casino," as it was popularly known, continued the policy of excluding women and locals. As his fortunes increased, Old Smoke, as he was then known, because of his cigar addiction, added a large gambling room on the Club House's east side.

Attempting to gain acceptance from the New York City "old money" aristocracy, Morrissey befriended Commodore Cornelius Vanderbilt and often bet large sums of money on Vanderbilt's stock picks, a move that led him to financial ruin. He had to sell his beloved Club House shortly before his death at age 47 in 1878.

Subsequently, in 1893, the building came into the ownership of Richard Canfield, the notorious "Prince of Gamblers," who expanded the grounds and gardens. The name Canfield Casino is now given to the building, which houses the Walworth Collection, the George Bolster Collection and the museum and offices of The Historical Society of Saratoga Springs.

The village of Saratoga Springs was growing rapidly by 1900, and strong temperance and anti-gambling movements were afoot. *New York Tribune* reporter, Nellie Bly, exposed much of the corruption and immorality that had crept into the summertime lifestyle. Reform pressure groups forced city government to restrict gambling in 1904 and, close down legal wagering entirely, except at The Racecourse, in 1907. Canfield left town after selling his property to the tougher new city government. By 1911, the building was used mainly for recreation, relaxation, games, drinking mineral waters and other social events. The road connecting Union Avenue and Broadway was severed to create a more peaceful Congress Park, which the upper classes seldom visited afterward.

Somewhere in all this activity, The Casino became a haven for ghosts. When the Walworth Mansion on Broadway was demolished, the third floor of the Casino was reconfigured to display many of the family's belongings. In 1977, Stuart Armstrong visited the newly-created museum and, as he walked up the stairs from the second to third floor, was thrilled to see a woman in period dress walking past the stair top. Looking forward to a conversation with a costumed guide, he was disappointed. There was no other living person on the third floor. Strange, he thought, doubting himself, I'm *sure* I saw a golden-haired woman in a long dress. Then, as he passed the Walworth bedroom display, there was the dress, splayed across the bed! It had belonged to Reubena Walworth, the famous nurse who had died of illness in the Spanish-American war, a woman whose portrait hung in the hallway, right beside him! Had her spirit somehow accompanied the heirlooms from the old home at Pine Grove? If so, he would have dearly wished to converse with her.

A museum volunteer has heard her name called out on the second floor, which houses offices and the gambling museum. Yet, at the time, that floor was otherwise unoccupied. Another guide on the second floor claims to have "received a warning" by a spectral voice, but would not discuss the matter further. And still a third guide claims to have smelled a peculiar aroma, maybe a cigar, when she works on the second floor alone. Museum guides downstairs sometimes encounter visitors descending the stairs, claiming to have seen surreptitious movements out of the corner of their eyes on that mysterious second floor.

In the summer of 1996, three Asian-American children went upstairs to view both the gambling museum and Walworth Collection. A short time later, the trio came scurrying downstairs. The two older children seemed scared and refused to go back upstairs, but the other child sought out a museum guide, seeking affirmation that he had really seen a scary old man wearing a hat upstairs. "I told the little boy that, 'It's okay, honey, nobody upstairs will hurt you,'" she said. Others claim to have seen the old man in a hat near the roulette wheel, and the guide figured this to be just one more sighting of Old Smoke, scheming to regain his beloved Club House, a possession that led the rich and famous of America to seek him out just yesterday in spirit time.

The Riley House

In 1839, Rensselaer Riley purchased the old Coon home on Gilbert Road east of the village of Saratoga Springs. The squarish old farmhouse was located in the center of a large farm. With his brothers Peter and John helping him, Riley hoped to be one of Saratoga County's gentleman farmers. The details of his life are rather sketchy, but we know he died in 1890, having married twice. A New York City real estate company then purchased the old farm and rented it to a succession of tenants. It is known that, between the 1920s and 1950s, it was a house of ill-repute, owned by a colorful woman named Lil. The old building became a family home again in the 1950s, and in the early 1970s, retired State Trooper Ray Kuchesky bought the house and is the present owner.

None of the above history, except Ray's name, was known to me or my associates when Michelle, a new acquaintance, told me of strange experiences that she had while smoking marijuana there when visiting the occupants before Ray's ownership. After hearing her tale, I argued with her, suggesting that a person might indeed have had strange visions while smoking controlled substances. Nevertheless, her story had an all too familiar ghostly ring to it.

Gathering about a dozen friends from our local parapsychology investigative organization, PSI, and accompanied by local psychics Millie Coutant and Gail Putnam, as well as nationally-famous Connecticut psychic Lorraine Warren, we descended on Ray's house on a cold December morning in 1976. Barbara Stone, local reporter for the Glens Falls *Post Star*, accompanied us.

Ray told us of purchasing the main house, a small servant's house, and a considerable tract of land behind it in the early 1970s. Shortly after moving in, he experienced the sound of music wafting through the house. When he checked his radio and television, he always found them turned off. At that point in his experiences, he was ready to hear our group's impressions. When our group began the investigation, by design, none of us had researched the house's history, beyond the brief information that Ray had provided.

As we entered the kitchen door at the rear of the house, Millie immediately looked to her left, and wondered aloud as to the identity of an old woman she saw in front of the sink. The rest of our group saw nothing, though Betty Jane (our photographer) took a Polaroid photo of the spot. A minute later, after the picture self-developed, we saw all the background, including the sink and window in focus. But there was a strange horseshoe-shaped disturbance across the photo, though nothing that resembled an old woman. Since that time, I've learned that such distortions can be attributed to energy fields. Several days later, Betty Jane took the photo to an expert who informed her that taking such a photo was impossible: either the entire picture would be *in* focus or *out* of focus—an enigma.

My job that day was to tape record all that our psychics "got." Gail suddenly exclaimed, "Oh, see the pretty lady!" We all asked where, and she pointed to the doorway out of the kitchen. She began following an invisible lady, and I was quick to stay with her, attempting to catch every word on tape. We wended our way into the dining room, then the front living room. Gail noted aloud that the woman had a large, bell-shaped maroon skirt and had her black hair beautifully styled. She came to a sudden stop in the front room, near the fireplace. As she did so, I smelled flowers, reminiscent of so many funeral homes I'd been in. I could see no source for the smell, as Ray had no visible bouquets of flowers—there was only an ambient smell of wood burning in the fireplace. I inhaled deeper, the better to experience the flower scent, but could smell nothing. Strangely, when I was *not* inhaling, my brain told me that I was smelling a floral scent. Simultaneously, Gail exclaimed, "Oh, smell the roses!" Gail continued narrating that the young woman was showing her a coffin in the southwest corner of the room, where her wake had been held. I suddenly comprehended that *I had smelled funeral flowers*. Then the scene vanished from Gail's vision.

Millie, the best psychic I've ever known, began wondering aloud about a coughing sound she heard. Turning around, (facing what to the rest of us was an empty living room) she observed a brass bed, its head propped up on bricks, and containing an old woman who coughed continually. Then, Barbara Stone, the reporter, perceived a stationary ice cold circle, located about six feet away from the fireplace. Everyone in our group took turns walking through the circle, from the warmth of the fireplace, into chilling cold, then back into warmth. Lorraine Warren informed us that such icy temperature drops were often indicative of a ghost presence, though none of us saw anything within the circle.

After roaming the downstairs, we assembled at the foot of the stairway to the second floor. Gail suddenly blurted out, "There! Did you see that? A naked lady just ran past the top of the stairs, trying to cover herself with a towel!" Apparently, the rest of us were too late for this unique ghost's display. Ray assured us that there was no living being upstairs.

As several of us then prepared to go upstairs, Millie restrained us. "We're walking through a marriage right here," she informed us. "The woman stands on the left in a white dress, wearing a Belgian lace veil. On her right is a man in a blue uniform." Nobody moved. What is the protocol, we wondered, for intruding on a ghostly marriage? With no clear answer, we finally chose to proceed up the stairs and, as we did so, Millie lost sight of the wedding.

We traversed the upstairs and several of the psychics got strong impressions. In the front southern bedroom, Lorraine went into a trance while seated on the bed. Closing her eyes, she seemed asleep for several minutes. Then, straightening and opening her eyes, she told of receiving the impression of someone being struck on the head with a pistol butt in the room, and of a man hanging, either just inside or outside the French doors that lead to the room's outdoor balcony. Later, I discovered that this was the room in which Michelle claimed to have had her strange experiences when she was in college. In retrospect, after learning more about the house's history, we determined that these events, if accurate, probably dated to the years of Prohibition, when Lil paid off law enforcement officers to leave her customers alone. Many never-recorded dark things, some violent, are likely to have occurred in and around the house.

After completing our tour of the upstairs, the group members stood leaning on the center stairway rail, conversing in an attempt to correlate individual experiences. Suddenly, I panicked—I couldn't breathe! Try as I might, I couldn't take air into my lungs. In distress, I turned to Millie on my right to notify her that I felt I was suffocating. She, as were *all the others,* was also experiencing great difficulty breathing. Gasping, Millie interjected, "It's okay. It's only the old lady from downstairs. She wants us to know how she felt when she died." Instantly, we all could breathe normally again. When I returned from the ghost hunt later, I phoned Michelle to ask specifically who had owned the house before Ray. She provided the name and phone number of a family who, it turned out, lived only a few houses from mine.

I called the number and found myself speaking to the young man who had been Michelle's friend. Apologizing for the abrupt question, I asked if he'd entertain a scenario. "Here's the image," I said, "an old lady coughing very hard in a bed in the living room." Quickly he responded, "Oh yeah, that's Gram. She died in 1970. She had emphysema so bad that she couldn't climb the stairs, so we brought her bed downstairs, and that's where she died." I then asked if her bed had been made of brass, and he answered,

207

"Sure, how did you know?" Here were two of Millie's sensations immediately verified! The man couldn't remember whether or not the head of the bed had been propped up on bricks, but I felt that much of our psychic communication had been validated. I then filled him in on the details, and we agreed that the old woman that Millie had seen in the kitchen and choking in the living room, was likely his grandmother's ghost.

One final visit was necessary before our team left the house—the cellar. It was appropriately cobwebby and dim, as a stereotypical Hollywood set would have required. Millie commented on the number of men dressed in blue uniforms lying on cots along the wall, almost as if the building were a military hospital of some sort. I knew this building couldn't date back to the Revolutionary War, but (because of the blue uniforms) supposed it could have been used during the Civil War. Later we learned that during Riley's tenure there, the 77th NY Regiment, a local Civil War outfit, drilled in the fields out back, and it is possible that Riley let them use his cellar as an infirmary during normal camp life.

In 1980, Ray and Diane, two teacher friends, announced their impending marriage. I asked Diane where they would be living and she told me of finding a cute house on Gilbert Road, in the days when there was little development along the road. "Not that big white house?" I queried. "No, the little one behind it. Why do you ask?" she responded. I told her about our group's experience in the Riley house four years earlier. I saw a polite but skeptical smile cross her face, and we both went our separate ways for summer vacation.

Eleven years later, Diane caught my arm on the first day of school, "Boy, have I got a story for *you!*" she said. "My sister came to visit us this past summer. We hadn't seen her since Ray and I married in 1980. And she said to us, 'I'm glad you guys no longer live in that little Gilbert Road house, or I'd never have come back. I never told you this, but, at the time I stayed with you, I was frightened by a woman wearing a lace veil floating *in the air* outside my second floor bedroom window.'" Both Diane and I laughed, remembering me telling her of Millie seeing the lace-veiled bride in Ray Kuchesky's house in 1976.

Attempting to gain as much information as possible about Ray's house, I discovered Riley's two marriages. He had married Irena in the early 1830s, soon after buying the house. The maroon outfit that Gail Putnam had seen on the young woman ghost certainly fit that pre-Civil War period of dress. Irena died at age 37 in 1849. Shortly thereafter, Rensselaer Riley married a second wife, Julia Ann, who eventually died in 1866. It is likely that the second marriage took place in the house. Who the blue-uniformed man on the stairs was, I'm not sure. Riley never served in the army, so perhaps it was Julia Ann's father, giving her away.

Research revealed that Lil's original establishment had been down at the northern end of Gilbert Road, and had caught fire mysteriously in the 1920s, when she was one month late in paying her "protection money" to local officials, so she removed her "business" to what later became Ray's house. I smiled, remembering the naked ghost.

Anna, a dear friend of mine, lived on a side road not far from Ray's house. She told me of a strange experience that she had in the area in 1995. As she walked her large dog, Sebastian, northward along Gilbert Road, she saw a man approaching her about one hundred feet away on the same shoulder of the road. For a moment she looked down at the dog, then returned her gaze to the approaching man. He had vanished! But there was no logical place that he could have gone, as the roadside vegetation was thick and wet with dew, and there were no trails or houses in between. There may be as-yet-undiscovered spirits beyond the City's east side.

At the end of our day of investigation in 1976, as we left via the back door, Millie peered into the dusk behind the house, toward what is now the polo field, and told us that a body had been surreptitiously buried there long ago. It was too windy and cold to stand and ponder *that* for long.

In the meantime, Ray keeps passersby reminded of the house's colorful past by placing a nude mannequin on the outdoor balcony, causing motorists to screech to a halt at all hours of the day and night.

A Man Freed?

Ghosts have been experienced in many ways throughout recorded history. Here is a tale of Saratoga in its early days, before thoroughbred racing and high stakes gambling edged out the quiet village life of the summer resort centered on the health-giving waters, a time when one might hear music from the great hotels wafting through the downtown area.

William L. Stone, a famous Saratoga author, published an article in the October 1878 issue of *Potter's American Monthly* magazine, detailing his first-hand experiences with spirits eighteen years before. Perhaps it was the rise of Spiritualism in America at that time that encouraged him to relate his adventure.

At the time of this ghostly tale in the late winter of 1860, Stone lived in a brick cottage near the downtown area, perhaps along Regent Street. It was a relatively new house, having been built by local artist William R. Freeman, who rented it to Stone while the Freemans visited friends in Georgia. The author records that soon after taking up residence there he and his family began to hear doors opening and slamming shut in the house, books falling from bookshelves, and footsteps in the hallway when no one was there. Night and day the interruptions continued, though upon investigation, the family members were unable to see any physical evidence of objects fallen or moved. Eventually, they tired of seeking the source of the noises.

To test their perceptions, when the Stones invited guests to the house, they did not warn the visitors about the phenomena, but chose instead to question them in the morning as to the soundness of their sleep. One after another, the friends told of footsteps scurrying through their rooms or on the stairways. They related sounds of rapping upon the headboards of the beds, or of hearing doors opening and noisily shutting after 1 a.m. Each person's disclosure was then followed by a lively discussion as to the potential cause of these events. None could be discovered.

There were no trees touching or near the house and the sounds persisted whether or not it was windy outside. There were no apparent animals or vermin in or near the house. The cause of the noises remained a mystery, leading the friends, in the absence of other plausible evidence, to suspect the disruptions were caused by a ghost.

Stone invited three friends, two ministers and a nephew, to join him during the summer when his wife and family were traveling. None of his guests knew in advance what awaited them. On the first night, Stone, reading in the library, heard his name called loudly and arose from his chair to seek out the caller. He went to the hallway, where he found the three other gentlemen, each coming from his room and wondering who had called *their* names. Then a servant called from the upstairs, seeking to know who had called *her*! Stone revealed his domicile's secret, and the group discussed the matter for a few hours before retiring.

Early the next morning, all were jolted awake by the sound of a very heavy object (perhaps a boulder?) crashing down the stairs. Arising in alarm, everyone assembled at the foot of the steps, though they found nothing which could have made the noise. On August 15, 1860 the four men sat relaxing in the cottage, listening to orchestral music drifting from the old

Union Hotel and the Congress Hall. It was a balmy summer evening, and before long, the conversation shifted to the recent events which had stymied them. Even as they discoursed, quiet, but audible, footsteps moved through the room, though no interloper was visible to the eye. Determining to get to the bottom of the matter, Stone took down an old alphabet board, a forerunner of the Ouija board, and the group prepared to contact the ghost.

To begin their spirit connection, the quartet seated themselves at a table and joined hands. The table immediately began to vibrate. Then came a loud series of sharp raps, both on and under the table, and upon the mantelpiece, and along the bookshelves. Stone began questioning the spirit by pointing to the letters in turn, and the spirit rapped in response as the correct letter was pointed out. Stone asked the spirit if it was an Indian, to which the shade responded in the negative as the "No" circle was pointed at on the board. Asked its name, the spirit gave a strange one—Leonard Lott Grow, an identity completely unknown to those assembled there. At this point, one of the men became fearful and withdrew his hands from those he clasped.

All of a sudden, the table began to vibrate more strongly, rocking in a macabre dance from leg to leg. Then, through the doorway, the four saw the table in a neighboring room levitate one foot above the carpet, then fall heavily to the floor, rattling the dishes upon it. This phenomenon was repeated two more times, greatly unsettling the quartet. Mr. Judson, the recalcitrant member, rejoined his hands with the others after Leonard Lott Grow's spirit communicated that he was deeply offended at the disrespect shown to him. By the appropriate number of raps, the entity indicated that it would behave if Judson would cooperate. As soon as all hands were rejoined, the house suddenly became quiet and remained calm throughout the remainder of the night.

Stone then asked Grow's spirit if his body was buried in the house and the ghost answered, "No." Asked if he had been killed in earlier times by the Indians, the entity again responded, "No." Asked if Mr. Freeman, the house's owner, had harmed him, the spirit again answered in the negative. "Then why do you haunt *this* house in particular?" Stone asked.

"Because I am at unrest, *unrest*! Communicate with Mrs…," Grow's spirit responded, suddenly breaking off the contact before revealing the woman's name. And the perplexed men could not ascertain how or why the connection had been abruptly terminated.

The next day, Stone's nephew, one of the four participants, told his uncle of having descended into the cellar that morning, and finding a boarded up room. After dinner that evening, the men decided to investigate the chamber. Lighting a candle, they negotiated the cellar stairs and, using an axe, pried apart the board wall. Suddenly, their candle was blown out, though the investigators pragmatically noted the cellar window was open and was the likely source of the breeze. They were quick to notice, however, that they were not in total darkness, as a glowing shape within the exposed chamber dimly illuminated their surroundings. The glowing and vaporous shape then began to flow, as a drifting fog, instantly chilling the men.

Astonished, the investigators could only gape as the vague mist began to sway, and then slowly coalesce into an erect figure without visible detail. Almost five feet in height, the apparition resembled a human form. When it moved slowly toward them, the men scrambled out of the cellar, aware that the shade was following them. In the brightly lit hallway, the apparition seemed to disappear, but when Stone turned down the gaslight, the phantom once again became visible, slowly swaying before them. The figure moved to the foot of the stairs, where they had previously heard the crash, and the men heard faint footsteps moving up the staircase as the mist dissipated. That was enough for Mr. Judson, who immediately left the house, taking a room for the night at Congress Hall, and returning directly to his home the next day.

Later, Stone commented that the phenomena of sound had continued throughout the remainder of his brief residence in the cottage, though when his family returned at summer's end, none of them ever saw the luminous presence. With autumn's arrival, the Stone family took new quarters in the village.

During that winter, Stone was introduced to a local minister, whose widowed sister and her two daughters were presently renting the Freeman cottage. The clergyman pleaded with Stone never to speak of his ghostly experiences, which were by now being widely rumored in the village, if he should encounter the widow or her girls.

Then, some months later at a party, William L. Stone did encounter the cleric's nieces. One of the girls asked Stone about his residence in the Freeman cottage, and whether he had heard any strange sounds. Stone dismissed his experiences as likely the result of mice or rats in the building. But the girl said, "*That* will not account for the remarkable sounds that *we* hear day and night!" She went on to describe the precise phenomena that Stone's family and friends had all experienced in the house. The young

212

woman also noted a new ghostly wrinkle: a sudden gust of air and the sound of rustling silk as the invisible presence whisked by.

After that meeting, Stone refused to categorize these events or even to explain them publicly. A careful historian, he chose to simply relate the facts to those who inquired. Three years later, however, while attending a party in New York City, the author was surprised to hear an addendum to his encounters. Mrs. Freeman, wife of their former landlord, was present with her husband, and was startled as Stone related to them his experiences in their cottage. As the author gave the purported spirit's name, Mrs. Freeman interjected, *"There*, husband, *that's it!"* Stone inquired as to her meaning.

Freeman's wife responded by relating her own experiences in Savannah, Georgia during the summer of 1860, when the Stones had rented their Saratoga cottage. She had encountered a Georgia woman who mourned the loss of contact with her brother, a gentleman named Leonard Lott Grow. Leonard, the woman explained, had gone north and had lost contact with his family in the South. The acquaintance had asked Mrs. Freeman to send word to her if she should ever meet or hear of her long-lost brother. Until encountering Stone at the party, Mrs. Freeman had never heard the unique name again. This seemed to identify the entity in Saratoga as the Georgia woman's lost brother, though the time and manner of his demise was never determined. Grow had apparently died of some misadventure and his place of death or burial never came to light. His death may or may not have taken place in the Freeman house, as spirits most often appear where there are sufficiently sensitive people to communicate with, rather than at the place of death. Grow's spirit had apparently roamed the Freeman's house, perhaps sensing the contact to his sister down South.

Many ghost stories leave the reader with more questions than answers, but it is always satisfying to know the earthly identity of those who now travel the highways of the inter-in-between world. Apparently, over time, Leonard released his desire to notify family of his fate, and slowly made his departure from Saratoga Springs to what the budding Spiritualist movement of that time called "The Summerland."

The Old Station

In the late 1800s, the better part of the Adirondack Mountains north of Saratoga was still a wilderness. Early pioneers such as William West Durant had taken notice of the vast timber and mineral resources in that region, however, and in 1884 he chartered The Adirondack Railway to bring the riches of garnet, iron and timber south to Saratoga and onward into the American economy. He built a big house at 117 Grand Avenue to serve as the southern terminus of the Railway. The High Gothic Victorian showplace is still there, squeezed within a bustling, gentrified neighborhood, though the tracks are long gone.

The Adirondack Railway merged with the Delaware & Hudson Railroad in 1902 and the long line didn't need two stations half a block apart, so the old terminal building was sold to raise capital for expansion of the merged lines. Over time, the building became a rooming house and, as the former immigrant neighborhood fell into disrepair and decay, so did the old station. The tracks were removed and re-routed to the west of the city in the 1950s. All memories of the railroad connection in the city's center vanished after the D&H station on Railroad Place was also razed.

Then, in the early 1990s, the Saratoga Springs Preservation Foundation was inaugurated to restore Saratoga's beautiful old houses that had fallen on hard times. Durant's High Gothic Victorian terminal was surely one of those. By 1993, the old station, looking brand new again, reopened with three apartments. Marvin Olick managed the property for the Preservation Foundation and helped install the first tenant in an upstairs apartment. He was quite surprised a few hours later when, shortly after midnight, he received a panicked phone call from the woman tenant. "Why didn't you tell me that the trains run at night?" she wailed. "I just got to sleep and that steam train came whistling and chugging right under my window!" Marvin did his best to calm the woman and tell her that there were neither tracks nor trains there any more. That marked the only known appearance of Saratoga's "ghost train." There was more to come, however.

A year later, another second floor tenant complained to Marvin that someone was slamming their apartment door most nights around 2 a.m., and then walking down the stairs, whereupon he or she unlocked and then slammed the street door. Finally, one night, the tenant attempted to catch the mysterious noisemaker in the act. He peeked out of his door right after the first slam and saw an older man dressed in a dark blue uniform and conductor's cap walking down the second floor hall, checking a large pocket watch, and then descending the stairs. A few seconds later, he heard the front door unlock and then slam. Only later did he realize that the other apartment wasn't rented at the time, and concluded that this was the ghost of a long dead conductor going to his punctual meeting with a night train.

Then, there was the attic apartment's "situation." Few tenants stayed there long, complaining about an incessant ticking sound. "Tick, tick-tick, tick." Even Marvin could hear it at times when he was summoned by tenants, but no source for the noise could be determined. Then, while researching former activities of the old railway station, Marvin found the cause: the attic had been a classroom for telegraphers in the late 1800s. Apparently a ghost telegraphy teacher or student was still on the job!

Many believe that *all* people have some psychic or intuitive ability, though few can muster it at will. It seems that, under the right conditions, many people can experience an opening of a "window to the past," events or persons that once occupied the space we live or work in today. It is as if we can be "time machines" on occasion, and may actually be reacting more to subtle vibrations created long ago in our space, rather than coming face to face with the spirit of a departed person or animal. The sensation can be the same.

Nikki's House

When I visited her house on Nelson Avenue in 1997, Nikki told me, "The real estate people didn't even want to show the inside of the house when we visited it in 1983. The former owners had attempted to modernize parts of the house and these changes clashed with the nice old Victorian style. It looked awful." Nevertheless, she loved the building for its potential and bought it, later learning that the house had been built in 1867.

Former residents of the house, Mr. and Mrs. Max, told of an elderly woman that they had met on Nelson Avenue, who remembered seeing the three old LaCross sisters seated on the porch of the house, wearing white dresses, when she was young. Mrs. Max also related an experience from the 1960s, when she had turned away from her sink, only to find herself face to face with an elderly woman wearing a white dress. Mrs. Max became unnerved and so frightened that she immediately put the house up for sale. "So it really sounded like a fascinating house that I had bought. I felt at home here, and was never afraid. I wanted to know more about the house's history."

A short time after she had moved her family into the house, Nikki's mother came to visit. The next morning her Mom came downstairs to breakfast and asked if Nikki was okay. "I heard you get up and go downstairs during the night," her mother said. "Is everything all right?" Nikki told her mother that she had slept soundly and hadn't gotten out of bed. "But I heard the downstairs door open and close when you went down, or…when *someone* went down," her mother countered.

A few years later, her stepson came home late. "In the morning he thanked me for coming to his bedroom door and saying goodnight, and I responded that I wish I had, but I'd gone to bed early and slept all night," Nikki said. "But," the boy argued, "I saw *some* woman out there in the hallway, who said goodnight. Aren't you the only woman in this house?" Nikki said that caused her to wonder.

Sometime later a woman friend came to visit and parked behind the house in Nikki's driveway. When Nikki greeted her at the back door, the woman expressed astonishment, "How'd you change your clothes so fast?" she asked. Puzzled, Nikki asked her friend what she meant by that question, "These are the same clothes I put on when I got up this morning." The friend scowled and responded, "Now listen here. I just drove past the front of your house and I saw you in the front window wearing a white dress when I pulled into the driveway!" Nikki mumbled something about white curtains moving, but deep down, she began to understand what was taking place; at least one of the old sisters was still around and watching who came and went on Nelson Avenue.

Strangely, Nickole and her children have never seen the ghosts that reside in her house, but so many of her visitors have! Her children have formulated a theory as to why. Nickole found some old photographs that show the original interior of the house during the occupancy of the LaCross family, the builders. "It's amazing really," she explained, "I have a certain style of furniture which almost duplicates the furnishings that they originally had, and many of the pieces are placed exactly where the first residents had *their* sofas or chairs. My kids think that the old lady or ladies are happy that I'm replicating the interior that they lived in, and don't feel the need to show themselves to *my* family, for fear they'd scare us into leaving, as they did with the Max family. I think they like life with us, as all they have to do is enjoy, while *we* do the work." And that sounded like as good an explanation as I could have imagined.

Spirits

In the 1970s, the PSI organization offered Saratogians monthly lectures on parapsychological subjects, and meetings were held in whatever local establishment would rent space inexpensively. At that time there was a somewhat rundown restaurant and bar on Union Avenue called The Lantern Lodge, with a wonderfully large meeting room in the front. In October 1975, our invited speaker was Rev. Penny Thorne, a Spiritualist minister from Albany who was uncannily accurate in the "messages" she seemed to get from the spirit world. Therefore, she was among our favorite speakers.

On the particular Friday night she was to again address us, the front door of the establishment was broken and closed for repairs, and all members and audience had to enter through the side door on Nelson Avenue. This entrance led directly into the bar, where our members then had to turn right and walk about thirty feet to the front meeting room. As program chairman, I arrived early and was eagerly waiting when I saw Penny enter through the side door. Moments later, as she entered the front room, she was very pale and said to me, "Don't you ever ask me to speak *here* again!"

Penny is a very good-natured woman and her pointed words surprised me. Readers should understand that Spiritualist ministers converse with spirits all the time; it is their stock in trade, and ministerial training provides techniques to help the minister carry on this process safely. So, why her anxiety? I asked her what was troubling her. "I had to come through that bar," she said, indicating the filled room behind her, "and do you know how many drunken spirits are in there? They are on the walls and even on the ceiling, and worst of all, they are standing behind those sitting at the bar, pushing themselves into the bodies of those who are drunk enough, and demanding more alcohol, which allows them to get high! And most of those patrons are ordering up another round without realizing they are being manipulated or possessed, if you will. These spirits are trapped in the earth because they will not or cannot end their craving and addictions without help."

This principle was new to me, but Penny explained that when a person is inebriated (or high on any substance) they lose some of their natural spiritual and physical protection against spirit invasion. Inebriated as these customers were, they were unable to prevent the possession and, with dulled faculties, unable to discern between their own desires and those forced upon them. The alcohol-addicted spirits, bound to the earth plane by their insatiable need for intoxication and its euphoria, were able to control living drinkers, fueling their demand for "just one more," so they could vicariously take part in the drunkenness.

Interestingly, two decades later I conversed with a woman whose alcoholic former husband had frequented *that bar*. Her revelations took Penny's analysis to another level. This husband, in denial of his alcoholic addiction, sometimes came home euphoric and expansive, as his nagging self-doubts, low self-esteem and inhibitions were deadened by drink. On other nights of heavy drinking, his emotional restraint vanished; the man was overcome with depression, resentments and anger.

Sleeping next to the passed-out, drunken man, the woman would sometimes suffer a panic attack, feeling someone, "something oozy and ugly," pressing heavily onto her chest while depriving her of breath. Almost paralyzed, she was unable to scream out for help for many seconds. As she began to pray for help, the ominous stranglehold broke, allowing her to scream in terror. Yet, the man never roused from his stupor.

The woman told how, after breaking the spirit's hold, she sat shaking, soaked in perspiration, pondering what could have sat on her chest with such malicious force. The experience and terror reoccurred several more times, causing the woman to conclude that the force or energy that threatened her, was emanating from the inebriated husband. Fortunately, in time, the man joined Alcoholics Anonymous and began working with a counselor. This did not preclude him, on one occasion, from attempting to drive his car—with his young wife inside—off the highway in a suicide attempt. His effort failed and he was hospitalized in the de-tox unit at Saratoga Hospital.

The location of the above incidents is of no significance today, as the old bar and restaurant has passed on to new owners and décor. But, the principle is important in a book of ghost stories, as it shows how spirits can find themselves unable to move upward and onward after death if they are chained to their earth life addictions and compulsions. Their "heaven" in death is the same as it was on earth, and it may be experienced as their "hell," where they remain until freed from enslavement by an outside force. For this reason, most religions urge their members to "make things right" before passing into death, or else find "more of the same" sorrow they have known while alive. This, I am told, is a powerful reason to pray for those who have died with "a problem," as a way to set these loved ones free when they, no longer having bodies, cannot accomplish the task for themselves.

Daniel

The Roman Catholic Church of St. Peter was erected on South Broadway in the early 1850s, and as the parish grew, a rectory was added in 1926, and then a school on Hamilton Street. Bishop Gibbons appointed Fr. Daniel Burns, later elevated to the position of Monsignor, as pastor. In 1953, the Catholic High School was built on Broadway. Fr. Burns was a true, kind manager, being on top of all matters twenty-four hours a day, and, as a result, parish members missed his firm guidance when he died in 1973.

Though pastors and assistant pastors have come and gone in the over quarter century since the Monsignor's death, most have had some experience that suggests Msgr. Burns has not left for good. In the early 1980s, the priests of the local deanery were invited to dine at the rectory and Mary, the cook, entered the living room to survey the group a final time. She had counted nine men dressed in their clerical garb and had set nine places. A few minutes later she called everyone to dinner and was surprised to see one empty chair. "Where is the ninth priest?" she inquired of the pastor. "There're only eight of us, Mary. We're ready now," he responded. Scratching her head in wonder, Mary removed the extra setting and served the meal.

A few weeks later, the pastor emerged from his study carrying an old photograph. Knowing that Mary's husband made picture frames, the priest asked if she'd have Doug frame this photo. Glancing at the picture, Mary exclaimed, "Hey, that's the priest that didn't come to the dinner table!" The pastor said, "That's impossible, this is a photo of Msgr. Burns," a man who had been dead for almost ten years.

Early in his career, Msgr. Burns had an elevator installed in the three-story rectory, and this elevator shaft seems to have become a focus for ghostly activity. Following Burns' death, several succeeding pastors heard the elevator operating at night, and one of these men, unable to restrain his curiosity, went to investigate whether his assistant pastor was roaming the building late at night. He never discovered the miscreant, though the sound of the elevator regularly squeaking to a halt on the third floor *was* a reality. The electricity that powered the elevator was cut, but for years since that time, the sound of a humming elevator that squeaks to a halt on the third floor, is still heard.

In the late 1980s, another pastor, as he sat reading at night, often heard the squeaky elevator noises but was unfazed by them. He simply yelled out, "It's okay, Monsignor, I'm taking care of everything!" That always did the trick; the noises immediately stopped and the pastor would resume his reading in silence.

This particular priest was sensitive to "the other world," and was troubled by the energies surrounding a particular chair, which he one day carried to the elementary school and placed in an office. Staff members say he mumbled something about "the activity going on with this chair," as he exited quickly. Whether he knew it or not, the chair was known to the staff as having belonged to Msgr. Burns.

In 1999, as I emerged from the church one Sunday morning, I mustered the courage to ask Fr. Tony, the Assistant Pastor, about Msgr. Burns' ghost. "It's no problem," Fr. Tony told me with a smile, "the Monsignor lives in the elevator shaft, and we live in the rest of the house. He doesn't bother us and we don't bother him." We both smiled.

Then, a year later, Fr. Tony took my arm after mass and informed me, "He's at it again!" I wasn't sure which "he" Fr. Tony was speaking of, as time had passed since our last discussion. "The monsignor!" he replied, "Now he's raising and lowering the garage door. I stand in the kitchen and look out the window, and the automatic garage door is going up and down, up and down. Right in front of me is the remote control, and I can see nobody is touching it." Up and down, I mused, such is the passage of our lives. The good Monsignor still retains his supervisory duties on South Broadway—at least until *he* goes up for the last time.

Lake Avenue Elementary School

One day after I retired from public school teaching in Saratoga, I received a phone call from John Stiassney, the head custodian at the Lake Avenue Elementary School. "I hear you're interested in ghosts," he said, "can you come over and listen to my story? I think we have one or two ghosts over here at Lake Avenue." Making an appointment with John, I was reminded of vague tales that Rita Finnegan, retired building principal, had told me about "strange goings-on" some years before. When I visited the old building a few days later, John showed me a notebook in which he had made records over the previous ten years. His anecdotal notations recorded the experiences that many of the night janitors had found scary or unexplainable. Many of the City School District's new janitors begin their careers at Lake Avenue, commencing on the less-desirable night shift, of course. And usually, when a man has gained enough seniority there, he will put in for a transfer to a day shift at one of the newer school buildings in the District. John informed me that most of the custodians had nicknamed the mischievous entity, "Henry," though nobody by that name had ever been known to work or die at the site.

John and his assistant, Paul, had pursued much historical research before I visited. They were truly concerned about finding a scientific explanation for strange sights and sounds that occur only on the night shift. There is no record of any daytime teacher or student experiencing a ghost there first hand, though some teachers have found puzzling results when they opened their classrooms in the morning. Kristen, a new art teacher who had gone to school there as a child, prepared her room the day before school started. The desk drawer seemed empty, as the outgoing teacher had cleared it completely. But, wait, what was wedged between the top of the drawer and the inside of the desk? She pulled out a single photo of a long-ago class picture, and which class? Kristen's! Coincidence, of course.

In their research John and Paul discovered that the building construction had been completed in 1925, two years after a previous structure, an old farmhouse, had been torn down. Capt. James Andrews, its builder, once farmed fields in the open country east of Broadway during the 1840s and for several decades afterward. Andrews, a staunch Abolitionist in the pre-Civil War years, used to secrete runaway slaves behind a false panel in his attic at night, before they resumed their northward trek to Canada on the

Underground Railroad. A photo of that space is still in the Bolster Collection at the Historical Society Museum in the Casino. Was it possible that the fears of the escaped slaves linger there on Lake Avenue? Andrews had named his youngest boy John Brown Andrews, after the famed Abolitionist who conducted the raid on the U.S. Arsenal in Harper's Ferry, VA, though later hanged for it. The two custodians also discovered that this son, John B., had died of an accidental gunshot wound in the house during the late 1860s, and was buried, along with the bodies of three sisters and an aunt, who had died earlier, in the back yard, probably along the margin of Regent Street. In later years, after Greenridge Cemetery was opened, all the Andrews family remains (at least as much as the diggers could *find!*) were transported to a new plot at Greenridge. Is it possible that they didn't get *all* of everyone?

Custodians Paul and John, as well as many past and present janitors, experienced and shared the experience of strange phenomena near the top of the stairway on the third floor: untraceable sounds, shadows and feelings of not being alone. They believe they discovered the identity of one of the ghosts—none other than young John Brown Andrews himself. "In 1995, we set up a video camera at the top of the stairs, loaded it with a six-hour blank tape, checked to make sure nobody else was in the building, then left for the night after turning the camera on. In the morning, when we came to work, we found the camera turned off at the switch. We rewound the tape and played it back. The picture showed just the normal empty hallway, but after about an hour, the picture began to vibrate strongly and suddenly went black. Someone or something had turned it off at that point.

"We did more research on the old Andrews homestead that used to stand here, then visited the family plot at Greenridge. We did a gravestone rubbing of John B. Andrews' inscription on the tomb and brought it back to school, placed it under the leg of the camera, and turned the video camera on again before we left for home. The next day we found that the camera had shut itself off after only five minutes. Guess we found our culprit," John smiled triumphantly.

The two men located the building's original 1923 blueprints and discovered that only the superstructure of the Andrews house had been knocked down. The cellar hole and foundation still remain beneath the concrete floor of the present auditorium. Paul took me in that room one evening after opening the left hand rear door. "Walk down that left aisle," he told me, "and see if you notice anything." I did a slow walk and, about twenty feet down the aisle I noted a slight shift in air temperature and smell. There was a distinct, if slight, musty smell. "Keep walking," Paul said, and in about another twenty feet I suddenly emerged from the smell. I turned around and retraced my steps and experienced the same phenomena again inside those invisible boundaries. Then the two men showed me where, over seventy years before, the architect had noted the exact location of the old cellar hole under the auditorium on the blueprints. The boundaries of the musty smell and cool sensation were identical to those I'd just experienced!

As the years went along, John's son, also named John, came to work on the night shift. Nowadays, custodial work is done by a single man on each floor, leaving each janitor without a buddy with whom he can share any experienced sights or sounds. A night shift custodian at Lake Avenue School needs to develop nerves of steel in order to deal with the eerie sights or sounds that he must occasionally confront on his solitary shift. Readers can understand why it's easier for the employee to stay mum and just hurry through his required work.

In any case, one evening young John's fiancée brought him a bag lunch when he was working alone on the second floor. She called to him from the hallway outside, informing him she was there. He responded that he was almost finished cleaning that room, and would join her in a minute or two. Hardly had John spoken those words than he heard his fiancée scream. He dropped his broom and ran out to find the young woman almost hysterical, sputtering about a man being there and then disappearing. Frightened, she headed downstairs, to exit the building through the Custodian's Room. John accompanied her, trying to make sense of what she said. In the Custodian's Room she stopped abruptly and pointed to an old photo on the bulletin board. "That's the guy!" she exclaimed. "That's the man upstairs that vanished!" John asked his dad about the man and discovered a tale of heartbreak that may well explain some of the haunting.

The old man had been the Head Custodian at Lake Avenue School in the 1950s or 1960s. After years of proudly doing his job, he was suddenly demoted. Worse yet, he was transferred to the distant Greenfield Elementary School. After only a few years there, he died of a heart ailment. "Likely it was a broken heart," John, Sr. told me. So now it appears that "Pie," as his friends called him, has returned to the halls of his beloved Lake Avenue School, perhaps observing the cleaning devices of modern day workers, and perhaps sharing inaudible reminiscences.

Paul told me of sweeping the old cellar locker room below the level of the rear parking lot during his first year at the school. As a young "new hire" on the night shift, he had been pushing his broom along when suddenly he became aware of a movement on his right. Looking, he saw a pair of boots (no legs!) walking beside him. "What was worse," he said, "was that they were striding about five inches *above* the floor! I dropped the broom, shot up the stairs right out into the parking lot, got into my car and went home. I completely forgot to lock that door!" Paul, with a developed Sixth Sense, is sensitive to ghost presences. The hair on his forearms stands out, and he gets goose pimply when in the company of invisible presences. Not all individuals with sensitivity think their gift is to be envied.

During the 1998 winter, I dropped by Lake Avenue to chat with Paul and John. Not much was happening because students, administrators and teachers were taking a vacation. As the three of us chatted, there came a loud scraping sound from upstairs. "That's up on second floor," John said. "We know nobody is in the building except us, but I'll go up and look anyway." A few minutes later he returned joking about "Henry's" antics. Paul and he had heard a woman's voice talking in the downstairs hall once, but nobody was there when they searched for her. On another occasion they heard a door slam upstairs, but found no one, again.

On another visit to the school in 2004, I chatted with Don, who replaced John, Sr. as Head Custodian. "You'd think that the construction that started here in 2003 would have changed things somewhat," he said, referring to ongoing renovations, "but it's been rather quiet lately. Sometimes I do smell cigarette smoke on the second floor, and of course, smoking is forbidden. But we know it's not one of us. On another occasion I headed up to clean the room of a teacher named Mary. Just outside her classroom door I felt a pressure on my chest, almost as if someone was forcibly pushing me away from that doorway. So, I decided *not* to push back, and just returned downstairs. When I came back later, nobody else was there and I got my work done and turned the lights off."

The students love the notoriety of a haunted school, though none have apparently glimpsed the spirits. In 2003, an eleven year old student told me, "The teachers are always talking about 'school spirit,' and I think they're talking about Henry!"

The Ash Grove Inn

"Is it ever going to reopen?" people ask. Nobody knows. The old restaurant sits at roadside on outer Church Street, with an empty parking lot. The sign has been removed and the place looks dismal. It is beginning to look haunted, people say, just reflecting the stories that have been told for twenty- five years.

Ed Ashton came to Saratoga Springs in the 1920s, hoping to partake of the glory of Saratoga's summer season, when the rich and famous of the world came to the thoroughbred races. For years he had dreamed of a great manor house surrounded by barns and fields filled with animals, much like the southern plantations of old. Then the American economy began to struggle, and Ashton found he could buy up the old farm fields along outer Church Street at bargain prices. Perhaps even *he* was not fully aware what a gold mine they would become. He purchased the old, almost abandoned, Waring Cemetery, from which most graves had already been removed, leaving many weathered old gravestones here and there. Just north of the present railroad overpass on Route 9N, he began creating a great estate, manor house and all.

The money to perform this transformation came easily, as the Delaware & Hudson Railroad, moving its tracks out of the city, sought a new route north, across Ashton's lands. Rather than sell the property outright, Ashton leased them the space, asking five cents for every railroad car that crossed his property. Thousands and thousands of railroad cars filled with minerals, forest products, paper, stone and passengers passed from north to south, making Ed Ashton a millionaire.

In 1931, his wife asked if she could build a small tea room along the road north of his house. Tea and sandwiches for summer visitors, however, wasn't much of a money maker, so Ed assumed control of the building after its first lackluster year, added a bar on the front, and converted it all into a major restaurant. He named it The Product House, a roadside establishment where all major food products (butter, eggs, cheese, meats, etc.) would be the harvest of his Ash Grove Farms, which spread out for a mile behind the restaurant.

The Ashtons began to move up in Saratoga society, buying another fine house on ritzy North Broadway. He became a director of the neighboring Saratoga Golf and Polo Club, and he became a director of the D & H, affecting an engineer's hat in his later years. He'd done it all by the time he suffered a heart attack (some say during a heated argument with a farmhand) and died in the field behind the restaurant.

Eventually, Mrs. Ashton sold the restaurant and some of the property to a Mr. Schurster, who operated the restaurant as The Ash Grove Inn. Schurster sold it all to Mr. Desidoro in 1954, and the building became a magnet for those seeking fine dining. Somewhere during those years, the ghost stories began. Desidoro told me he'd never seen any ghosts (as if seeing was the only way to perceive them), but then he paused. "You know, I wonder. Look at the paving stones in the bar floor. Do you see the squarish white ones? Know what they are? Ed took the abandoned headstones from the Waring Cemetery and installed them amid the flagstones." Desidoro wondered if "something extra" had come from the cemetery along with the stones. Of course the epitaphs were turned face down. And it is in the bar area that so many of the stories later took place.

In 1997, I met Sally, who was a former waitress and bartender at the Ash Grove. "I saw many strange things happen repeatedly there," she said. "One of those involved the main door on the east side of the building, which had one of those double springs, so you could push it open from the inside and the outside. But sometimes it opened by itself!" It was physically impossible for such a door to remain open, but it did, she said. Most of the regulars heard and saw it open and stay open in its impossible position. Especially in the winter when cold air came in, someone would always shout, 'It's cold in here, Ed. Close the door!' And sure enough, one hundred percent of the time, the door would close. "All the old timers were used to it—that it was the ghost of Ed Ashton who opened and closed the door. But one night a newcomer, a pretty drunk young man, came in. He had a beer or two, and then the door opened itself behind him. The regulars, without turning, watched the door move in the back bar mirror reflection, and just shouted, 'Ed—the door!' The young guy was dumbfounded, and when the door closed, turned white and staggered to his feet, slurring defiantly that he didn't believe in ghosts."

Sally continued, "Suddenly I saw movement on the back bar. All the shot glasses lined up there began to rise, levitating above the countertop. Then slowly they paraded to the edge and fell, shattering, one after another, on the stone floor. I panicked and said to the young guy, 'Mister, you'd better tell the ghost you *believe* or we're going to be out of business in a few more minutes!' By now, the guy was round-eyed and wild looking, trying to understand it all. He threw some money for his drinks on the bar and yelled,

'Okay, ghost, I believe!' and he staggered out. We never saw him again. All the glasses dropped back down to their former place on the back bar.

"I *told* you there were lots of strange goings on," she grinned. "One night, I looked in the sink and saw blood in the water. I thought perhaps I'd cut myself and looked all over, but no, it wasn't *my* blood, and I never discovered where it originated. Another evening, I went out back of the building to get some supplies from the storeroom. As I went out the back door I was lifted five or six inches up into the air by someone very strong. Whatever it was that held me, it was *cold*!"

I wondered aloud if perhaps Sally hadn't been *very tired* that night, and maybe imagined it all. She retorted, "I felt the soles of my shoes *slap* on the stone floor when I told Ed to drop me, so I know I'd been held in the air." I couldn't think of any rejoinder. She also told of tending bar one night and seeing a shadow dart up the stairs to the second floor. She's pretty sure it was a ghost because she watched those stairs for the rest of her shift and didn't see anyone descend.

Mike, now in the law enforcement field, tended bar at the Ash Grove for a few years also and testified that it was always cold around the bar, even during the summer's heat. "And there was a strange blue light that reflected off the walls, but we could never find where the light originated."

In the 1980s, Marlene Mangino McKinney bought the old restaurant and business improved. She began an advertising campaign, hiring local photographer George Bolster to take a nice publicity photo of the property. George set up his camera on Route 9N on a Sunday morning when there were no staff or customers inside. Bolster was puzzled, however, when the finished photograph showed the silhouette of a man inside a dining room window. And on the man's head—what seemed to be an engineer's hat!

"When I bought the restaurant I had all the locks on the upstairs doors replaced," Marlene said. "After the man installed them, he was unable to pull the keys out. He pulled really hard with no results. Then *I* walked over, touched the keys, and they came right out! I guess Ed favored a woman's touch, eh?" she grinned.

After Marlene sold the restaurant in 1984, Sally continued to work there, and noted that no matter who owned the Ash Grove, the phenomena persisted pretty much as usual. Tommy, a regular, sat at the bar one night and watched the door drama unfold three times. Determinedly, he stood, paid his bill and left, saying, "Well, that's enough for even me!"

Eventually, Sally found another job. The new owners were unable to make a success of the business, though they tried. During those struggling later years a man named Ian did the cooking at the restaurant. He told Dan, who became the next (and present) owner, that he used to keep his plates on the shelf above the range, to keep them warm. On several occasions, he saw plates rising from the warming shelf, move forward, and fall, crashing to the floor, yet they never broke!

The Ash Grove closed in the early 1990s, and Dan has faced daunting legal and procedural difficulties with the city, trying to get his restaurant reopened. In 2003, Ithaca college film student Christian Clark, from Saratoga Springs, produced a successful short film drawing on the many ghostly phenomena associated with Ed Ashton, his love of railroads and, of course, haunting. It was a prize winning story, offering a fictional explanation for Ed's desire to stay "in business."

Siro's

One of the most successful restaurants in the city is Siro's, on Lincoln Avenue, just outside a west gate of the Thoroughbred Racetrack. Open only during the summer season, Siro's has become "the place to go" after the races for the rich and beautiful people of the world who visit the city during Racing Season. Dinner reservations are often made months ahead of time.

Originally an 1850s house, it was converted to a restaurant in 1938 by Ralph and Philomena Nunziato, who called it *The Maranese*. Two years after, they moved the business to Union Avenue, leaving the old house abandoned until 1945. Then Jimmy Siro from New York City opened it as "Siro's Steakhouse," and the public made it the place to go during the 1950s. Harry and Eleanor Kirker bought the restaurant from Jimmy in 1975, and at the closing, Eleanor remembers Jimmy casually saying, "By the way, this building comes with a ghost." They all laughed and the Kirkers didn't think much about the story...at first.

Ten years later, the Kirkers sold the restaurant to Davis Mead and his partners and, according to Courtney Reid in the 1985 issue of *EYE on Saratoga*, the Kirkers gave the same friendly advice to the new owners. Mead said he chuckled as he was interviewed by Reid just a few months after taking possession of the establishment. "There are undefinable noises at night—too many unexplainable noises and happenings, not like the slamming of a car door outside or a sound that we know, and it's definitely not a cat! There *is* always something screwy here, but, if it's a ghost, it is a very nice ghost—one who enjoys the good life."

When locking the building at night, Mead often took six or seven steps away from the door, before hearing the door click open again behind him. Apparently, this locking-up effort had to be performed several times before it "took," and he could go home. This phenomenon has happened less frequently in the last few years.

Mead went on to tell how he would make sure the television in the bar was turned off each night, though he many times found it turned on when he opened up in the morning, and it was always tuned to the Arts & Entertainment cable channel. Sometimes the chef, working alone in the kitchen during the morning, would hear the television come on out in the bar, change channels and finally come to a stop on A&E. They began to realize their spirit had good taste, which is only fitting in a city which hosts the New York City Ballet, The Philadelphia Orchestra, the National Museum of Dance, the National Museum of Racing, and a Cultural Arts Center, as well as other cultural treasures.

For several years I worked at Saratoga Travel and Tours with Amy, also the bookkeeper at Siro's. She gave me strange looks and expressions of doubt when I first related this story. "I *work* there, you know, and I've never heard or seen a ghost," she said with an air of finality. Then, about a year after our conversation, she spoke to me with a new look in her eye. "I *now* know you're right," she said. "I do Siro's books on Saturday mornings, and because I'm going to be working there alone, I bring my police dog for protection and company. I always lock myself in and go upstairs to the office. Last Saturday, my dog and I both heard the front door on Lincoln Avenue being unlocked, then heavy footsteps plodded through the bar and then the dining room, and *then* out the back door, which closed loudly. Dog looked at me and I looked at dog, but neither of us went down until we had to. By that time, there was nobody there." Many times a ghost is better seen than heard.

Scott

In the late 1960s and early 1970s, the City of Saratoga Springs began a growth spurt. Off Route 9N, north of the city, new houses were constructed for the increased number of U.S. Navy families coming for training at the West Milton Submarine Base. One of the earliest of these houses, built in 1969, was a place of sadness for a brief time. The Schaively family, consisting of mother, father and son Scott, was transferred by the Navy to Saratoga. Soon after the move, it became apparent that young Scott was gravely ill and would need an organ transplant. The father's military insurance would not completely cover the surgery costs, and as the call went out for a transplantable organ, local groups began to seek donations to help the Schaivelys.

Donation containers were placed at most check-out lines in area stores, each one adorned with a photo of young Scott, hairless because of the medical treatment he was receiving. Then the good news came: *The Saratogian* notified its readers that a suitable organ was available, and the transplant could be done almost immediately, the following day. But that day also, young Scott died. There was much grief in the community, as this had been a huge cooperative community effort. Some time after the child's funeral, Mr. Schaively was transferred to the Sub Base at Groton, CT, and the parents sold their home on Kirby Road and departed.

Warren and Sue, the new owners, were happy to have their first home on such a quiet street. Soon after moving in, however, they began to experience strange occurrences. Warren often heard their large bag of recyclable aluminum cans crashing to the floor and being kicked around in the garage, though the overhead door was securely down. Upon investigation, they found cans strewn all over the floor. Soon after, as they relaxed in their living room, they heard the soft patter of a child's bare feet on the hardwood floor of the downstairs hallway. In the master bedroom upstairs, they began to hear creaking or movements, and sometimes, what sounded like a child playing, though upon investigation they found nothing. And the couple lived there alone, not having children.

In 1992, they decided upon interior renovations including repainting of wall surfaces. As Warren worked in the bathroom, taking down the fixtures, he found the name "Scott" scrawled on the wall in a childish hand behind the medicine cabinet. What does a conscientious couple do? They were well aware of the Schaively's sorrowful departure; everyone in Saratoga knew of the boy's struggle and eventual death. Was there something wrong about removing the handwriting that might be the last remaining physical remnant of the boy's short life? After much consideration they decided to paint over the signature.

In succeeding months, as they related their experience to friends, Sue learned that little Scott had died on Mother's Day in his mother's bed upstairs in the master bedroom, where they'd heard so many noises. But the room no longer had its playful sounds, and no longer was there the patter of a child's feet in the downstairs hallway. Likely, with his signature eradicated, Scott's last mental and spiritual hold on his loved ones' house had been broken. His spirit had departed, hopefully now liberated into perfect health from a shortened existence filled with painful medical procedures. Old earthly struggles ceased for one family and a new family's life went on in the house on Kirby Road.

Unfinished Business

"This place was in rough condition when we bought it in 1999. The previous owners had lived here for two generations and there were a number of small rooms in what had been constructed as a two-apartment building. We decided to open up the interior space, take out some non-bearing walls and doors and revamp the interior," said Suzanne Moore. She referred to what is now an attractive cottage at 120 Catherine Street. The 1876 house sits at the corner of East Avenue. As so many ghost investigations have confirmed, if a ghost inhabits a building, it usually makes itself known as soon as renovation starts.

Shortly after moving into the house, Suzanne entertained a friend one afternoon in 1999. As the woman climbed their stairs, she told Suzanne that there was a ghost there, but Suzanne and her husband, Joe, and their children had never experienced anything "strange." Almost two years later they finally got a surprise.

Two teen daughters, Lyndsey and Lauren, slept in an upstairs bedroom and were usually joined by their Dalmatian, Livie. On that particular night, Livie had moved from her accustomed position on Lyndsey's bed onto Lauren's. Lights were out and the two girls slumbered. Suddenly, the two were awakened by Livie's shrill baying. "We'd never heard her make that sound before," said Lyndsey, "and it frightened us. We looked over and saw Livie staring intently at the corner of the bedroom. And we could see that *nothing* was there!" Lauren interjected, "Besides, the dog is *deaf*! What could have awakened her? Certainly not a sound. We called Mom because Livie wouldn't pay any attention to my sister and me."

Suzanne added, "We sure didn't get much sleep that night. Our sons, Joey and Jonathan, felt more secure sleeping in my bed for the rest of that night, as they weren't ready for encountering Livie's cornered ghost." Suzanne was tantalized by this mysterious event.

Many times, families do not immediately associate a strange episode with the paranormal, and only as the experiences become more frequent or intensify, do they realize they're "not in Kansas anymore." Livie's baying was a "wake-up call" for the Moores. Suzanne remembered that, two years before, her friend had sensed a ghost in the house. Suzanne's daughters also recalled that, only months before this raucous incident, Livie had whined *at that particular spot* in the bedroom, but the family had not thought it extraordinary at the time.

Hearing of this newest incident, another of Suzanne's friends, Katie, asked, "Well, if you have a ghost, who do you think it is?" The two women agreed to look into the history of the house, and began a laborious research. "We spent many long and grueling hours searching records at The Saratoga Room of the city library and at the County Clerk's Office in Ballston Spa," Suzanne told me.

Research showed that the house had, indeed, been built in 1876 by Thomas Lee and his wife, Margaret. Shortly thereafter, there had been a few deed changes within the family, then, for quite a few years, the house and land were owned by the Westcotts. Elizabeth Westcott sold the property to the Joyce family who lived next door on East Avenue (then called 3rd Street). The addition on the house where the girls' bedroom is located had not yet been added by 1888, suggesting that the resident ghost must originate during the occupancies of the Westcotts or Joyces.

Eventually, Mrs. Bridget Joyce passed the property on to her son, Joseph, in 1907, and he, in turn, sold it to his sister, Catherine, who supported herself by taking in boarders for many years. Catherine never married, and when she died childless in 1942, the property passed by her will to nephews in Williamstown, MA. As I listened to all the research the women had done, I was filled with admiration.

Suzanne and Katie also found a filed copy of Catherine's will and discovered that she had left money to the two Catholic churches in the city, as well as to a local bank, and requested burial in the Joyce plot in St. Peter's Cemetery on West Avenue. "We thought it would be nice to pay our respects to Catherine and went to the cemetery. We found the large Joyce memorial stone but, at first, couldn't find a headstone for Catherine. The big marker is a foot thick, and only as we passed its side did we find her name inscribed on that part, almost unnoticeable. She was inscribed as the daughter of Bridget Whalen and Patrick Joyce, and we discovered that nobody had ever engraved her date of death beneath her name! Surely, after leaving all the money to a bank and two churches, *somebody* must have had that responsibility to honor that just-ended life by completing her gravestone. So, we went over to St. Peter's Church and talked with the priest, an assistant there, but he told us that tombstone engraving is the responsibility of the family." She concluded, "I'm now trying to contact those nephews in order to get them to do their duty."

I told Suzanne that I'd read in ghost folklore that a spirit which cannot find the date of its body's death on a gravestone, or cannot find a grave marker of some sort, can remain in denial that its death has taken place. This may be most common among those who avoid recognizing their mortality. Note that, in *A Christmas Carol*, Scrooge *had to be shown* his inscribed name and date of death on a gravestone, before he comprehended that his actions and inactions really mattered. The spirits of Christmases Past, Present and Future had to teach him to become conscious that the process of life and death has a transcendent function in the cosmos. Thus, a ghost in denial of its death can continue to roam the earth until awakened by an outside force.

The spirit in the Moore's house, most likely Catherine's, isn't harmful. "Outside, we began tearing out a big willow tree stump so that our lilac bush could grow," Suzanne told me. "Joe did much hard yard work, grading and pruning, and constructing a brick sidewalk." Brush and overgrowth were cleared and, where they had not been perceived before, wild yellow roses bloomed, planted by some long-ago hand, and now possibly restored by a grateful Catherine.

A Tale of Two Houses

What follows is an odd story, one that combines ghostly manifestations and the intuitive abilities of the two women who experienced them.

Two young professional women rented a house on the east side of the city in the early 1980s. Both were counselors for troubled teens at Kaydeross House on the city's south side. I have given them the names, Karyl and Cathy, to permit them anonymity, as I do in many stories where maintaining privacy is important. Their rented home, not far from St. Clement's Church, was a small bungalow, built and occupied by one man until just before they moved in.

Karyl had a bedroom in the basement and Cathy slept on the first floor. Sometimes Karyl complained that Cathy's incessant walking overhead kept her awake, though in the morning Cathy looked puzzled and usually denied having been out of bed during the night. Karyl retorted that she could also *hear* the kitchen cabinets being opened and closed all night. In the end, Cathy's sincere refutation led the pair to realize they might have a ghostly presence. As they analyzed their unwelcome guest's habits, they reasoned that the slow, heavy footsteps sounded much like an older person—likely a man. His mission seemed to center on maintenance or repairs, judging from the noises. They needed a name for this workman and came up with the name "Ben."

Karyl enjoyed sleeping in on weekends, when she didn't have to go to work; it allowed her to catch up on the week's nights of interrupted sleep. In May 1985, she remembers waking up in the morning, rolling over, and noting her clock radio read 8:45 a.m. Too early, she thought, and rolled over again to resume sleep. At that point, she vaguely heard what she presumed was Cathy, awake and walking in her room upstairs. The steps began to descend the stairs to her bedroom door, so she rolled over to say, "Good morning" to Cathy.

The door opened, and a blast of icy air announced the appearance of an old man in the doorway! Almost paralyzed, Karyl panicked, crying out "You need to get *away* from here!" Instantly, she felt herself engulfed by an invisible awareness that seemed to transport her, and the next minute she found herself beside a creek. "I had read about out-of-body experiences, but this time, *I was experiencing one*! I was *really,* physically, alongside

234

that stream," she said. "Before I could get my bearings, I found myself back in bed!

"The scenery kept shifting from bedroom to streamside, and back again, each time as if I were *really* in that spot. All at once, I wasn't on the shore of the stream, but in the prow of a rowboat of some kind! All I noticed was the back of the man who rowed the boat as if he was intently searching for something or someone up ahead. With this last shift, I found myself back in my bed, chilled to the bone, as if I'd just come out of a freezer. My body was still almost paralyzed, and it took all my will power to get it awake."

The thought crossed her mind that she hoped that the episode was ended, but again she found herself seated in the boat, this time gazing at a handsome young man who now stood in the prow, as if to guide the boat's journey. "For some reason I concluded he was a 'warrior angel' who was there to protect me on the strange journey I was making. This made me feel safer, and I asked the man 'Why are we on this creek? Where are you taking me?' He ignored me, so I sat back to let things unfold. Suddenly, the boat's movement stopped in mid-stream, and I found myself thrust back into bed.

"Boats, 'warrior angels,' streams—what did it all *mean?* And why was *I* being shown all this?"

She shifted her gaze about the bedroom, to regain her bearings. The old man, Ben, and the angel now stood in (or was it outside?) her bedroom. It was difficult to discern, as the images became superimposed, visions flickering upon one another. It was all too much, and she screamed, "Get out! Get out!" Then, she sensed the spirit, Ben, grudgingly comply and withdraw.

As in a dream, she visualized herself running upstairs and calling her mother on the phone to relate all the bizarre occurrences. "Even today, I can't make heads or tails out of what happened next: I could hear myself screaming, 'You'll never get away with this in Texas!' I figured I was going nuts." As she felt herself fully returned to her physical body, she shot out of bed to actually run upstairs, grabbed the phone and dialed her mother. Her mom patiently wrote down every detail of Karyl's experience, something she was grateful for later, as she now has the written record. As she stood talking on the phone, she glanced at the kitchen clock, which read 9:40 a.m. All the journeying had taken only an hour—it seemed like days!

"This was the strangest morning I've ever had," Karyl laughed, though her eyes conveyed the great respect she had for the incident. Her mother suggested the two young women visit a psychic woman in Albany to unravel the significance of the vision.

When they met the psychic, they produced a Polaroid photo of their bungalow, wanting to get the woman's impressions about the building *before* they related their tale. Slowly, the psychic studied the picture, and then offered an impression of an old man. "He either committed suicide or was hanged in some manner. I keep getting the throat, as if he died choking." The psychic paused, before adding, "His spirit wants you to help him move on." She encouraged Karyl and Cathy to ask questions of their neighbors, to determine who the man might be. The psychic felt sure that the neighbors could shed light on the mystery.

It turned out that a neighbor was a relative of the former owner, and informed the young women that the old man was named George, but that his middle name was *Benjamin*! He had built the house in the 1920s and lived there for years with his son and the son's wife, after his own wife had died. When the daughter-in-law died, the son was no longer able to care for his father, and had placed him in an eldercare facility on the city's south side, a place called *Kaydeross House.*

The young women were shocked. This was the very building in which *they* worked each day! No longer a residence for the elderly, it now served the needs of adolescents. The relative sadly revealed that, one day, old George Benjamin just wandered away from the facility and drowned. Searchers found his floating body in the Kaydeross Creek. Karyl had to sit down to steady herself. She had just been on the banks of that creek in her vision experience.

What next? Astounded at the psychic's insights, coupled with this new information, and the many seeming "coincidences" of Karyl's visions, the pair decided to do as much as they could to sever Ben's tortured hold on the physical plane.

Not long afterward, Karyl had the distinct impression that Ben was hovering close-by in the downstairs of the house and, speaking to him carefully and lovingly, affirmed that his earthly work was finished. She promised that she and Cathy would take good care of the house he had built, so he was now free to move onward. She instructed him to seek The Light and his perception of God. Ben seemed reluctant to make that move right then, as they continued to hear him rummaging through the house at night. Perhaps he was torn between the house *he* had made, and a new house in the world beyond. He then disappeared for that day.

A few days later the women heard him moving about in the kitchen, opening and closing doors and drawers as usual. Entering the room, they assured him that everything was truly okay now, and that he could simply walk into The Light. That seemed to resonate with the man's spirit this time, as the house became strangely quiet from then on. When the two women had the opportunity to sleep uninterrupted at night, it was difficult at first to do so. They were surprised that they missed their old friend. But sending Ben onward had been an act of love that they didn't regret.

Today, almost a quarter century later, the two have married and have homes, husbands and children. New residents live in the bungalow on Saratoga's quiet East Side. Except for Karyl and Cathy, nobody would know about the strange events that spanned one man's life and death, and peaceful passage into The Light.

TOWN OF SARATOGA

H'RE SLEEPS AT LAST IN QUIET REST
HE FILLS A SOLDIERS GRAVE.
HIS LIFE A SACRIFICE HE GAVE
HIS COUNTRY'S FLAG TO SAVE.

Miner F., Co. C, 14th Reg. VT Vol.
Died at Fairfax Station, TN 2/7/1863
AE 24 yrs

Town of Saratoga

A large town in eastern Saratoga County, the Town of Saratoga was formed in 1788, and from it sprang parts of Greenfield, Northumberland, Malta and the City of Saratoga Springs. Any American town would be proud to have this town's past. Here is part of The Saratoga National Historical Park, site of the two battles of 1777, the field on which Burgoyne's army grounded arms in surrender, a beautifully restored battle monument and Gen. Schuyler's plantation house. The Gerald R. Solomon National Veterans' Cemetery was added in recent years, permitting the town to become a final resting place for thousands who have made our nation free.

The Schuyler House

Philip Schuyler was quick to recognize the economic potential of the fertile flat lands along the Hudson River above Albany, and by 1745 he had erected many barns and outbuildings to surround a magnificent mansion located just south of today's Village of Schuylerville. Employing both slaves and free laborers, he grew vast fields of wheat and other grains, and exported these southward to the river port at Albany, where he had a more genteel mansion.

Then, in 1777, when it was apparent that Gen. Burgoyne's invasion route was certain to overrun his estates, Schuyler was commissioned a general in the revolutionary army and moved to defend his new state, though he knew the British attack would destroy his plantation.

Burgoyne did order the mansion and mills burned when he reached Schuylerville, but within months Burgoyne's campaign was defeated. Ironically, after his surrender, he was feted by American commanders as a captured officer in Schuyler's Albany mansion. By early 1778, Schuyler had begun a slow rebuilding of his estate. With a new, if smaller, farmhouse almost rebuilt, he left military affairs and returned to the business of agriculture, which functioned on the property until 1839.

241

Today, the National Park Service administers the old house as an historic site, offering history lovers a chance to see how the upper classes lived and worked. It also offers unsuspecting visitors or guides a chance to meet some of the estate's former workers.

There is the legend of "David, a former slave or servant in the Schuyler House, whose ghostly essence usually appears at nighttime, when visitors and staff have departed and the building is locked. Romantic legend has given the spirit the name "David," a name that is almost certainly not accurate, as no one by that name is listed among Schuyler's slaves or dependents. Legend has him in love with a servant lass, who was sent from the Schuylerville mansion down to Albany, to work in Schuyler's mansion on Catherine Street. Allegedly David was broken-hearted and, after the death of his body, has continued to remain in the Schuylerville house awaiting the return of his true love.

This particular ghost, thought to be male, is blamed for the glow that several witnesses claim to have seen inside the windows, making it appear that someone is puffing on a pipe or cigar after the house has been secured for the night. One former Park Service ranger claimed to have smelled cigar smoke in the building when he opened the house for daily tours. Of course, smoking in such an old, historic house is strictly forbidden.

Might there be a second, or even third, ghost there? On occasion lights are seen in second floor rooms after the building is closed. Occasionally, candlesticks are found overturned when the staff opens up in the morning.

In order to provide visitors a feeling that Gen. Schuyler has just stepped away from his desk, a colonial newspaper is left open on the desktop, next to Schuyler's spectacles. The Park Service didn't have an authentic New York Colony newspaper to use in the display, and uses a Pennsylvania paper instead. So the masthead doesn't show, the paper is open as if the reader is only partly finished reading. But, many times, in the morning, the paper is found turned to its front page again, as if the ghost is highly incensed that the paper is not authentically New York.

On one occasion a tour guide heard three loud bangs on the rear wall of the house. Surely someone had thrown something or perhaps a bird collided with the house, she thought. However, investigation showed nothing amiss—nobody and no thing was there. The house has ancient "crown glass" windows, creating a swirl pattern, and one visitor claimed to see faces from a costumed era when she looked into such a window. The ghostly being seems to be sensed most often on the second floor near a closet, and in the small space under the roof where servants once slept. A former ranger, described by his partner as "hard as nails," heard footsteps in the old servant quarters upstairs in the attic, and knowing nobody was there, went to investigate, as was his job. His partner remembers that the ranger, with ashen face, returned quickly downstairs, walked straight out the front door, went to the headquarters building, and resigned. Nobody ever learned what he had seen.

Many area volunteers staff the old mansion during the spring to fall season, and one of these women told me of feeling pushed from behind when she walked near the "ghost closet" upstairs. A local man, with heightened psychic perceptions, visited the house, took the tour, and noted that the hair on his arms rose at several locations in the house. This is his body's individual reaction to a ghostly presence. When this man descended into the front living room and stood before a portrait of Mrs. Schuyler, he received a strong psychic impression that the woman did not like the artist's rendering of her, though she could do nothing about it now but resent how the rendition didn't flatter her.

Another house tour guide, after routinely finishing her shift and checking out at the Battlefield office five miles south on Route 4, then used to retrace her route back up the highway toward the Schuyler House on her way home. Just after exiting the Battlefield gate, on two different occasions she looked to a bluff on her left, where historical interpreters have placed three cannons. On each of these occasions, she spied a figure in a red uniform standing motionless near the old British fortifications.

The events of 1777 surely left a dynamic imprint on these lands, from the village of Schuylerville to the Town of Stillwater. Much blood was shed by British and American armies, and it may take several more centuries before a spiritual calm settles once more over the banks of the Hudson River.

The Other House

Not far away from the Schuyler House, on lands that formerly were owned by the Schuylers, sits a more modern home. Adorned with hanging flower pots in the summer, it looks so much like other riverside homes that few would suspect it of harboring its share of ghostly characters also. The owner, well versed in local history, told me that there was a massacre of some early settlers on that spot in the early 1740s, and felt she had identified some of her spirits. Also, not too far away, Frank Lovelass, a famous Tory spy, was hanged during the Revolutionary War. Political feelings ran high in those days, and though they buried his body, his executioners kept poor Frank's head as a trophy. For years the blanched skull was paraded through the village, it is said, with a red, white and blue ribbon woven through the eye sockets. Eventually, the New York State Department of Health demanded the skull's burial, and it was interred. Can Frank still be upset over his body's post-death treatment?

In any case, the house near Schuyler's was built in 1992, and the woman owner hoped for many years of peace there. But such peace has not been forthcoming. In August of that year, she awoke during the night to see a bearded man silhouetted in her bedroom doorway. Saying nothing, the man seemed to stare at her intently. "I panicked and my heart raced very fast," she said, "so I closed my eyes. When I opened them again he was gone. I lay there shaking and wondering what kind of a housebreaker *that* was. In the morning I checked my locks and, thankfully, everything was still secure. But how could that be? I wondered."

Then, perhaps a week later, as she slept, she became aware of voices. "There she is," she heard. Opening her eyes, she saw the same bearded man from the week before, only this time he was accompanied by a woman dressed in a high-necked dress and bonnet. "Then, just like that, they vanished!" she said. Sometime after that, her sleep was interrupted by the feeling that she was not alone. She roused to see a small girl in Colonial style dress. "As I concentrated on her clothing details, she just fizzled out," the woman told me.

She added, "Sometimes when I am watching television I feel a coldness overtaking my body from behind the chair. One of my Irish-American friends told me this is how ghosts often show up, and she taught me to say, 'In the name of Jesus Christ, what do you want?' And ghosts have to respond, but they can't, so it always gets rid of them. My friend is descended from the famous Fitzgerald family (the old Fitzgerald Brewery) and learned this technique from her Irish family. Old Mrs. Fitzgerald awoke once to see her dead husband (who had loved peppermint patties) leaning over the baby's cradle. She asked the ghost 'In the name of Jesus Christ what do you want?' and she saw her dead husband disappear. But then, in the morning she found a foil-wrapped peppermint patty on the windowsill beside the baby's cradle! Love goes on."

244

On occasion, guests at her home walk the short distance to the Schuyler House, but one of them will no longer stroll over there, because she is afraid of the emotional or psychic sensations she receives on the grounds of the historic site. The homeowner's daughter, also, has had difficulties in her mother's house. "Occasionally, she comes over to vacuum my rugs, only to experience the vacuum electric cord jumping out of the wall socket! On another occasion, the owner found her television set turned on when she came home from work. The only other person to have entered her house during the day was a building inspector, and she knew he was too busy to watch television during the day.

"The ghosts help me out sometimes. One day I came home, unlocked my door, and found my kitchen table partially set, with forks and spoons, but no knives, carefully arranged on napkins. Maybe I should have waited an hour longer and the ghost would have had supper ready too," she said with a grin.

Another time, she discovered that she had lost an amethyst ring that her grandmother had given her; it was a keepsake and she was very upset. Literally turning her small house upside down in a search, she didn't find the ring. She couldn't understand it—she always placed the ring in a special holder on her dresser when she went to bed at night. Totally frustrated after the fruitless search, she yelled out, "Spirits, if *you* took my ring, please return it!" Then she went to bed. In the morning, when she swung her bare feet off the bed and onto the rug, they came right down on the ring, which she was certain hadn't been there the previous night.

"Another time, in the summer, I looked out my window to see my hanging flower planters blowing in the wind, and I could hear my wind chimes tinkling. I opened the door to see it all, but found that, though everything was swinging in the wind, there was *no wind* at all!" she told me.

Her job allows her to work among historians and she sometimes has shared her experiences with them, and they, being experts in many fields, help her understand the significance of her plot of land. "My ghosts don't mean any harm," she concludes. "They are something that still intrudes into the present from the past. And that takes most of the fear out of it for me," she laughed.

The Holmes House

This is a short tale, but it takes place in one of the oldest houses in the Town of Saratoga. South of the Schuyler House is Coveville Road, connecting Route 4 and Route 32 through some beautiful farm country. Cherrie Weinstein, reporter for *The Saratogian* in October 1991, wrote up an interview she had done with a former resident of the beautiful old Greek Revival house on the western section of Coveville Road.

The woman being interviewed told of often awakening at night to hear a "whirring sound" in her dark bedroom. It immediately scared her because, she learned from experience, the sound was a prelude to having all the blankets snatched from her bed. And every time these events took place, her hair stood straight up on her head because of her fright.

The woman had moved into the old 1840s house in 1961, but by 1986, could endure the phenomena no longer. She moved out. She never divulged whether or not other residents experienced anything similar. My understanding is that today, the house is peaceful. This anecdote, however short, points to the very individual reaction that different people can have in the same building.

The Séance House

Not far off County Route 70, in the southwest corner of the town, sits an old square house on a knoll. A long time resident of the area told me that in the late 1800s the building had been used as a gathering place for Spiritualists, who conducted séances there. As in many séance connections, some of the spirits that are invited into our realm are recalcitrant when they are asked to leave. Such a case may account for the incidents here.

A man who lived in the house during the 1960s recounted the ongoing phenomena that his family experienced there. Often they heard the sound of breaking glass emanating from the living room, but upon inspection they never found anything amiss. "We never quite got used to that," he told me. "My children sometimes saw smoky-type people or figures on the stairs, though these soon faded out." He had heard that ghosts in a formerly "quiet

246

house" can emerge when renovations or construction are underway, and he thought some home improvements he'd made might have precipitated the events. The man also noted that a small local cemetery is not far from the house, and wondered if everyone buried there was peaceful.

"But we enjoyed living there," he exclaimed, "and we found it exciting rather than scary. We never knew what would happen next."

The elderly lady who shared this part of the tale, her experiences from the 1920s, identifies herself as "a Christian woman that doesn't believe in ghosts." Nevertheless, she still has difficulty in explaining events that occurred in the house when she was much younger. "I remember hearing a tapping on the headboard of my bed," she said, "so I pulled the covers over my head and hid!" was her response.

Metaphorically, this is the tactic taken by many sincere people who encounter what appears to be a ghost. Rather than accept that a personality has survived death, and yet, has not found the end of its journey in *either* Heaven or Hell, these individuals have no accommodation in their thinking for souls "in transition."

Society and traditional religions have not provided clearly-defined rules of etiquette for compassionately dealing with ghostly encounters. Hiding under a blanket obscures what many others perceive as an *obligation* to help such lost or struggling souls, though their distress causes us alarm. This woman was unaware that Christians (and members of every other religion) have encountered ghosts at various times in history, events mentioned in the sacred texts of each. Apparently, the secret is in what one *does* about these appearances that is the true measure of their faith.

When I queried the present owner of the house, a Saratoga Springs merchant, he said, "I've not had one single strange experience there since I've been in the house." So, I guess we'll have to give him the last word on this formerly haunted house.

Spook Hollow Road

In 1995, WGY Radio morning show host, Don Weeks, brought Spook Hollow Road to the public's attention. Don, famous for his Halloween gags and remote broadcasts, has had some truly memorable personal experiences with ghosts in houses where he has lived, but not here. Hoping for some spectral monkey business, Don was disappointed after interviewing several local residents. It was a quiet place on the day of his broadcast. Nevertheless, in a ghost book on Saratoga County, no author can omit mention of this unique and potentially scary place name.

There is a generic ghost story about the spirit of a dead pack peddler that can be found in almost all states of the U.S., and probably in many other countries too, just like the "phantom hitchhiker" and "the ghostly phone call." Allegedly, a pack peddler was murdered in a house along this stretch of road in the early 1800s, and it is rumored that the ghost still haunts the thoroughfare. Tom Wood, now the Town Supervisor, gave me one version of the story, and Paul Griffen, an old timer who lives nearby, provided the other.

When one ventures along the short road, it's easy to see that there is no genuine hollow in the road surface. There is an old cellar hole off to the side, and perhaps that stimulated the locals' imaginations, if the murdered peddler is fiction. Tom Wood says that in the early 1900s local people used to walk the road, and many of those were youngsters walking to the nearby one-room school. Those who traversed this road, especially around dusk, claimed to see "spooks" emerging from the cellar, sometimes with lit pipes in their mouths. Others claimed to hear strange sounds wafting from the old foundation. Tom, a former Town Historian, thought the sounds were made by startled wild animals, suddenly put on guard by the noise of passing children. And, as far as a visible "spook" goes, he hypothesized that it may have been a tramp or dispossessed immigrant farmer (and there *were* some around, back then) might have sought temporary refuge there, emerging at the sound of children's voices.

Paul, who lives near the end of Spook Hollow Road, says his father remembered when there actually was a rundown house atop the stone foundation, but it had vanished by the time Paul was born. "There was a canopy of elm trees overhanging that road, and this alone seems to have created a spooky atmosphere as night drew near," he said. Originally, he told me, (and Tom concurs) that the small rise in the road was called "Spook House Hill," but when Saratoga County renamed many old roads, now requiring official names, the politicians who interviewed the locals misunderstood the local name, and just called it "Spook Hill Road," a name that has stuck.

Henry's House

There is an old house on the bend in Hanehan Road, which was built in the early 1850s, which is likely the second building on that site. The original owner and builder had been a Revolutionary War veteran, but his home vanished before this story begins. In the 1920s, Henry Mulligan and his wife bought the old 1800s farmhouse and lived there. It was a part of his job to occasionally be away on business and, at such times, he warned his wife, for safety's sake, not to go into the horse barn until he returned.

One fateful day, when Henry was gone on business, his wife did go into the barn and, passing a box stall, was kicked and grievously injured by a horse. With internal bleeding, she suffered for days, having only a neighbor woman to nurse her. She died of injuries just a few days before Henry returned. He was inconsolable and lost interest in keeping up the farm. When a new family bought the place, they discovered they had purchased more than they counted on.

Soon after moving into the house, the new owners heard sobbing in the cellar. Investigation revealed nothing. Also, when milking a cow in the barn one morning, the new owner suddenly felt a touch on his shoulder. When he turned, nobody was there—yet, he knew it was a human touch. The owner's relative, Shirley, lived in the old Mulligan house around that time. She told me that she once experienced someone blowing down her neck when she was upstairs. "The first time it happened I tried to make myself believe I imagined it. But the second time, I ran down the stairs! My husband looked over at me and asked, 'What's the matter honey? You see a ghost?'"

Mary, a relative who also lived in the house during that period, told me that each time she went upstairs she got chilled at that stair top landing. That might be explained away, but one day, while standing there, she heard a woman calling for help in a weak voice. "Henry, Henry," the voice pleaded. "I knew we didn't have a Henry in our family, so I figured it must be something left over from the dead woman. I had a little dog then, and he so hated to cross the top of the stairs that, when he had to, he'd skitter across to hide under the baby's crib whenever I left the house," Mary added.

"The longer I lived there, the more the strange things occurred. Once, at the top of the stairs, I ran into a man with very black eyes and who wore boots. He just crouched there staring, and didn't move. Then, slowly, he just faded out." Mary continued, "That spot was very strange. We had very cold spots there where they shouldn't have been...especially in summer. One night, as I passed that spot, I felt the touch of a hand, gently brushing across my face, and I just didn't know what to make of it. All in all, I was ready to believe we had at least *one* ghost."

The barn presented even more problems for her. "I always had an ominous feeling whenever I had to go over there and push hay down from the loft for our animals' morning feeding. Everything inside me was saying, 'Don't go up there!' but of course I had to go; I had work to do," she added.

When Mary's niece, Debbie, was twelve and sleeping in a downstairs bedroom, the girl often heard the steps to upstairs creaking in the night, as if some invisible person was ascending. For a while she thought maybe she imagined it; then her mother said *she* heard the sounds also.

Years later, as teenagers, Debbie and her cousin, Gail, slept upstairs and, once felt someone pull their hair during the night. Debbie told me, "We ran and jumped in bed with the grown-ups!"

Debbie remembered that they had an old antique pump organ in a back room, which was always closed off in cold weather to conserve heat. "I was always edgy about that room, and once I heard random notes of music being picked out on that keyboard. It couldn't have been a cat or other animal in there, because it was closed up tight. And, in any case, what form of energy was supplying the air for the organ? Like her Aunt Mary, Debbie disliked climbing the stairs because of the strong presence that she felt there.

Debbie had as much difficulty with the barn as Aunt Mary did. As often as she was able, she'd go across the road and knock hay down for the animals during morning feeding. But, one day it was late in the evening before she got the opportunity to perform her chore, and she had to cross after dark. To enter the loft, one had to slide open a large door to get into the stairway to the loft. When she did so that evening, she encountered a white mist that continually changed its shape. It seemed quite thick and she wondered if she'd be able to get through it, but that quickly became a moot point, as it darted away.

"We had pigs, two ponies and a horse in that barn," she remembered, "and originally the barn had box stalls, but one of those had some energy in it that frightened every horse that we tried to put in there; they just wouldn't stay and sometimes were terrified of something we couldn't see. My father had to knock that stall down eventually. After he died, I was sleeping in a bedroom on the opposite side of the house from my mother. During the night I had a vision or dream in which I saw my Dad walking across the front of our property carrying two pails. Suddenly I heard my mother yell out in her room, and I jumped up to go to her. When I got there she told me she'd just had a dream about Dad walking along carrying two pails!" That synchronistic dream has stayed with them both for years.

"Dad was part Native American and he shared so many of his own telepathic experiences with me. I miss him," she sighed. Had her Dad become another, albeit protective, presence in the house?

Nobody lives there any more, though Debbie now owns the place and recalls many of the good times she experienced in that house. "As a kid, I learned to dowse for water, and I wanted to understand the paranormal events I experienced when I lived there, so, as a young adult, I joined PSI in Saratoga Springs. They used to have fascinating meetings each month, and I learned some things about ghosts.

"You know, I've been thinking that someone ought to fix up that old place," she concluded. "Though I had some strange experiences there, I have lots of good family memories too." Seven years have passed since I interviewed Debbie and, when I recently drove by the old Mulligan House, it was further dilapidated and boarded up. It doesn't look as if it can be restored, and maybe it's for the best.

The House on Pearl Street

An old brick house that predates the 1866 map of Schuylerville was filled with mysterious happenings during the 1970s. A young couple suddenly found one of the two apartments in the house available, as the husband's friend had suddenly moved out. The husband told me that he and his wife felt fortunate at the time to secure a spacious apartment near the center of the village. "In the end, we didn't stay much longer than my friend had," he reflected, "just three months!"

The early happiness of finding the cozy apartment downstairs in a nice old house on a pleasant street slowly evaporated. The couple noticed that each experienced a mood shift whenever they returned home. "It felt like a kind of inner darkness overtook us," the man said, and his wife interjected, "Both of us would wake up at night, convinced that someone had just grabbed or jabbed us. We became afraid and I feared for our child."

They had only briefly met the upstairs older woman tenant, a widow, who pretty much kept to herself. Apparently, she had lived alone in her apartment for many years. The husband told me, "Once the widow went away for a couple of weeks and left her key with us, so we could water her plants from time to time. But, for some reason, she cut short her trip and returned home before we could venture up there and see the interior. We later found out she returned home to find flower pots overturned, with some plants and soil strewn about the floor. She never complained to us, however, and it was only through a mutual acquaintance that we even *heard* about the mishap. Why didn't she ask us about the vandalism, did she know something that we didn't? Eventually, we recognized that the upstairs was also afflicted, perhaps by her husband's ghost."

The downstairs couple always knew when the upstairs tenant left the house, as they'd hear her descending the front stairs and exiting onto the front porch. Many times they were stymied to hear her toilet flush and her rocking chair moving noisily upstairs, though she was definitely out of the house. Recent research has determined that she was likely the widow of a man named Oliver. There is a story on Pearl Street that, when Oliver neared death in the 1960s, he demanded to be carried to another house, one that he had built further down the street, because there was too much tension in his family upstairs at the duplex. So, he died in "his" house, and may still be contributing to quiet disturbances at *that* address today, also.

All the unexplained goings-on, and the mood of desolation, caused a rift between the young couple to widen, and many upsetting arguments took place. The wife finally had enough and, after only two months residence, took their child and went to live elsewhere. The husband, however, intrigued by the phenomena and feeling an emotional attraction to the apartment, stayed on. "His moods continued to darken," his wife told me, "and he didn't seem to want to change his outlook. I know it sounds strange, but I had come to think the house didn't like him, and was overtaking or destroying him in some way," she explained.

Her husband countered, "For some reason I felt I *needed* to stay, even after she moved out. But, eventually, even *I* started to notice the bad shape I was in." After a month alone, and missing his family, the man agreed to move out and gave his notice to the landlord.

"When he returned to living with us again," his wife said, "he was his old happy self once more. After we had left the house we heard a story that a boy had once died of spinal meningitis in our old apartment. I reflected that when I was there I felt the presence liked *me*, but was trying to get rid of my husband—sounds silly, doesn't it?"

The couple learned that one of their old friends was now renting the apartment on Pearl Street. Though they warned him of the "hostile" atmosphere, the man laughed at them. Then, perhaps a month later, the pair ran into him in downtown Schuylerville, and found him to be an emotionally and philosophically changed man because of *his own* experiences in the old house, which he too had left after only a short tenure.

Some individuals are more sensitive than others to "the other world," just as people can vary in their perceptions of color or sound. One individual can have a ghostly contact in a building and, a few minutes later, another person can pass through the area with no extraordinary experiences. The husband in the story above, we determined after some conversation, was indeed sensitive. He had lived in a house on Burgoyne Street when he was single, and had awakened one night to see an amorphous figure at the foot of his bed. As the form advanced toward his face, the man could make out the image of a beard with sunken eyes. Feeling the ghostly breath upon his face, the man quickly jumped to his feet and turned on the lights, at which point the figure vanished. "I remember the night my Dad died, too," he told me. "When I returned from the hospital, I was deep in thought at home, and suddenly someone I couldn't see shoved me off my seat and onto the floor. I believe it could have been my father, letting me know he still existed beyond his body." Perhaps this was another example of a loved one joyfully finding that existence continues.

Such experiences are fairly common when a loved one has passed over and finds a continued existence, with the capacity to think and reason outside the physical body. Love for the living causes the spirit to seek to communicate the good news to relatives or whoever is sensitive enough to listen.

The Stewart House

A woman came to the old Stewart property on Hanehan Road in the early 1980s, set up a mobile home, and began the renovation of the ancient farmhouse that some neighbors, remembering a past owner's family name, called "The Bugli House." She heard from these neighbors a legend that the small hill behind the house had once been an Indian burial site and, after a short time, she began to wonder if the legend was true, as she occasionally heard soft foot stomping and bells jingling at night in the hill area. Shining a flashlight into the trees didn't identify anything out of the ordinary there, though her dog was constantly on guard and growling when the phenomenon occurred.

She and her husband had a tense marriage, but she was not aware at that time that the marriage was about to end. He traveled on business often, and when he was traveling she began to notice another strange occurrence. Two or three days before her mate returned from his trips she smelled a powerful odor. Eventually she connected the two events. "It was a very predictable thing," she told me, "so I always knew when to expect him." As she made a connection between the stomping, jingling and odor, she wondered if some energy from the Indians remained upon the land, perhaps guarding the graves and now her, warning when her fractious husband was about to return home.

As work on the old house progressed slowly, she made the acquaintance of neighbors who told her other legends about the hilltop property. According to one legend, long ago the farmer owner of her house had gone back to the mound area and cut a large tree. The next day his cow died. He chalked it up to coincidence and, the next day, went to the mound to cut another tree. The next day his horse died. He shared his worry with a neighbor who accused him of being a superstitious fool. Taking up an axe, the neighbor strode to the mound, where he cut a tree. When it fell, however, the scoffing neighbor tripped over his own feet and was unable to escape the falling tree; it fell on him and killed him.

Following her divorce, work on the woman's old house progressed more quickly, and when she had completed the renovations, she moved into what some other neighbors called "the old Stewart House." Before long she began to hear a woman crying softly in the front of her living room. She always checked, though she lived alone. No one was ever there. The suggestion of a female ghost was partially confirmed a few months later, when a visiting female friend told of seeing an old woman enter the house's back door as she drove up.

In time the owner made a new male friend and, when he came to visit her one evening, she was surprised that, as he pulled into the driveway, he had seen "part of a man in overalls, walking near the barn." "Funny thing," the friend said, "he was only visible from the waist up."

Before long she heard another tale from a neighbor woman who came visiting. The lady told of seeing an elderly woman in a rocking chair in the living room. "Strange thing, though," the neighbor said, "only the upper part of the rocking chair was visible." The owner reflected that she had raised the floor about eight inches during the renovation. To see the bottom of the rocker, one might need to see through the new floor surface. The woman correctly hypothesized what is known to many ghost researchers—ghosts continue to walk on floors that existed in *their* time, not ours!

Now a quarter-century resident of Hanehan Road and the old farm, the woman has settled in nicely, secure that only friendly former residents are around, Indians and whites alike.

The Assistant

Businesses have come and gone over the years in the Village of Schuylerville. One of these old buildings was renovated during the 1980s so that a new printing business could move in. The present owner, whom I'll call Pat, believes that one of the old factory employees has stayed over to lend a hand with her manufacturing business. She is not sure, however, just who the individual is, as the structure once housed a combination funeral home and morgue, and another section of the building was used in the paper making business.

"In the early years much of my work was done at night," the owner told me, "processing photographic film in the darkroom so that my customer orders were ready for delivery in the morning. The film boxes weighed about twenty-five pounds each and took quite a bit of effort to lift from the table where we kept them. Soon after we started our operations, we would smell a distinct odor from time to time. When the smell started, we learned, one or more of those boxes was going to start flying! This continued until we stopped using photography for our work. Another prank of this ghost, a man I think, is that he turns on the water in the sinks upstairs when nobody else is up there. There are times when I come to work in the early morning and find the sink faucets running full blast as I come in."

As far as Pat is concerned, she's never alone there. There are footsteps that are heard occasionally on the stairs. "Maybe he's checking up on us or maybe he's still in his time zone, doing what he did when he worked here or ran a business," she suggested. Pat notes that the old darkroom was torn out in the mid 1990s to make room for business expansion, and maybe that excited the ghost. "But whenever his antics get too much and begin to threaten our production schedule, *and* if I'm all alone in here, I talk to him...quietly. And, whenever I clue him in to what's going on, the mischief stops."

To make up for his antics, the ghost apparently opens factory doors, sometimes when a worker is lugging an object toward the door, but at other times, when nobody is near—a door will just open, stay open for a minute, then close. Pat wonders what the ghost's work schedule is and what he thinks *he's* producing.

The Brisbin House

When David and Joan Riebel bought the large old frame house in the early 1990s, they were prepared for an adventure. At the time of sale, the girls in the Porter family had told them of "an old man in a blue coat" that kept a ghostly watch over the old farm. Nevertheless, ghosts weren't a big topic in Saratoga County in those days, as almost nobody talked openly about them, and the Riebels considered the tales fantasy or folklore.

Sylvester's History of Saratoga County, published in the late 1800s, shows the large old farmhouse and outbuildings as belonging to the Brisbin family, prosperous and influential farmers at that time. The drawing does not do justice to the beauty that the builder must have seen when choosing this site on the sweeping hillside that offers a wonderful panorama of the Green Mountains to the east. The large two-story Shaker style farmhouse is flanked today by two barns, a restored corn crib, open fields and a quaint hollyhock garden outside the kitchen door.

As the Reibels began renovation of the old farmhouse over a century after its construction, they discovered there had been a house on the property as far back as 1764, and discovered an old brick oven in the rear section of their home that must date from the early house. They figured that the larger, front section of the house dated from the early 1800s, as it showed many characteristics of Shaker architecture.

The task of renovation and restoration was daunting, said Joan. "There were many layers of wallpaper in the downstairs hallway, and one day while I was stripping these off, I got the idea that I wasn't alone. I looked up to my left on the stairs, and saw a man in a blue coat with tails, typical of men's fashions in the 1840-1860 period. He just stood smiling on the landing for a while, then faded away. I felt he was blessing my hard work and kept on with the difficult task."

This experience led Joan to ask questions of old timers in the Town of Saratoga, about the previous families, the Brisbins, and other major events in the neighborhood over the years. She also tentatively sounded out the neighbors about their understanding of ghostly phenomena. One of these, a woman, claimed to have some mediumistic ability and offered to contact the ghost man for them. Joan was dubious about such an event, but nevertheless invited the woman for a little "communication session." The pair sat in the dining room and the woman prepared a little prop for the affair—an inflated balloon. Loosing the string on the balloon, the woman spoke to the spirit, "If you like these people (meaning the Riebels) move this balloon." Joan was amazed that the balloon then zoomed through the room, into the other rooms and throughout the house. There was no breeze blowing and certainly no wind that could propel it.

The old man in blue seems to be a quiet ghost, Joan says, and he seems to enjoy the hard work and expense her family has incurred in restoring the Brisbin house. To observe the continuing restoration work, descendants of the Brisbin family have periodically popped in for visits. On occasion, these relatives have dropped by to share treasured historic photos of the old domicile in past decades. Joan and David have created a scrapbook of their work in the house, and included these pictures of the interior scenery and past inhabitants. Now, the living can appreciate the progress as much as the old man in blue.

One day recently, Mrs. Porter brought a photo to Joan that had been taken of her in the kitchen doorway some years ago. In the top center of the picture is a small, filmy image, which Mrs. Porter had enlarged. It shows what appears to be the bust of a middle-aged woman with, what might be wings or outstretched arms. Curiously, Joan had recently hung a small sign at that very spot; on it was the inscription: "Ghost Crossing."

In between the Brisbin and Riebel occupancies, during the 1980s and 1990s, other folks lived there. One of them, Wendy Porter, lived there with her parents, sisters and brother. She was naturally sensitive to other dimensions and, at first, had difficulty getting other family members to accept the fact that *she* could see others walking about in the house. At one time she had heard a baby's cry, which drew her to a small upstairs bedroom, where she saw a ghostly man rocking in a chair while holding a baby. She had a hard time watching the scene fade in, then out, and trying later to explain the experience to family members who insisted it was all her imagination. On another occasion, Wendy met a man who, when visiting the house, had seen a ghostly woman on the premises. But Wendy was puzzled: she had seen the man in blue and a man rocking the baby, but no female.

Of course, she also saw the man in the blue suit as he walked through the house, and she was often the object of jokes that he played on family members. Game pieces left on a chess board were suddenly and inexplicably upended. A stereo that had been turned off at bedtime would suddenly erupt in loud music during the middle of the night. Comparing notes with one of her sisters, Wendy discovered that both of them had experienced someone sitting down on their beds during the night, and had awakened to see a smiling man in blue. Because of these events, the blue man got the blame for bedroom lights that suddenly illuminated or extinguished without apparent cause. Because the school bus came early in the morning, Wendy carefully laid out her next day's outfit before going to bed, but many mornings, she awoke to find them strewn all over the bedroom floor.

Wendy's sister, Stacey, was continually frustrated by a different ghostly man—an individual wearing a tan suit from the early 1900s. The brown-haired man used to mess up her homework papers and posters in the bedroom she shared with Wendy. She had a poster depicting monkeys, which was usually turned upside down each day by the time she returned from school, even though nobody had been home to move it. Many times, the sisters felt victimized by one another because the ghosts couldn't be caught in the act.

Stacey remembers hearing voices after they went to bed at night, seeming to emanate from the attic. There was also what she characterized as "old time music," apparently from a music box, that also seemed to issue from the attic, though they never went up after dark to investigate.

When old timers came to visit and share their memories, the Porters learned that several children had died in the big house before the 1980s, suggesting the identity of the next spirit. "One morning I awoke to find a small red-haired girl standing beside my bed," Stacy remembered. "Wearing a lacy white dress with pearl buttons, the child sported high-buttoned shoes and a matching white hat." Before she could bring the little girl fully into focus, the child faded away. "That settled the matter of whether or not we had ghosts for *me*," Stacey recounted, "I jumped out of bed, resolving 'I'm not imagining *this*!'" *Now*, she knew Wendy was right.

On another occasion their family took down their artificial Christmas tree, disassembled it, and placed it in its storage box, which was then hefted to the upstairs. All of a sudden the box became animated, zooming across the upstairs hallway and down the stairs. The girls remember being mystified, but also how quick they had been to scatter out of its way. "Another problem I had was with my new radio, which turned itself off and on whenever *it* wanted to," said Stacey. "I told my Dad about it, but he said it was probably just a short circuit. Nevertheless, I also had a tape player that wouldn't work right either, and between the stereo, radio and tape, it was just too much of a coincidence." The tape player offered her another bonus of sorts. Instead of writing down each day's events in a diary, she quietly recorded her day's experiences on cassette tapes. One day, while playing back one of these reminiscences, she heard a loud stomping in the background, a sound she is certain wasn't present when she recorded the session.

Both well-adjusted parents today, Wendy and Staccy still puzzle over the meaning of these childhood events. If there was some information the ghosts wanted to communicate, what was it? Many times the girls became brief opponents because of the ghostly antics, though today they laugh good-naturedly about the mix-ups.

Readers should be aware that one need not *see* ghosts, as they can also be heard, felt, or even smelled. "From time to time after we moved in," said Joan Riebel, "I would enter the present day dining room in the morning, and smell cinnamon, coffee and, sometimes, bacon cooking. It was always a delight to share in the aromas of the past." Her husband, David, agrees that the ghostly smells also extended to an upstairs bedroom, where he inhaled smoke one night. He arose from bed and checked the upstairs, there was no fire and nobody was smoking, (the Riebels do not smoke). But the scent, it became clear, was definitely tobacco. Walking back into the bedroom, he clearly smelled an old-fashioned strong tobacco burning, such as was smoked in the days of unfiltered cigarettes around World War II. "On another occasion, early in 2004, when I was alone in the house," he offered, "I smelled a wonderful perfume. When Joan returned, I asked her about it, but the fragrance didn't match any of her scents. Perhaps it was just an old time resident popping in to say that they were there for a visit, or that they remembered their years here fondly."

Ghosts can also be apprehended by touch. On another recent night, David had settled into a deep sleep, but was roused by the feel of the blankets being pulled away from his back by a very cold force. He awoke and turned to the other side of the bed, but nobody was there, though the cold remained for another minute or so. When he slept in another upstairs bedroom sometime later, he also felt an invisible hand moving the bed sheets, though no culprit was discovered.

And, of course, ghosts can be heard. Joan was startled at nighttime a few years ago. "I heard a woman's voice calling, 'Ernie!' and I searched the house," she told me, "but nobody else was around. When I checked the Brisbin family records I couldn't find anyone by that name, so we're still puzzled as to Ernie's identity."

Then, perhaps a month later, his identity came to light. The Ketchum family on Burgoyne Road told of an "Uncle Charlie" who lived in the farmhouse before the Porters. "Uncle Charlie Ketchum wasn't well, and hired a French-Canadian housekeeper named Eva to oversee the cooking and cleaning. It was hard for us to understand her," Daisy Ketchum said, "because of her heavy accent. She had a tall, thin son named Ernie, who occasionally came around, and Charlie gave him a small bedroom over the kitchen. He usually didn't stay around long, but he was an occasional resident there between the years 1944 and 1965. Very likely, both he and Eva are dead now." So, there was another little mystery apparently solved.

It is no wonder that this array of ghosts is in no hurry to depart. The old building, surely destined for decay and demolition in the near future, was rescued by the Riebels. Not just saved, but meticulously and faithfully restored to its patrician appearance of 150 years ago. New roofs and a spacious addition have been added to the house and outbuildings, and mammoth restoration work of the interior of the large barn is well underway, so that, one day soon, it can resume its past function as a splendid barn dance gathering hall. David and Joan Riebel have taken on the task, as a labor of love, of restoring the estate to true museum quality representing the Shaker Period of American architecture. They have yet to tackle an old covered well outside the kitchen door, a structure that also may be filled with mysteries.

If one objective was on the mind of James Brisbin, the original owner, and likely the man in blue, it could have been to lead the occupants of his farmhouse to a higher level of understanding about the world of spirit. In that effort, he sure succeeded!

The Ghosts of Burgoyne Road

Burgoyne Road follows, in part, much of the old Indian Trail between the Hudson River (at what is now Schuylerville) and the lower reaches of Fish Creek, which empties into Saratoga Lake. Long before the Europeans came to this area, the Mohawks contested with the Canadian Hurons and Abenaki for the right to hunt and fish these forests and streams. Recent archaeological studies of the area have turned up countless arrowheads, net sinkers, hide scrapers, etc., all remnants of the Late Woodland Period of Indian occupation. In later years, after the whites arrived, a railroad paralleled this aboriginal path. It may be the friction between the races over land ownership or the vastly different beliefs about spiritual matters that has created a residue of energy that often becomes visible to modern people who have abandoned the old ways.

"It was Halloween in 1991, and I was just twelve years old," Lisa Westcott told me, "and we were expecting the Trick or Treaters in a few hours. A movement outside the front window of our house on Burgoyne Road caught my eye, and I thought what a marvelous costume the person was wearing. He had red hair and a red goatee and his face was chalky white. Where his eyes should have been, there were just black holes. He was just passing the first front window and I waited for him to come past the second one, but he never did. He must be waiting outside, I thought, and opened the door to see, but nobody was outside. Suddenly, the back door of our house flew open, even though there was no wind outside. But nobody came in and no one was outside when I went to look."

This strange experience led Lisa to relate the event to her mother, Alma. "Well, I told her that a *lot* of strange things had happened in that front part of the house," Alma explained to me. "When my husband, Gerald, was alive, he once saw a soldier walk right through the front living room wall. Gerald asked him if he was lost, and the ghost disappeared. Lisa,

261

also, had seen a soldier carrying a rifle, walking down the hill behind our house. All of a sudden, he just disappeared. We never heard of any battles this far north of the Battlefield, but, of course, these men could have just been hunters from the past. When Gerald was ill, before he died, he saw many strange things, like ghost children in the house—and two soldiers wearing what appeared to be *togas*! These men that Gerald saw looked in our front window, and then disappeared."

Lisa remembered a time about 1996, when she had just put her little niece, Desiree, to bed. "I sat on the edge of the bed patting her back. I glanced up and was scared to death. Hovering in the air over the bed was a woman with no feet. She had brown hair, a brown blouse and a flowered skirt. I yelled out and the lady disappeared. I sat there wondering just what it *was* that I had seen, and began to see faint tiny white streaks crossing the floor. I never did learn what they were or what caused them."

Except for the exterior sightings, almost all the ghostly experiences took place in the front section of the Westcott house. Alma told me that part wasn't original, that it had been transported to its present location from an old farm south of Schuylerville, along the River Road, about ninety years ago, placing its relocation during the early 1900s. Quite possibly the ghostly entities inside the house are remnants of that farm family. And perhaps the soldiers were somehow attached to the house, as its original location was quite close to Burgoyne's line of march and deployment at the time of the Battles of Saratoga in 1777. It never was clear whether the soldiers were British, Canadian, German or Americans. Readers should understand that physical objects, including houses, can many times retain the energy of some powerful emotions from past owners or occupants. Used or owned in their lifetimes, such physical objects can carry the emotional energy of a spirit that cannot free itself from this present physical plane.

Alma had a number of anecdotes about their house, centering on a rocking chair and bedboard that had been given to her. She believed these objects, containing consciousness from days gone by, under their own power, changed location from time to time, threatening to trip her as she walked by. "In the end, I just gave them away," she said.

"I tried to soft-pedal the excitement I felt about the ghosts, so the children wouldn't be alarmed but, when Desiree was four, she and her friend, Samantha, ran excitedly into the house, saying they'd just seen two women walking in the yard and looking at the flowers. Desiree had never seen my mother, but her description of the women matched perfectly my memories of my mother and grandmother. They loved to look at the flowers."

262

She remembered seeing a white mist in the doorway between the old and newer parts of the house when her children were little. Again, she hadn't commented at the time, but when Lisa was 21, Alma asked if her daughter had ever seen anything strange around the doorway when she was little. Lisa answered, "You mean that little white thing that used to run across the doorway?"

So, energies or the consciousness of long-dead individuals seem to have permeated the old building brought to Burgoyne Road. But, there are other stories to be told.

Warren Ketchum, whose father was an early farmer near the eastern end of the road in the 1940s to 1970s, remembers seeing a foot-deep path running from DeGarmo Road along and over Burgoyne Road, then climbing the hill into the Larmon property. Boy Scout groups and other school children in the early 20th Century were told these were old Indian trails. It would not be surprising, then, that in 2002, a woman named Maureen observed a filmy shape, which she took to be an Indian spirit, traversing the old Ketchum property.

"We used to find musket flints and arrowheads whenever Dad plowed the fields in the spring," Warren said. Across from the old Ketchum farmhouse is a large boulder whose surface is worn down. It was a "samp mortar" used by Indian natives to grind their corn. The stone was located near a spring that surely was a landmark for Indians moving along the old trail. Archaeological excavations conducted during the 1980s along Fish Creek have established that there was a sizeable summertime Indian population in the area, which dug mussels and fished along the creek, drying the catch for later transportation to the Massachusetts and Connecticut area. How much of the Indian energy remains in the region?

Mary grew up near the western end of Burgoyne Road, and supplemented her teenage allowance by babysitting. One nearby family, the Grouts, hired her to sit often for their girls. "I was curious about their house, to begin with," Mary told me. "Throughout the years I could remember, the old farmhouse had one family after another. None of them stayed long, and after I'd met the girls living there, they began to explain: the house had a ghost. Well, maybe, I'll see, I said to myself."

The girls were adamant, telling Mary of a boy who often appeared in their yard, with hair matted down, and drenched to the skin. Mary's father, Armond, well versed in the early history of the Saratoga Lake region, told her of an early settler and his son living near Fish Creek, who were attacked by Indians. The settler father was killed, and the son was drowned in the creek by the marauders. Mary wondered, could this be a ghost boy from over two hundred years ago? And if so, what did he want?

"One thing I remember vividly about that house from the first time I entered—a horrible musty odor. That family seemed to be forever remodeling, taking out walls or building new ones, but they couldn't get rid of the smell." The Grouts had Siamese cats which, one night when she sat with the children, became quite agitated. The musty smell seemed to become more intense and a chill filled the room. The combination of mustiness and coldness was almost intolerable. The cats continued to be upset, and thinking somebody had come to visit, Mary looked out the window. A figure stood unmoving outside. It wasn't a full grown man, but more of a youth. He seemed dripping wet, and as the youth's head was indistinct, Mary could see no hair matted down on his face. "And that was it for me," she exclaimed. "As soon as the parents returned that night I told them I couldn't work for them anymore! I didn't explain, but I think they knew. In any case, just a few months later, they moved out and the house sat vacant for quite a while afterward."

In the late 1980s, Barbara and Pat contemplated building a home on high hilly acreage they had just purchased south of Burgoyne Road. They decided to meditate on the land and built a nighttime campfire for their dedication ceremony. Peering intently into the mesmerizing fire while reflecting on their hopes to build a home on their beautiful land, Barbara told a Burgoyne Road neighbor that she saw a motion on the opposite side of the fire. Focusing into the darkness, she observed that an Indian man had silently come up from the woods, drawn to their campfire and sincere meditation. Standing with folded arms, the figure was accompanied by another man and a woman. All three stood unmoving and mute, surveying the two women and their fire, seeming to analyze their hearts and intentions, before walking soundlessly back into the forest. Barbara and Pat felt that it was a great blessing by Indian spirits who *still* protect the sacred lands along Fish Creek and throughout the region.

Warren Ketchum and Daisy, his wife, know of a young woman named Judy, who was strolling one evening up Burgoyne Road, then onto Cemetery Road. In her peripheral vision, Judy noticed another girl about her age, dressed in white or light violet, walking along with her. Somewhat nervous about the other girl's sudden appearance, Judy picked up her pace; the other girl did likewise. A short time later, as they passed the cemetery, the figure suddenly vanished.

264

A gentleman named Mike drove eastward on Burgoyne Road a few years ago and, before reaching its end, passed by the cemetery. As he slowed for the upcoming intersection stop, he saw a woman floating about three feet off the ground emerge from the cemetery on his left. In mid-air, she sped to the window of his car, looked in, and then vanished.

The expanding Saratoga Springs homebuilding market is rapidly claiming much of the quietness that used to exist west of Gen. Schuyler's plantation. Speeding cars careen carelessly past the old Indian paths and farms alive with memories of years gone by. Farms which are rapidly going out of production are being subdivided for building projects. If an old spirit lingers, it is likely because its essence still seeks the beauty it responded to in life, and which will soon be no more.

The Old Wilbur Place

In the early days of Saratoga County the Wilbur family owned a large tract of land in the Town of Saratoga. The original homestead was a log cabin built in the 1700s, though it was replaced by the present large frame house in 1875. Eventually, the Wilburs and their descendants gave up the place and sold it to another family, the Pascales. The new owners burned down the fallen remains of the old log cabin.

The newer 1875 frame house is large and solid and was a happy place to raise children in the 1950s. Sitting on a grassy knoll, it offers views extending east into Vermont. One summer, the peacefulness was threatened, when Mrs. Pascale's sister came to visit, bringing her three children.

The rambunctious youngsters were shown to their sleeping quarters in a large bedroom at the rear of the upstairs. In the morning, the Pascales were astounded to find these children downstairs, asleep on the living room couch and rug! When awakened, the wide-eyed children gave the same incredible explanation: someone or something, perhaps an angry old woman, had appeared in the door to their room demanding, "Get out! You're not wanted here." The Pascale family had never had any paranormal experience in the old house.

Mrs. Pascale's sister considered herself a logical and fearless woman, and refused to believe the childrens' tale. She decided to prove to her progeny that it was all a product of their vivid imaginations—*she* would sleep in the room!

But like her children, in the morning the mother was found, somewhat shamefaced, on the living room couch, scratching her head over the same impossible, scary event that had occurred in the middle of the night, this time to *her*.

Though similar experiences awaited many who stayed overnight in that rear bedroom on the second floor, Mr. and Mrs. Pascale and their children never encountered the wraith. When I first interviewed one of the Pascale daughters, she told me the house had just been sold, and the new owners were intending to open a bed and breakfast there. The two of us were tantalized by the prospect of a series of guests experiencing the angry woman upstairs—would she reappear?

On my last visit in 2004, I found some beautiful restoration taking place: old doors replaced, walls moved, and the exterior modernized with a pool. If ghosts are there, *this* should bring them out, I thought. As the renovations neared completion, however, the new owners have had no ghostly experiences as yet. I cautioned them that it is usually the *visitors* who seem to do so in that house, so they, too, are eagerly awaiting their opening night. The woman smiled and told me the opening is projected for the fall of 2004 or early 2005. She grinned, "We'll see."

TOWN OF STILLWATER

A flower in the garden
bloomed
With foliage fresh and gay.
Its worth,
its beauty was entombed
before meridian day.

MOST PATIENTLY
HE DID SUBMIT
WAS TO GOD'S WILL RESIGNED
HE BID ADIEU
TO WEEPING FRIENDS
AND ALL HE LEFT BEHIND.

S.Kelly 05

Town of Stillwater

T he lands of this town were a major part of the region called *Sar-agh-to-ga* by the Iroquois natives—a "place of many waters." Countless streams, as well as the Hudson River, drew the first European settlers to what became Stillwater long before the Revolutionary War. Much of the Saratoga Battlefield lies within the town whose placid Hudson River waters Gen. Burgoyne hoped to reach. When independence was established, in 1791 the Town of Stillwater was demarcated, followed by the incorporation of a village government in 1816. In later years, canals and railroads added to the "transportation" theme of the town, supporting a mix of farming and industry.

Travelers

Years ago I heard this tale from Bill Dixon of Malta Ridge. He had forgotten how or where it had come to him. I have heard the theme repeated many times, and in each rendition, the particulars and location change, though the outcome is identical. This story is of the genre of "travelers surprised by a ghost," and like the "murdered pack peddler" tales, a popular theme in American folklore.

Sometime before 1900, the legend goes, two weary travelers—a husband and wife, stepped down from the train at the Saratoga Springs station. Hiring a carriage, they set out for a destination somewhere to the east of Saratoga Lake, perhaps in the area of Bemis Heights. The sky grew ominously grey, then black, and the wind's fury grew. The man applied the whip, urging the horse faster, though the couple soon realized that they couldn't outrun the storm. Visibility grew worse, and the road turned muddy as the rainstorm pelted them. Through the downpour they spotted a light—a farmhouse that might offer them a haven!

The husband stepped out of the carriage and into the storm, approached the door, and knocked. An old man bearing a kerosene lamp opened the door and urged the pair to come in. "I'll put your horse in the barn later, but please come in—you're soaked," he added. The farmer told them he'd seen the storm brewing in the west all day and knew this one

269

would blow and rain all night. He offered them a cold supper and showed them to a room upstairs, where the couple spent a dry and comfortable night.

Awakening at sun-up the next morning, the pair dressed and went downstairs to take their leave of the owner. No one was about, and the place seemed deserted. Even the dinnerware from the previous night had disappeared. Thankful for the succor provided by the stranger, the husband took a shiny silver dollar from his pocket and placed it atop a small table in the hallway in compensation for their host's generosity. Then, making their way to the barn, they hitched the horse and drove away.

A short time later they arrived at their destination in the Stillwater area and were greeted by their hosts. After pleasantries, their host inquired how the pair could have arrived so swiftly that day from Saratoga, and the travelers told of their stay in the old farmhouse near a turn, up on the heights about five miles west. Astonished, the friend, who knew the township very well, responded that there was no such farmhouse in the place the travelers described. The guests, however, were adamant that they knew well how they had been sheltered the previous night and, besides, they were not given to fantasy. To settle the dispute, the host offered to help his visitors backtrack to locate the old house and settle the matter for good.

As the trio approached the familiar area, the husband seemed disoriented. Certainly the trees looked the same and the configuration of the road was familiar, but they could not find the house or barn. Asking his guests once more for a description of the house, their host remembered a likely old farmhouse that once stood in the field to the left, but stated that it had burned to the ground *over twenty years earlier.* How could all these discrepancies be reconciled?

Stopping at an old overgrown foundation pointed out by their host, the trio peered into the cellar hole. The interior was greatly obscured by briars and years of overgrowth on top of charred timbers. Suddenly, the wife gasped and pointed into the depression. There, on an old weathered and charred remnant of a tabletop, was a shiny silver dollar!

Fields of Battle

Debbie, who works in a Stillwater restaurant, regularly drives to work from her home in Schuylerville very early in the morning, as she has done for years. In 1999, on a clear night, she hastened down Route 4, past the Coveville Marina sign. Rounding the curve, and perhaps with eyes still filled with sleep, she *ran into*, or over, a kneeling man in buckskins, who pointed a long musket. Horrified, she slammed on her brakes, exited her car and walked back along the highway. There was no body, no blood. Adrenalin pumped through her body, and she shook, knowing on some level that, though there was no corpse, this was a *real* event. It is easy to understand how and why she repressed the entire episode, however. There was no physical evidence of a collision, so it all had been a matter of her imagination. Or was it?

Then, in early 2003, again driving south, and at the same time and spot in the road, as she rounded the curve she spied a red-uniformed man seated on a large horse. Right in the southbound lane, the man who sported a British grenadier's hat, and with a drawn sword, became her second casualty. "I couldn't stop and just plowed through him. Strange thing though, I know he had blue eyes, but I don't understand how I could have seen *that* at 4:30 a.m.," she told me. Again, leaving her car parked on the shoulder, she sprinted back to find the victims. She experienced an awful sense of *déjà vu* after the eerie event because, this time also, she had felt no impact from hitting the mounted man. As in her previous experience, she found no evidence of injury or death. Fully awake now, she continued driving south, deciding to get some advice. *Something* had to be going on. Twice at the same spot!

This woman didn't understand that there have been ghost stories circulating at the Saratoga National Historical Park for perhaps a hundred years or more. Hundreds of people pass the famous historic site each day, not recognizing that the battles continue in the world of spirit and in the unquiet souls that struggled there. Ghost sightings are quite common at places where great numbers of people have perished violently, as many of the dead cannot or will not accept that they have died. Some fight on in spirit, attempting to do their military duty, not realizing that their bodies have died.

In 1777, Gen. John Burgoyne advanced south from Canada along the Lake Champlain-Lake George-Hudson River route, hoping to conquer Albany. Aided by an army from the west and a fleet from the south, the British hoped to divide the northeast colonies from the rest of British America. Gen. Philip Schuyler was among the first to understand that Burgoyne's army must not advance beyond the high bluffs south of Schuyler's small community that is known as Schuylerville today. Bounded by the Hudson River to the east and a small escarpment to the west, the river road would certainly be Burgoyne's path of march. The colonials began the fortification of the heights and put out a call for volunteers to march to Saratoga (as the region was called) to defeat the British army. Readers know that they did just *that* in two major battles that autumn, causing the events at Saratoga to become the "Turning Point of the Revolution."

Once the British had surrendered and moved south to prison camps, the upper Hudson Valley became relatively quiet again, and with Independence in 1783, the area grew in both agriculture and industry. Farming spread onto fields where blood had been shed, and New York State sought to preserve the core lands on which the struggles took place. Today the battle site is administered by the National Park Service.

Through the years, local residents as well as Park Service personnel have experienced strange phenomena in that area. One weekend in 1984, uniformed re-enactors set up a camp to show park visitors how colonial armies lived and fought. At dusk, one of the women participants saw a strange, greenish light moving slowly across the site of the Balcarres Redoubt, one of the British fortifications. Discussion around that night's campfire centered on a longtime legend: General Fraser's ghost. British General Simon Fraser was killed during the fighting and his corpse was hastily interred in The Great Redoubt, an earthwork fortification. Since that time, however, no one has been able to locate the grave.

Michael, a Park Service ranger in the 1980s, became consumed by the mystery and, hoping to discover the location of Fraser's grave, sought out a reputable psychic to provide new information in his off-duty hours. Deep in trance, the woman uttered these words in a husky, male voice, "You can't find my body, the wolves got it." This event was very unsettling to the ranger, who had hoped to discover and protect one more historic feature. Stories persist of lights that are most often green, moving aimlessly about the battlefield, and Fraser is considered the most likely source.

There are many strange sightings in daylight, also. In the 1980s, a group of junior high school students from Ballston Spa visited the battlefield on a field trip. Jimmy, one of the 8th Graders, noticed something strange as their guide spoke to the group at the Freeman's Farm overlook. The lad looked to his immediate left, where a motion caught his attention, and saw a man in dark colors, perhaps buckskin, lying on the ground amid the scrub brush. He whispered to the man, "Are you okay?" and the man answered softly, "I'm alright." Jimmy turned his attention once again to his teacher and the guide commenting on the first day of battle. A minute later, he turned to see what the prone man was up to. Nobody was there. Jimmy is sure he would have seen or heard any movement on the man's part to leave.

At the same spot, where British, Hessians and Americans collided almost 120 years before, a touring couple took in the line of trees and the expanse of field, reconciling these with the terrain map display showing the movement of armies there in September, 1777. Their attention was caught by a red-uniformed figure striding from the tree line at the left. The apparent British soldier crossed in front of them and then turned left into the trees that once marked the American positions. Grateful for this bit of realism the pair complimented the ranger at the Interpretation Center at the end of their tour. "Uniformed actor?" the ranger inquired, "We have no actors out there. Our budget was cut by Congress and we can't afford to have such staff, as much as we'd like them." Another mystery.

Reenactment groups perform at the battlefield almost every year, and in 1997 a group depicting the American militia was encamped not too far from the Neilson House on the southwest section of the National Park. Families rolled into their sleeping bags in the crisp autumn weather one night, and lights were extinguished. Suddenly, the group was startled to hear the rapid approach of galloping horses and the jingle of chains. The ground shook beneath them as they heard vague human voices urging the horse teams onward. Somebody was racing with wagons or cannons straight for their bivouac. Some families stood; others turned on flashlights. Nothing could be seen as the din moved straight through their encampment and vanished to the north. They called out to one another and, as it was apparent that no one was injured and there was nothing they could do, the camp settled once more into an uneasy sleep. Upon investigation in the morning, no hoof prints or wagon wheel ruts could be discovered. Is some colonial cannon battery still attempting to turn the tide of battle by repositioning their guns?

In all my ghostly research on this historic site, perhaps the eeriest tale comes from two Park Service rangers themselves. Remember that these men are charged with keeping peace and order, as well as enforcing federal rules for national parks. Such employees tend not to be "true believers" or to fantasize.

In the late 1980s, the two rangers moved their patrol cars toward Route 32 on the western boundary of the site. Sitting along a ridge, about a mile apart, they were able to scan the road, from which poachers often love to take potshots at the white-tailed deer that populate the battlefield, and which are protected by federal no-hunting laws. Each man was to observe his area and, though the two-way radio was available, there seemed little need to use it that pleasant afternoon.

Jim remembers being parked in the autumn sunshine, with his windows rolled down. "Suddenly there was a murmur of conversation all around me, as if I was in a meeting or gathering of some sort. From time to time, the noise was punctuated by loud outbursts that were clearly human voices, though I couldn't make out their words. I looked every direction out my windows. Nobody else was there! The hubbub moved toward a crescendo and, suddenly, I heard a man's voice scream out, 'Oh, no! Not the leg!' Believe me, I turned every which way then, scanning all around my patrol car, but there was *nobody* visible—the fields were calm and unoccupied. Eventually the noise subsided, leaving me scratching my head. At 4:45 p.m., I picked up my mike and called Jamie, 'Let's get together at the road intersection and we'll drive back in to headquarters.'" As he moved eastward toward the rendezvous, Jim wondered how he would explain the events to his partner, or if he would even try.

At the meeting site, the two patrol cars swung door to door, but before Jim could say a word, an excited Jamie said, "Jim, you're not going to believe it. I was sitting in the car and all of a sudden it was like a big party going on all around me. All kinds of voices talking and yelling, and I couldn't see anybody!"

When they returned to ranger headquarters, the pair noted that this day was an anniversary day of the Second Battle, which had proved decisive in defeating Gen. Burgoyne. But how do two federal employees enter such events in their day's report?

Sometime later, they gained more perspective on the situation when they met a local couple who lived near the battlefield. They often walked the quiet fields, but were especially drawn to an abandoned old barn that has since been demolished. Part of the old Burdyl farm, the structure was left

274

open to the weather after the National Park Service bought the lands. The husband told Jim and Jamie that he and his wife were continually fascinated by the barn because it was like a "spirit loudspeaker." Almost any day, they claimed, they could enter the structure and hear voices and the moans and groans of suffering men. "The barn itself almost certainly didn't date back to the time of the battle, but archaeological excavations nearby indicate that this was once the site of a barn that *did* serve as the American field hospital, where many amputations were certainly done," Jim related.

The turning point in the American war for independence came here at what some call "Old Saratoga." The fledgling rebel army had never won such a victory since the war began, and the American victory lured the French to assist what our founders called "the united states." While the Spirit of '76 continues along the bluffs and rolling pastures beside The Hudson, so do the determined and unquiet spirits of many who made our nation free.

TOWN OF WATERFORD

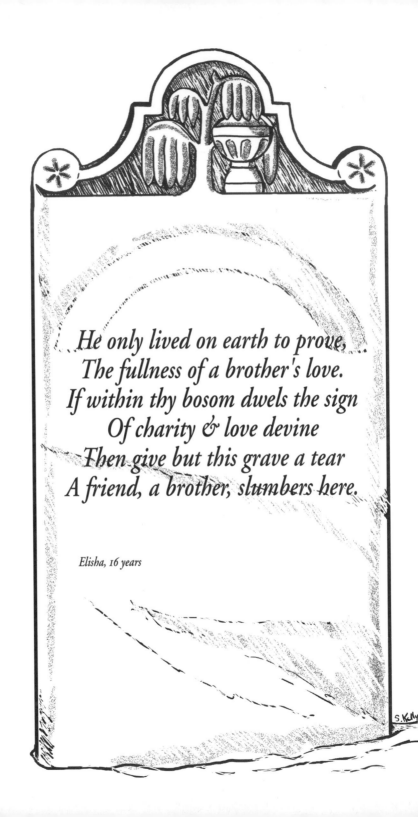

He only lived on earth to prove,
The fullness of a brother's love.
If within thy bosom dwels the sign
Of charity & love devine
Then give but this grave a tear
A friend, a brother, slumbers here.

Elisha, 16 years

Town of Waterford

Early Dutch explorers and, later the British, recognized that the confluence of the Hudson and Mohawk Rivers held a strategic importance, and several small forts were built along those shores. After the Revolution the communities of this town, now called Waterford, funneled farm produce and manufactures into the new nation's economy, moving them downriver to New York City. One of the first long bridges to span The Hudson was constructed in 1804, permitting the produce of the Empire State to move past the Village of Waterford in all directions on the road networks, as well as the Erie and Champlain Canals. Much of this history is now preserved at the New York State Historic and Nature Park on Peebles' Island and in the Waterford Historical Museum and Cultural Center.

The Carpenter's House

Many hard-working people lived along the intricate lock system in Waterford. Immigrants and people down on their luck were drawn to the village in hopes of making a prosperous life. Among these was a poor carpenter who hoped to support his family with his craft. He contracted tuberculosis, and found it increasingly difficult to work enough hours to provide for his wife and children housed in the spare frame house near Lock #2. Eventually, the man became totally disabled and, in order to keep a roof over his family's head, agreed to sign the house over to his avaricious parents who promised the family could remain in their home. Perhaps knowing his parents too well, the man extracted a promise from them that his wife and children could continue to live there *after* his imminent death, and to enforce their agreement, he threatened to return from the grave and haunt them if they reneged. His fears were well founded. Soon after his death, the parents evicted the carpenter's wife and children, hoping to rent the house for their personal wealth.

Among the many tales collected by Dr. Louis Jones at the State University in Albany, this one is recounted in his classic book of folklore, *Things That Go Bump in the Night.* Jones notes that the parents first needed to make repairs to the run-down house if it were to be attractive to tenants.

While they accumulated funds for renovation, they closed and shuttered the house. Already in poor shape, the blinds and barred door created an air of mystery about the place, and soon, passersby claimed to see lights moving about inside the structure. A neighbor, remembering the carpenter's curse, circulated the old tale, and perhaps embellishing it a bit in the process, created such fear that the haunted house was avoided by local folk. As the building gained more and more of a fearsome reputation, nobody even considered renting from the parents, no matter how cheap the price. Neighbors were known to go out of their way to cross the street instead of passing in front of the house.

Unable to stanch the local gossip of fear, and unable to muster the necessary repair funds, the parents were unable to capitalize on their ill-gotten gains. Over the years the weather and lack of upkeep took a toll, and parts of the building sagged and then collapsed. True to his word, the carpenter's ghost (probably seen as the nocturnal light) kept his parents from profiting from their greedy gain.

Mr. Munson's House

In the 1800s, Waterford grew to be a town of mills and manufacturing, employing many newly-arrived immigrants. Clouds of smoke drifted across the Hudson into Rensselaer County and the canal repair basin shops did a thriving business as America moved westward on the Erie Canal.

One of Waterford's many mills was owned by a Mr. Munson, whose plant manager suddenly and mysteriously disappeared early in 1912. Though the two men had often exchanged angry words, no one, at that time, suspected foul play. Then, the mill manager's wife also turned up missing, an event equally inexplicable. Meanwhile, Mr. Munson appeared to live contentedly in his mansion on Broad Street.

As a little girl, Gertrude Myers' mother used to dream of one day living in that beautiful house, and whenever walking past Munson's house she was filled with longing for the gracious life that it seemed to embody. She was startled, then, to see a strange scenario playing out at Munson's as she walked home one late afternoon. A dormer window suddenly flew open and a white-capped woman frantically waved a white cloth to attract a passerby, as if seeking help. Though no cries reached her ears, the girl felt sure the woman was yelling or screaming. She had never associated such crisis with the elegant house and, afraid, she scurried home.

At dinner, she related the strange incident to her family, who told her she couldn't have seen such a sight, as Munson was a bachelor and lived alone. The family discussion turned to Munson. His disappeared manager had been his business partner, but with the man's disappearance, and now, that of his wife, old Mr. Munson seemed to be the sole owner of the prosperous mill. They reminded one another that Munson was outspoken in his hatred of religion, especially Christianity. They had heard that the local Catholic Church, seeking to build a grand church building, had several times offered to buy Munson's property, only to have their agent told, "No Christian will *ever* get my property!"

Eventually, the story of the little girl's experience spread among the neighbors, and many began to suspect that Munson was involved in some form of mischief, or even worse. Some postulated that Munson had made off with his manager's wife and was holding her against her will in the Broad Street mansion. Others, noting Munson's increased prosperity, suggested that the mill owner had covertly murdered the manager *and* his wife, or paid someone to do the dirty work, as well as hide their corpses. Those of this opinion began to suspect the white-capped figure in the dormer window was in fact, the vanished mill manager's ghost, crying out for justice.

In a mill town, such powerful businessmen had great status and no police official dared to launch an investigation on a little girl's vision. The years passed and Munson grew more crotchety and isolated in his big house. Then, before 1920, Munson suffered a seizure and died.

As there were no close heirs, the large house on Broad Street, as well as Munson's other earthly possessions, were put up for public auction. A Jewish family bought the estate and, a short time later, as if pre-arranged, re-sold the old house to the Catholic congregation. If Munson's spirit was outraged, he didn't immediately register a complaint.

The Munson house was torn down by the parish and the Church of St. Mary was constructed on the site, after being properly blessed by the priest. No bodies were found buried in the Munson cellar, though the construction crews weren't especially looking for them either. From time to time in the early 1940s, however, neighbors along Broad Street claimed to see a shadowy figure with indistinct features standing before St. Mary's Church, shaking his fist at all devout parishioners who entered. Today, all is placid on Broad Street.

Physical evidence of much of Waterford's great industrial history has vanished, due to the closing and demolition of many old mills. Without the excellent historical interpretation done by village museums, memory and understanding of the working peoples' struggles would be unavailable to today's members of an "easy come, easy go" consumer culture. Stories such as the above remind us that greed and mystery have gone hand in hand throughout human history.

The Moving Crew

Before St. Mary's Church was built, there was another house behind the Munson mansion, that locals called "The Quigley House." As with so many old buildings that have ghostly reputations, renters came and went in rapid succession, usually after only a month or two. It was well known in the village that tenants complained of their furniture constantly re-arranging itself within the old house. Objects, both heavy and light, were moved during the night, or when the tenants were away. Couches, chairs, tables—nothing was too difficult for the ghostly moving crew to lift and re-arrange.

It is said that the landlords eventually gave up trying to rent the house with such a scary reputation, and the old building sat and sat, unoccupied until around 1930, when new owners had it torn down. Now, upon demolition and excavation, in *this* building's cellar, human bones *were* found! Few, at the time, connected these corporeal remains with the disappeared mill manger and his wife. There was speculation, instead, that some long-ago tenant had saved himself the price of a funeral by burying a relative in the cellar. Others wondered if the bones might not belong to a "rum runner" from the early Prohibition days; and even others suspected the unrecorded death had been an outright murder. All of this, in any case, was in the days before DNA analysis, and no attempt was made to identify the victim(s).

Dr. Louis Jones recounted this cellar discovery in his book, noting that in the 1930s another house was built on the opposite side of that rear lot, but at the time Jones' book was printed, in the late 1940s, no ghostly events had occurred in the new building.

TOWN OF WILTON

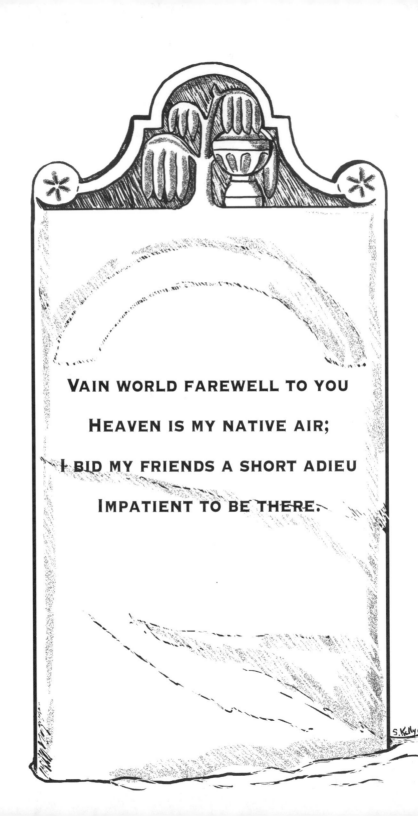

VAIN WORLD FAREWELL TO YOU

HEAVEN IS MY NATIVE AIR;

I BID MY FRIENDS A SHORT ADIEU

IMPATIENT TO BE THERE.

Town of Wilton

K nown as Palmertown on the earliest maps, the small settlement at the foot of Mt. McGregor, dating from the late 1700s, eventually became known as Wiltonville. Small businesses abounded, including mills, shops and the ever-present farming. A great hotel, The Balmoral, graced the mount before it burned in the late 1800s, leaving just the Drexel cottage, where retired Union General Ulysses S. Grant wrote his memoirs and died. The Metropolitan Life Insurance Company built a TB hospital there after the turn of the century, and after successive uses as a veterans' rest facility and a school for the disabled, the facility became a state prison. Wilton is the fastest growing town in the county today, with countless housing developments and several large shopping malls.

The Stiles Tavern

Perhaps the most powerful influence in the Town of Wilton's ghost world was the Battle of Wilton on February 19, 1693, during the French & Indian War. This ferocious battle, unknown today except among local history lovers, was fought out under blizzard conditions for three days along the general route of Parkhurst Road and present day Route 9. Hoping to inflict great casualties on the English settlements near Albany, a large force of southward-moving French and Indians were met and repulsed by Lt. John Schuyler and the Albany County Militia, with both sides suffering heavy casualties. The only evidence of the slaughter today is a solitary New York State historic marker near the junction of Route 9 and Parkhurst Road.

Following the Revolution, in 1798, Benjamin Phillips built a barn and house at the site, near the junction with Greenfield Road, enlarging the structure a few years later. Shortly thereafter, perhaps because of family issues, Phillips sold his property to Ruben Stiles, who opened a tavern on the busy thoroughfare in the 1820s. Stagecoaches stopped regularly at the inn, which was a favorite gathering place for hearing the latest news, getting mail, joining political discussions and attending social functions. Shortly after 1900, the Stiles family sold the building to a Mr. Clark, who re-converted the structure to its present use—a home.

In the 1950s, attorney Theodore Grey and his family purchased and renovated the home. They didn't immediately realize they had "others" living with them. Entering the house upon returning from school, the daughter passed by the old innkeeper's room, within which she heard the unmistakable sound of a button dropping on a hard surface. Who could have done it? She was there all alone. Then another fell, and another. Buttons appearing from nowhere was quite an exceptional experience. Not knowing how to respond, and her mother being a button collector, the girl decided to pick them up to save.

Not long afterward, she and her sister made a new discovery. The Stiles Tavern once had a large, functioning upstairs ballroom, which subsequent owners had partitioned into two bedrooms. When the two girls went to bed at night, just before dropping off to sleep, they'd sometimes hear the tapping of feet and faint music, as if a dance from long ago was continuing all around them. "It happened too many times for it to have been our imagination," the sisters assured me.

Michael, a family friend, often house-sat for the Greys when they were away on vacation. A young man with strong intuitive tendencies, he also experienced some strange events during those stays. Electrical problems that never troubled the Greys were common experiences when he stayed there. Lights he'd turned off would later be found illuminated, and lights he had switched on would unaccountably be turned off, as if a ghostly innkeeper or considerate maid were still present. When he went upstairs to bed at night, Michael sometimes found his sheets and blankets turned down. Maybe because he hadn't responded by thanking the ghost maid, or perhaps because he never left a tip, sometimes he'd also find the pillowcase removed from his pillow and tossed into a corner. Michael enjoyed the interplay with the ghost and, if its activity lagged, sometimes would yell out, "I'm enjoying what you're doing, please don't stop on my account!" These words apparently frustrated the impudent ghost, who then ceased its capers.

One of the Grey daughters became engaged in the 1970s, and the family hosted their future son-in-law at Christmas time. Gathering around the tree on Christmas Eve, ready to exchange presents, the Greys were hopeful that the young man would like the expensive cigarette lighter they had bought, wrapped and placed beneath the tree for him. Present after present was handed out that night, but it seemed the lighter had vanished. When all presents had been distributed, it was nowhere in sight. The parents made a diligent search of the entire tree, and apologized, but there was nothing for the man, only what sounded like a flimsy excuse instead.

Again apologetic on Christmas Day, the family gathered around the tree, and suddenly heard a rustling in the boughs. From high up in the branches, a small present was slowly bumping and sliding its way, bough by bough, down to the floor, whereupon the parents delightedly presented the gift to their daughter's fiancé. Perhaps this was the best introduction for the man, as he was about to live part-time in a house where the mischievous ghost often spirited objects away, only to return them another day.

Perhaps it was the open electrical or chemical energy of the Greys, or those who visited the family, that caused the ghosts to manifest. However, after the house was sold, the new owners just didn't get any "vibes." Oftentimes, the addition or subtraction of just one person in a household can change the energies dramatically, causing much head-scratching and doubt that a place ever was "haunted."

Nothing of note has happened now in over fifteen years, leaving the new family to speculate that perhaps the servants of the old days have now moved on to a higher calling in the world beyond. In any case, they have now placed the old tavern up for sale. The old house sits, awaiting new residents for its third century.

It seems that each individual or family has its own collective energy, which can assure the spirit being that its communication (whether positive or negative, hostile or friendly) will be received by the living. Perhaps the new owners will interact happily with the "long time residents."

Stiles Corners

One woman told me of passing the historic marker and observing an old man searching for something along the road. "I've seen him several times, and he doesn't look quite real," she said. Neighbors can't place such a person. Another time she observed a man with no apparent legs sitting at roadside, studying passersby.

Sometimes, local people approach me and ask if I know anything about "The Corners," as many receive strange impressions or see strange sights when passing through the intersection. Not far up Parkhurst Road is an old house in which two strolling neighbors saw a little girl looking out

287

the window. Dressed in a formal white dress (a burial dress?) the child just stared, and the women knew that the owner had no children.

Since I began collecting Wilton stories in the 1970s, I have heard local people tell incredible tales about The Corners area. Could some vibrant energy linger at the crossroads and stimulate the visions of so many Wilton people? Might this energy be a residue of the old stagecoach days along the north-south road? Or, might some of it result from a farther-back period, when the Great War Trail wound its way through that area between Canada and Albany? Conceivably, the spirit energy released at the time of a 300 year-old battle may still emerge to amalgamate at times with peoples' consciousness. Many who study this matter believe that this is exactly what is transpiring in a locale such as Wilton, so charged with historic contention.

Sandy's House

When former town historian Lorraine Westcott wrote about this house in *The Saratogian*, she named it after the owner at that time, so I've retained the title. Here is another curious case in which the prior resident or residents didn't completely abandon the house after they physically departed.

About a mile north of Stiles Corners, Sandy began to experience very cold drafts in her house. Her dogs reacted as adversely as she did to the anomalous chills. Sandy determined to get to the bottom of the matter and contacted a psychic. When the gifted lady came to Sandy's house, she sensed an unhappy older woman's spirit on the premises. At that point, Sandy remembered having found some personal effects and jewelry from a prior owner in the attic when she moved in. The documents indentified the former owner as Agatha, so Sandy transferred that name to the chill that she now realized was a ghost. At the time of Lorraine's article, Sandy had just sold the home and, as the young new owners weren't very curious about the house's history at the time of sale, she neglected to mention the indwelling spirit.

The couple, a young contractor and his wife, who bought the house, soon noticed little things, strange things, even before moving in. The man came to install some wall-too-wall carpet in the entryway and other interior floors. As he completed the job and was about to install the trim, he heard a male voice demanding, "What the hell ya doin'?" Thinking it was the voice of his father on a surprise visit, the contractor looked outside. His father's truck was nowhere to be seen; the driveway was empty. With no human being to respond to, he continued installing wood trim around the doorway and again was startled to hear the same critical query. "I checked the whole house again," he told me, "and nobody was there. I said to myself, that's enough of *that*! And I left quickly, not really wanting to believe I'd heard the voice."

A few days later, as he worked inside the house, he was interrupted by the arrival of Sandy's car. She had brought a bottle of champagne to help celebrate the new ownership, and perhaps to help the couple "loosen up" for the tales she felt impelled to tell. The young couple heard the "Agatha stories" and learned that the old woman had died of cancer, leaving many of her belongings in the attic, those discovered by Sandy. Among her anecdotes, Sandy related the experience of hearing a very loud BOOM one day when she was alone. She had explored her house inside and out, she said, but never found a cause for the seeming explosion. When she had questioned the neighbors, she found that none of them had heard the explosive sound. In the end, when combined with other subtle phenomena, Sandy attributed the episode to Agatha, but couldn't explain how an old lady ghost could make such a blasting noise. No one, at that time, ever considered the possibility that it was generated in a battle three hundred years ago.

After hearing Sandy's revelations, and as his own experiences accumulated, the husband came to understand they were dealing with things he'd never believed in before. He remembered that their family dog had growled and stared at a certain part of the living room soon after he and his wife moved in. This additional space at the end of the living room had been gained by walling off a section of the garage. Was some strange force from the garage's history now present in his home?

On the other side of that living room wall was a kitchen cabinet that also played a key role in other strange episodes. Avid fans of the Adirondack Red Wings hockey team, he and his wife kept their season tickets in that cupboard. One winter night, they rushed home from work, hoping to get to that night's hockey game before it started. Eating quickly, the husband showered and the couple climbed into their truck. Then, the wife remembered she'd forgotten the tickets in the cupboard and, dashing inside, she reached into the kitchen cabinet where the tickets were kept. Nothing was there! She searched high and low inside, but the tickets were gone. By the time they got to the Glens Falls Civic Center, bought new tickets and took their seats, the first period was already half gone. "We were upset and sure felt like yelling *that* night," the wife said with a wry smile. The next day they heard on the television news that a serious accident had taken place on Route 9 near Glens Falls, and by being late to the game the previous night they had just missed the collision scene. At that point, they had to ponder if Agatha or a guardian angel had their safety in mind. Nonetheless, their precious season tickets never reappeared.

At one time, the wife had seen a stack of her dinner plates, stored in the mysterious "lost tickets" kitchen cabinet, move horizontally from their shelf and fall onto the kitchen counter and then onto the floor, where some of them broke.

As I discussed these curious events with the couple, it occurred to us how close they lived to Parkhurst Road, with its history of violent activity between Indians, French, British and American warriors. Considering the topography, the site of Sandy's house was almost certainly in the midst of the fray on the last day of the battle, when French and Indians were making their retreat northward. Could there still be some remnant of that historic violence present along the old War Path?

The wife exclaimed, "Oh my, all the unkind words I leveled at Agatha that day my dishes crashed! I must have blamed the wrong ghost."

Col. French's House

It is tempting to name a ghost house after its present owners, but in this case the powerful personality of the builder may explain most of the events that took place on this part of Parkhurst Road.

Col. Winsor Brown French, commander of the famous 77th New York Infantry Regiment in the Civil War, built Apple Tree Farm upon his return to civilian life. French's regiment is memorialized by a large statue in Congress Park in Saratoga Springs. After his passing, the Colonel's large frame house passed to new owners. In the 1980s, the McMasters owned the house, then, sold it to its present owners, the Butlers in 1993. Wayne and Kathy Butler and their children smiled when the departing McMasters said, "Oh yes, did we mention the ghost?"

It didn't take the new residents long, however, to discover that the former owners knew well of what they spoke. Kathy, alone in the house one day, had just stepped out of the shower when she heard a noise. Knowing that she was all alone in the house, she was put on guard, but then tantalized as she recognized that the noise was coming from *all the upstairs bedroom doors* opening and closing almost in military precision! Her ferocious watchdogs slept through the entire episode.

In her large bedroom, which must have been the house's master bedroom at one time, the twelve year-old daughter had a unique introduction to what must certainly have been the Colonel. Soon after moving in, at 4 a.m., the girl awoke to find her bedroom lights shining brightly and all the bedclothes missing! She recovered the blankets and pillows, which were neatly folded and placed in a row on the floor, almost like a reveille inspection in an army camp. Her bed sheets lay neatly folded in a perfect square at the foot of her bed! Even a sleepwalking teenager would have found executing this precision difficult, and the girl didn't sleepwalk. "We heard quite an outcry from our daughter, who woke us right up," Kathy said to historian Lorraine Westcott.

Kathy also related that their seven year-old son had experienced a strange incident. The doorknobs on his bedroom doors began to rattle as if someone outside wanted to enter, but when he opened the door he found the hallway empty.

Wayne remembered a time when, walking through the upstairs, he saw the back of a woman at the other end of the hallway, and assumed it was Kathy. He went downstairs and was startled to find Kathy working down there. Who was upstairs?

After 1994, there has been little ghostly activity in the old house. Col. French was undoubtedly testing the mettle of his new regiment and, finding them good and trainable recruits, he has retreated to quieter dimensions where he can study peace maneuvers, instead of war.

Christine's House

Many years ago, one of my Ninth Grade students had difficulty completing her homework assignments. Teachers hear all kinds of excuses such as "the baby ate it" or "the dog shredded it," but Christine had a different tale: "The ghost kept me up all night." I gave her a little leeway for creativity on that one, but not much. Then, years later, after Christine and I had forgotten one another, I read a *Saratogian* column by Lorraine Westcott detailing the story of a house on Route 50, north of Saratoga Springs, in the Town of Wilton. I asked Charlie, one of my fellow teachers, if he'd heard of a haunted house up there, as it was close to his home. "Sure," he said, "Christine's house. Don't you remember, one of my Science students that often didn't have her homework done because of a ghost in her house?" I was dazzled, and instantly remembered the excuses that I'd felt were a "cop-out" on the girl's part. For the first time in years I had found a student's excuse that, bizarre as it was, had credence!

Though it took weeks, I finally located Christine, who is now a mother and housewife in Arizona. She informed me that her parents live near Albany today, so I was able to interview them also. When I interviewed Christine's mother, Barbara, she remembered how icy cold the master bedroom had always been in that "haunted" house.

David, her husband, interjected that, "It was just a bad luck house for us," and went on to enumerate the many experiences that had brought him to this conclusion. "I stood in the stairwell one day and heard a male voice call out my name. I knew I was alone in the building—at least I *thought* so!" He recalled awakening one morning to a bat biting his hand. After several days of anxiety and doctor visits, they determined the creature wasn't rabid. He related having a huge pine tree fall on their house, and another incident in which he fell through the roof surface when attempting repairs on the shingles. Bad luck for sure!

Barbara recalled being startled by an apparition of a bald old man standing on the second floor. Upon questioning neighbors, she was told that a former owner was alleged to have hanged himself upstairs in the house. With the series of troublesome events assailing them, Barbara decided to invite an area psychic to delve into the mysteries surrounding them. The intuitive woman, who knew nothing of the house's history or reputation, sat in meditative silence before she spoke, "I see a hanged man being cut down

292

up there, and taken to (pointing) *that* bedroom." Christine remembered that the indicated room had always been an uncomfortable place for her. She had called it "the red room," though she wasn't certain why she chose that color. "My aunt had a miscarriage when she stayed in that room, and I was always afraid of it from the time we moved in. I was ten at the time," she added.

It was a very active house—something going on at all times. David said, "It was a regular circus. The washer and dryer sometimes turned themselves off and on, and things were always disappearing, though they always reappeared—usually on the back of the toilet." "Right," added Barbara, "and that old man's spirit walked around upstairs, always humming to himself. I remember my brother calling the old man 'Popeye' because he was bald. And when my dad was renovating some of the upstairs, he found a bone-handled knife stuck into a stud inside the wall. We often wondered if that knife had been used to cut down the hanged man. The sounds got louder and louder while we lived there," Barbara sighed, as if remembering incidents too numerous to recite.

Christine remembered her fright over an invisible person who used to sit on her bed at night, wrinkling the coverlet when she was in bed. "I was *so* scared," she said, "but one evening I had a vision of The Virgin Mary watching over me, so I knew nothing would hurt me and I'd be okay. Sometimes we would see wet footprints on the bathroom floor when nobody had been home all day. I laughingly called it 'The House from Hell' to deal with the frustration of never knowing what we'd experience next."

Barbara recalled that one night she thought she was dreaming and, in the vision, saw a woman enter her room shouting the name 'Gilda' or something similar. This name tied in with her hunch that the hanged man had been of Germanic origins. Barbara believes that the ghost man and ghost woman remained in the house after she and her family moved away. After interviewing their family, I spent time at the County Clerk's Office researching former owners of the house. Between 1940 and 1943, I discovered, the house had been transferred between two men who had German family names. Unfortunately, property deeds often don't tell who the wives were unless they were co-owners of the property. Barbara may indeed be correct in her intuitions about the ghosts, and a Gilda may have been there during that time.

After Christine's family left, the rundown house was purchased by an energetic young couple who did extensive renovations inside the house. I stopped by one day and asked if they had experienced anything strange during their brief tenure. They just couldn't believe such goings-on were a part of their house's history, as it was so quiet and peaceful. So, perhaps the old man and woman have now passed beyond Route 50 and have gone to a place of peace. Let's hope so, because the young couple sure didn't need the excitement that Christine and her family experienced!

Okay, Christine, I finally believe you! I imagine that doing homework with all those sideshows must have been very difficult. What trauma your family might have been spared with a simple house blessing to send the former residents on their way. Perhaps, in the future, when the reality of troubled spirits gains greater public understanding and acceptance, there will be more publicity on certified professionals that families in need may call.

The Old Carr Place

"David, I remember that my kids said you were interested in ghosts," Karen Campola said when she called me. I had taught her two children in school, where "strange things" often surfaced in our class discussions about world cultures and religions. Karen was refurbishing an old house just off Gailor Road, a building originally constructed after the Revolutionary War, perhaps about 1789. At one time an old stagecoach stop, it had been in the Carr family for many generations before being purchased in the 1930s by another family in which the father allegedly hanged himself in the garage. Around the time of World War II, a plumber and his wife lived there, hoping to operate a tourist home (what would be called a bed & breakfast today). Then, in the late 1980s, Karen and her family purchased the old building and decided to restore some of its faded elegance. At the time Karen was Saratoga County Historian.

When she called, she hoped that I might help her understand some of the occurrences taking place during the renovations. She said the building contractor had come downstairs during a break one day and said to her, "Mrs. C., I really like the plans you have for upstairs, and I enjoy doing this job, but would you please ask the old lady to back off?" Karen couldn't comprehend his question; what old lady was he talking about? "My husband and I live here alone," she told him, "there's no one else."

294

"There's an old lady in a flower print dress who is always looking over my shoulder, and I'm afraid she'll get hurt if she gets too close," the carpenter responded, a bit irritated. Puzzled as to her invisible guest, Karen invited me to come over and "look around."

I took Wildy, an intuitive man with an interest in the paranormal, with me, hoping he might assist in resolving the puzzle. In the hallway, Karen, Wildy and I shared our intuitions about the downstairs, after admiring the renovations, especially the old bricks with cat footprints in them that Karen used in rebuilding her fireplace hearth. There was now a sparkle in the old hardwood floors.

When we went upstairs, we entered the bedroom that had troubled the carpenter, finding it to be bright and not at all ominous. The walls were shining from a fresh coat of white paint, and there were, as yet, no furnishings and no curtains on the windows. Nevertheless, something in me did not want to enter the room. Wildy felt nothing, and pointed out that the room was visibly empty.

In an instant, my perception of the room changed from a sunny scene to a dismal and gloomy interior. I saw thick curtains on both windows and in the far corner I saw, or imagined I saw, an old-fashioned, spool crib or child's youth bed. Inside it, curled up beneath a blanket, was a small child. A woman in early 1900s dress sat in a chair at the foot of the crib, reading from a book, probably a prayer book or Bible. The words, "Margaret prays" came into my mind. Then suddenly, the brightness reappeared. Gone were the gloomy scenes that I accepted might have come from my imagination.

I asked Karen if there ever was a Margaret in the house, and she said she didn't know, but the Carr burial plots were just down the road in the Brick Church Cemetery. "Let's go see," she suggested. South of the house, about one hundred yards away on Northern Pines Road, we found the old cemetery, no longer well cared for. Among the Carr burials, we found two headstones with the name Margaret, though neither had a family name. It was coincidental, and offered some evidence that indeed a Margaret had attended the illness or death of a now-forgotten child in the house long ago. In the end, Wildy and I weren't able to answer the questions that Karen wanted answered.

We saw no lady in a print dress, though Karen later informed me that neighbors, hearing the carpenter's description of the old woman, said the ghost was a dead ringer for the World War II era plumber's wife. When the renovations began, she seems to have returned to investigate the new appearance. After the contractor left, she appears to have vanished for good.

In investigating another house, I was told by the psychic assisting me, that, as a departed soul reviews the experiences of the ended life, or when a bond of love is momentarily re-established, perhaps by the passing thoughts of a living person, the spirit can manifest in his or her old surroundings. Humans who are sensitive to such visions may see the entity for a short time, though it would be wrong to term the phenomenon as a "haunting." Such is perhaps the explanation in this story.

In any case, the former county historian has had her brush with genuine historical characters and loved having had them appear, if only for a time.

Mt. McGregor

In 1882, Joseph Drexel, a wealthy Philadelphian, opened a narrow gauge railroad to the summit known as Mt. McGregor, in the Town of Wilton, where, with partners, he had recently opened the Balmoral Hotel, offering summer visitors luxurious surroundings in the foothills of the Adirondacks. Three years later, he loaned a small cottage near the hotel to his dying friend, ex-President Ulysses S. Grant, so that Grant could finish writing his memoirs. Perhaps healed temporarily by the house's breathtaking vistas of the Hudson Valley, Saratoga Lake, and Vermont's Green Mountains off to the east, Grant completed the task in six weeks. Shortly thereafter, he died in the house now known as "Grant's Cottage," a national historic site. In 1897, the hotel burned and, for the next few years, the summit and "Grant's Lookout" lay deserted except for the small cottage.

In 1913, The Metropolitan Life Insurance Company opened a thirty-building sanatorium complex on the site, offering rehabilitation to its employees from the New York City area who suffered from tuberculosis, a contagious disease that afflicted innumerable urban Americans at that time. Provisions for the patients were grown on five farms situated on the mountaintop. The grounds were beautifully landscaped with ponds, trees and flowers, in the hope that clean mountain air, fresh food, and natural beauty would revivify the patients. And many *were* cured of TB there, though others died and were cremated in the on-site crematorium.

With the introduction of new medicines, an isolation facility was no longer needed by the mid-1940s. The State of New York then purchased the hospital complex as a Rest Camp for Veterans after World War II ended in 1945, offering veterans of the World Wars a healing place. Within a decade, as fewer military service people needed treatment, and with the advent of the VA hospitals throughout the nation, the buildings were then placed under the jurisdiction of the Rome State School. A few years afterward, it was renamed The Wilton State Hospital, and still later, The Wilton Developmental Center, a place of treatment for those who were mentally handicapped.

In 1976, after moving the mentally and physically handicapped patients to a new facility, the new Wilton Developmental Center on Ballard Rd., the vacant older institution was transferred to the NY State Department of Correctional Services, which operates a medium security prison there today. All of this makes an interesting local history lesson, but why is it in a ghost book?

Employees who worked in the Veterans' Rest Camp, as well as in the Developmental Center, whispered about the little girl seen staring from a fourth floor window in the building now designated as "C Dorm" by the Corrections Department, where no inmates were housed. This child of perhaps eight years of age was often seen staring through the latticed window, but when officers went to that floor, no one was ever there. This perplexed the prison staff, as the space (at that time) was unused and locked. Nobody could identify the child, as her clothing gave no indication of her historic origins, and she gave no other expression of her purpose than simply to appear, then disappear. Barry Hildebrandt, an employee from the Rome State School and State Hospital days, remembers several incidents when people went to check on the girl, but found no one. "It was a bit creepy up on the fourth floor, so we seldom went up. One of my co-workers often heard the moans and groans of former patients when he ventured up there, though the space was certainly uninhabited."

The little girl continued to appear in the window after the grounds became a prison but, according to prison Deputy Superintendent Paul Garcia, "we eventually decided to use that space as a mosque for our Muslim inmates, and after the conversion to a worship space, there have been no further sightings of her in C Dorm. They now see her *next door* in *D Dorm* attic!"

The fourth floor of D Dorm is likewise unused, except for storage and, for a time, as housing for prisoners with discipline problems. There are a half-dozen doors to be unlocked before a person can reach the fourth floor, but the child's spirit is heedless of modern restrictions. Gary, a corrections officer, checking that floor one evening, turned after locking a door and saw a pre-teen girl in a long white dress peering intently at him from a side storage room. Then, she disappeared. Another corrections officer, patrolling the same space, checked the security unit door, found it locked, and turned to see the little girl, who quickly disappeared. "She's just suddenly *there*. The girl doesn't interact with us—she doesn't seem happy or sad, but just seems to solemnly observe our activities," corrections officers say.

"It's hard to guess who she might be," said Hildebrandt. "These buildings have housed children during the TB hospital days, children as patients during the State Hospital days, and children of the families who worked at Mt. McGregor. She might originate from the Drexel or Grant families. Not all children on the grounds were severely ill during sanitorium or State School days, either. In earlier times, children who were somehow 'different' or perhaps an embarrassment to their families, could be institutionalized, and how sad it would be for an almost-normal child to be incarcerated there, in spite of the gardens and ponds. It might create a really troubled spirit that would have difficulty understanding and leaving when her life was over."

Prison officials were cordial and gave me a thorough tour of the facility, hoping that my experiences with ghosts and ghost stories could help them understand, not just the little girl in white, but others who, for the most part, have been simply puzzling and not frightening. Prison Building 10, the old hospital infirmary, offered newly-hired Correction Officer Regina quite a shock on her first night on duty there, though. In her first floor office, she noticed that her AM/FM radio began to turn on and off, as if someone wanted to contact her. She jokingly spoke aloud into the semi-darkness of the empty room, "Come on now," she chided, "we all have to get along here. You're not going to scare *me* out of here!" Several weeks later, when making the rounds and climbing the old staircase to Floor 4, she unlocked the glass-windowed door and looked around inside. Everything seemed to be okay. Having been taunted by officers about ghosts on Floor 4, and with a smile on her face, she left the room and locked the door. As she was about to withdraw her key from the lock, the center of the glass panel before her exploded outward, "almost as if someone inside had punched a fist through the glass at me!" she said. Covered with glass shards, and suffering small cuts, she reported the incident to her supervisor and went to the Hospital Clinic for first aid.

A few days later, when she told Deputy Superintendent Garcia of the incident, he smiled. Now *he* could tell her of *his* experience there. During his own night patrol of Building 10 in 1988, Garcia had signed in at the office desk, as is standard procedure, then heard a strange noise. It didn't seem to emanate from Floor 1, so he went up the staircase to Floor 2. Nothing. Ascending to Floor 3, he began to hear a clinking sound, almost as if someone were striking chains together, but nothing was visible on the third floor. Checking Floor 4, he found nothing out of the ordinary there and, securing all doors behind him as he descended, returned to his office post. He had puzzled for years as to what had caused the jangling or clanking sound. Now, Regina had suffered a more intense "close encounter." Perhaps the two unexplained incidents were related in a way that neither one understood.

There is much good humor among employees at the Mt. McGregor Correctional Facility. "Often, we're just puzzled," said Katie, an office secretary in the Administration Building, which is one of the old hospital buildings. "We look at one another and grin when something strange happens. One day, while working in my office, out of the corner of my eye, I saw a man dressed in dark clothing enter Deputy Garcia's office. A few minutes later, I heard the customary squeak of his office chair, as if he'd sat down." However, a few minutes later, Garcia passed her doorway and headed toward his office! "Wasn't that *you* that just went into the office?" she queried. "Not me, I've been at the other end of the corridor," the Deputy said. Katie remembers the figure wore a longer-than-usual dark garment, of the old frock-coat type.

Kim, Deputy Garcia's secretary, told me, "On another occasion I heard his phone ring. I always give him two rings to get to his phone before I pick up and answer his calls. That day I heard no chair squeak, indicating that he'd turned toward his phone, so I answered, as I always do, but there was no one on the line. On other occasions the phone has rung and I've heard the squeaking chair in Garcia's office, but the phone continues to ring. Dashing to his office to find out why he's not answering, I've found Mr. Garcia *not there*, and I leave the room pondering who or what made the squeak. And then there are the ice-cold drafts that we sometimes experience in that area behind his desk..." she teased with a smile.

Other old buildings, now converted for prison use, also hold their secrets. In the Administration Building and in Building 21, doors seem to open and close themselves continually. Building 6, a counseling building, is often discovered with its lights burning long after the civilian employees, who are certain they have shut them off, have left. And on the other side of the campus, through the trees just off prison grounds, the night perimeter patrol officer sometimes sees the lights on in Grant's Cottage. And, it is a certainty that no one is there, as the staff leaves before 5 p.m.

Several volunteers who have worked at Grant's Cottage testify to cold drafts and the feeling of "being watched." None of them has suggested that the spirit in residence is President Grant. Many suspect it may be Mrs. A.J. Giambino, a long-time dedicated caretaker of the site, who died (like Grant) of throat cancer in 1984. A devoted overseer of the historic site, many believe it may have been difficult for her to "let go" of the dedication and responsibilities.

There have also been visitors to the Grant Cottage who have taken photographs of the building that elicited strange images when printed, images that could be interpreted as a face or two peering from the upstairs rooms. However, those rooms are not open to the public and the photos were always taken when the guides were all downstairs. Who or what was upstairs?

On the winding drive up Mt. McGregor, Barbara, another Corrections official, has several times encountered a woman in Victorian dress near the powerhouse building. Her first experience, of running right over or *through* the wraith, left Barbara's heart pounding. The original road to the summit didn't follow its present-day route, so it is puzzling why the ghost lady would appear there. It is tantalizing to consider, however, that the road, at that spot, borders the old crematorium from the TB hospital days!

Modern employees continue their service at the two facilities on Mt. McGregor, despite the occasional incorporeal annoyances. As in most phantasmic episodes, there is little, if any, fear on the part of the experiencers. Many of the employees are inspired that former residents or patients continue "living" in this most beautiful of prison sites in New York State. Most often they are simply puzzled as to *what it all means.*

The Wilton Academy

This last tale, set in a long-gone Wilton landmark, is rich in phenomena that tantalize the student of the after-death state. Ghosts from the historic past mingle today with spirits from recent times.

The little hamlet of Wiltonville expanded after 1859, as the railroad moved north through the valley. Stephen Fradenburgh came down from the Town of Moreau to found a small, though short-lived, elite academy on what is now Parkhurst Road. Offering a superior education to those who could afford the fees, Wilton Academy was the envy of many neighboring towns. Fradenburgh's chief instructor was a Miss Boice, who made academic excellence in all subjects her priority. When she died suddenly two years after the opening, however, the fortunes of the academy quickly declined. Fradenburgh moved to Vermont, leaving his hopes and dreams wafting through a boarded-up building, and died soon after moving away. The old school became a private home for a succession of owners, though few of those families stayed very long, because there was something eerie afoot at the old Wilton Academy.

A local man remembers driving past the old building in 1960 and seeing it abandoned, as it had been sporadically during the century following the Academy's demise.

Sometimes, other passersby noted a glow in the building's cupola, even though electrical power to the old school had been shut off. When dawn's early light began to illuminate the façade, the light would no longer be visible. Local youngsters used to break in and hold impromptu parties whenever the old academy was uninhabited, and many locals preferred to believe that the light was somehow connected with teenage pranks.

Retired rodeo rider, Harry Rusk, and his family came from a southern state in 1967, and set up housekeeping in the old school building. It seemed appropriate, as Harry and his wife, Donna, were openhearted and many times sheltered youngsters who were estranged from their families. They also took in foster children, so, at times, there were as many as ten busy inhabitants in the old structure. "The Rusks were idealistic folks," said a local woman, "and they hoped to restore the old building to the magnificence envisioned by the builder before the Civil War."

301

The Rusks seemed to take it all in stride: the restoration projects, their children, the foster kids, the mix of personalities, each with its own joys, sorrows and problems and, to top it all off, *the ghosts*. This combination of energies made life at the old Academy lively.

Harry sometimes told of seeing an old man standing in the cupola, which brought chills to the spines of visitors who could not see the figure.

"There were French doors at the foot of the stairs on the first floor," one friend of the Rusks remembers, "and they just would *not* stay closed. Harry got so frustrated that one night he nailed them shut. In the morning the nail was found in the middle of the room and the doors stood wide open."

Another day, when Harry was away and the children were all in school, Donna, relishing her solitude, began whistling a happy song as she worked in the kitchen. Momentarily distracted by something, she left off whistling, and from somewhere else in the house came whistled notes to complete the tune. Just more of the same, she figured.

Don, a family friend, was intrigued by a light phenomenon that could be experienced when he stayed overnight in a second floor bedroom. When one sat on the bed in the dark room, within ten to fifteen minutes, a faint glow began to appear. The halo, about 6 x 9 inches, first appeared on the inside of the closed bedroom door, and then would travel about the perimeter of the room. Concluding its "search," the light always disappeared through another closed door of the room. When there was nothing interesting on evening television, family members could go upstairs to the bedroom and be entertained by the mysterious light.

Trying to comprehend the phenomenon, Don once left the bedroom door open approximately one-half inch in an experiment, and through the opening, he could see a tall bald man, walking through the hallway outside the bedroom, as the light vanished into the other door. Don didn't recognize the strange man and told no one about the sighting at that time, as he didn't think the others in the room had seen the figure. A few days later, one of those friends phoned to ask "Who do you think the guy was out in the hall?" The friend gave the same description of the phantom that Don had witnessed.

A few months afterward, Harry told Don that two of his boys had awakened one morning and had seen two men arguing at the foot of their beds in the "light room." From the description the boys gave, Don immediately recognized one of the figures as the man he'd seen in the hallway.

During Christmas week in 1967, Harry shouted downstairs to Donna that he had just seen two male ghosts arguing beside *their* bed.

As Harry played his electric guitar while sitting on one of two opposing living room sofas, a series of interwoven events commenced. The big round mirror that hung on the wall between the sofas began a pendulum-like swaying. It gained momentum, swinging in larger and larger arcs. Just as suddenly, it slowed to a stop, but instantly there came a loud BANG at the foot of the center stairway. No sooner had the echoes of that vibration faded, than Harry heard racing footsteps upstairs, rapidly crossing from the top of the stairs to the foot of the stairway leading to the third floor. At first Harry thought Charlie, a friend who often stayed overnight with them, was cavorting, and Harry went upstairs to check. Nearing the top of the first stairs, he heard echoing footsteps racing to the third floor and called out, "Charlie, that you?" Charlie lay in a bed near the stair top on the third floor and, as he later told Harry, "I thought that was *you* coming upstairs. I heard those pounding steps crossing the hall on the second floor and coming up here and stopping outside my door. There were three more stomps, and then there was nobody—nothing! And when I heard you calling me from down the stairs, I freaked out and hid under my bed covers until you got here!"

Maybe the building's ghosts sensed the upcoming conflagration and were more active than usual that winter, perhaps even trying to warn the family.

In the midst of a heavy snowstorm, a fire started during the early morning hours. It spread rapidly in the old tinder-dry structure, and later on, the fire chief speculated that the cause of the blaze was a faulty kerosene heater. Everyone apparently slept through the early stages of the fire, and it was a Deputy Sheriff passing by on patrol who spotted flames shooting from the roof. Area rescue and fire departments hurried to the scene over snow-drifted roads, but there was little to save. The building was engulfed in flames. Three children actually escaped, but Harry and Donna and two of their biological children, as well as the four foster children perished in the flames. Gone was a loving family and an historic building.

A new home now occupies the former site of Wilton Academy. The owner has seen what he thinks is the shade of Harry Rusk in his office at the rear of the house. A female presence (Donna?) has been experienced near the staircase and in the baby's room upstairs. "There have been instances in which my wife and I have seen others, but we're not sure who they are. Sometimes, we don't see the entire figure, only parts, maybe just an arm or shoulder appears, or a leg is seen going out a door," he explained.

In this house, as in so many others on Parkhurst Road, a phantom soldier sometimes appears, this one along the rear boundary of the property, perhaps still reeling from the carnage of the long ago Battle of Wilton. The owner of the new home has also had tools disappear from his tool box, and on one occasion, as he worked repairing a fence, he reached for a nail and found the box was gone! It had been right at his feet as he worked, but suddenly had vanished. He later found the box of nails on the opposite side of the paddock, where he hadn't been that day!

He and his wife sometimes hear mysterious voices conversing inside their house, and once there was a loud scream from the downstairs that abruptly woke all the sleeping occupants. From time to time, the family also experiences strange phenomena involving the telephone, as well as the radio and television sets turning off and on, unaided by a human hand.

The owner is also fascinated by the great number of similarities that he has discovered between the Rusk family and his own. Both sets of parents are approximately the same age. They have the same number of children. The new owner, like Harry, raises rodeo horses and is active in the rodeo circuit.

Perhaps the spirits of the Rusks, and others who perished there almost forty years ago, are happy to intermingle with living folks much like themselves. It is possible that they seek to experience, albeit vicariously, the completion of a happy life, which ended with the tragic fire.

It is possible that the Rusks have opened their big hearts on The Other Side, and have offered shelter to other spirits in need of "parenting" or friendship. Perhaps Harry and Donna's family management skills are being fine-tuned in overseeing the horseplay of the young ones once committed to their earthly care. Readers should not be surprised that drama and sadness and mirth may still be playing out on that part of Parkhurst Road that borders The Other Side.

KILLED INSTANTLY BY
THE KICK OF A HORSE.

May 16, 1844
AE 20 yrs. 6 mos. 9 days

Acknowledgements

The following individuals have my gratitude for sharing their stories, energy and time, allowing me to create this book:

Peg Adams, Mr.&Mrs. Lamar Alsop, Judy Anderson, Doris, Don and Stuart Armstrong, Robertson Baker, Sr., Georgia Ball, Kathleen Bango, Bill Bayard, Clyde Bell, Richard Beresford and the National Park Service staff, Patty Berrigan, Paul Biggie, Davis Bixby, Lawrence Blanche, Don Bowman, Barbara Breyer, Kathy Briaddy, Bruce Brownell, Wayne and Kathy Butler, Maria Bucciferro, Mrs. Bugli, Mr.&Mrs. Ray Bussing, Mr.&Mrs. Robert Cackener, Mr.&Mrs. Christopher Cady, Elizabeth Cady, Bob and Rosemary Carney, Mr.&Mrs. John Christman, Sandy Cheney, Kathy Cicero, Ernie Clothier, Anna Coker, Doris Cole, Will and Christina Connelly, Agada Craig, Gail Cramer, John Cromie, Caren Crootof, Christine Cuttita, Rebecca Cushing, Rev. Tom Davis, Pat Delay, Mary DeMarco, Angela DePaul, Andrew Desidoro, Nancy Dragonette, Jean Driscoll, Mr.&Mrs. Leslie Dubb.

Also: Jay & Priscilla Edwards, Smoky Eggleston, Jessica Ehlinger, Al Eisenhauer, Ralph Ellsworth, Theresa Ellsworth, Lee Erb, Claude Everts, Ron Farra, Mary Fassett, Gerry Ferris, Russ Fitch, the Freiburgh family, Joanne Fuller, Tom Gamache, Wendy Gamache and Stacey, Eileen Gannon, Paul Garcia, Andy Gaudreau, Bud&Alice Gaudreau, Martha Gilgallen, R. Gilligan, Debbie Gilmore, Shirley Gilmore, Amy Godine, Faith Groy, Phil Griffen, Sharon Hack, Mr.&Mrs. Hammond, Eileen Hannay, Sue Haswell, Margaret Hayes, Walter Hayes, Chris Heidorf, John Himmelrick, Jennie Himmelrick, Mr.&Mrs. Richard Hunter, Penny Jewell, Brock Johnson, Cathy Judge, Phyllis Keeler, Mike and Ann Kelley, Ellen Kennedy, Warren and Daisy Ketchum, Rachel Kitchen, Chuck Kish, Jason Komorny, Mike & Robin Kravetz, Ray Kuchesky, Charlie Kuenzel, Tim Lagoe, Wanda LaRock, Carol Lathers, Cathy Leggett, Janet Levine, Herbert Loeffler, Kathleen Lombardi and Trish Lyell.

Thanks also to Fr. Tony Maione, Fr. John Malecki, Stan Malecki, Mary Mangino, Mr.&Mrs. Robert Marcotte, Richard Martin, Lee McConchie, Dr. John McFadden, Mary McFarran, James McKevitt, Marlene M. McKinney, James Melanson, Tony & Nancy Merlino, Mr.&Mrs. Mark Milanese, Nickole Mook, Joe & Suzanne Moore, Keira Moore, Scott Morgan, Elizabeth Morris, Jennifer Moss, Pat Niles, Mike & Maeve Noonan, Barbara

O'Brien, Claire Olds, Marvin Olick, Mary Packer, Jim and Kerrie Pascale, Debbie Peck, Pat Peck, Sharon Peck, Joseph Pitkin, Katie Porter, Jean Raymond, Mary Reed, Chuck & Midge Reib, Mr.&Mrs. John Rice, Dick Richards, David and Joan Riebel, Shelley Riley, Elinor Riter, David Roberts, Marshall Robinson, Ruth Roerig, Keith Ruehmer, Lynn Ruehmer and Dorothy Ryan.

Also, my appreciation for the assistance of John Scherer, Rosemary Schultz, Bill Schwarting, Anna Serafini, Mr.&Mrs. Sexton, Bill Shaw, Mrs. Sherman, Dale & Karen Shook, Joyce Spence, John Stiassney, Martha Stonequist, Doris Stauffer, Walter Taras, Gail Taras, Tim Taylor, Frank Thompson, Mr.&Mrs. John Tranka, Mrs. Tretiak, Shirley VanArnum, Genevieve VanAuken, Alan VonStetina, Vaughn Ward, Mike Waring, Alma and Lisa Westcott, Lorraine Westcott, Linda White, Phil Whitney, Jeff and Lori Wodicka, Mike & Donna Wilcox, Sally Wintersteiner, Irene Wood, Tom Wood, and Jeannine Woutersz.

Many thanks to Pat Meaney and Joe Zarzynski for their valuable advice and encouragement in launching this effort.

Special thanks for help and advice from Ellen DeLalla and Jean Stamm, and especially to Victoria Garlanda, who has been an enduring research help, all at the Saratoga Room of the Saratoga Springs Library, and also to Virginia Humphrey at the Ballston Spa Library.

In the end, my hat is off to the countless individuals who supplied leads or recounted personal experiences on subject matter that proves that the grave is not the end.

Index